The Art of Demotivation™

E. L. KERSTEN, PH.D

The Art of Demotivation™

MANAGER EDITION

DEMOTIVATORS® ILLUSTRATIONS
BY KEVIN SPROULS

DESPAIR INK
WWW.DESPAIR.COM

:-(°

JACKET AND BINDING DESIGN BY MARK MELNICK
UNDERCOVER™ JACKET DESIGN BY DESPAIR, INC. & MARK MELNICK
BOOK DESIGN CONSULTATION BY BTDNYC: BETH TONDREAU & SUZANNE DELL'ORTO
WITH CHARTS, GEARS, GEWGAWS & ADDITIONAL PACKAGING DESIGN BY DESPAIR, INC.
ILLUSTRATIONS BY KEVIN SPROULS

ISBN 1-892503-40-9

This book is dedicated to
the unsung heroes who occupy the
corner offices in companies throughout
the world. Though routinely misunderstood, taken advantage of, and maligned
by those they support, they tirelessly bear
the brunt of an economic burden that only
a few can even begin to understand.
Your tribulations have not gone unnoticed.
I encourage you to keep hope alive.

Help has finally arrived.

Warning

This book was written for executives.[1] If you are not an executive, do not intend to become an executive, or have no hope of becoming an executive, **DO NOT READ THIS BOOK.** Early feedback from focus groups comprised of typical business book readers have repeatedly evidenced that non-executives find its contents confusing, controversial, and on occasion, offensive. Negative reactions have been particularly acute in two key groups: employees who are in the early stages of their careers but have none of the qualities to suggest that they might one day become executives, and employees near the final stages of their careers who have squandered any potential of becoming executives. If you are not an executive, do the investors in your company a favor and give this book to your boss. In so doing, you will do your part to increase the longevity of your organization and may even guarantee your place within it.

If you are an executive, congratulations! Your position of leadership is an acknowledgment that you possess rare and valuable gifts: discipline, vision and perseverance foremost among them. Though I've no doubt you've accomplished many things worthy of commendation prior to this moment, I am confident that your greatest glories lie ahead, as the book you are about to begin has the power to transform your organization in ways you dared not dream possible. Increased profitability and decreased attrition are but the first of many benefits already being enjoyed by early implementors of this radical new management philosophy.

This work is revolutionary in the truest and most radical sense. It is a repudiation of the tacitly held assumptions that inform, constrain, and render impotent contemporary "theories" of management. As

---

[1] Note: If your title includes the word "Executive," but you serve a trivial, non-managerial function in your organization (e.g., "Account Executive"), you are not an executive.

such, you will not encounter the wisdom and insights contained herein in either previously heralded management books or in the best business schools in the country. In fact, it is all but inevitable that the celebrated "experts" of management theory—whether they be best-selling authors, motivational speakers or tenured academics—will vehemently disagree with my thesis and instinctively criticize those who dare to follow my advice. This is not because my book is untrue or because the measures advocated do not work, but because disruptive ideas are always rejected as heresy by the high priests of the status quo (Kuhn, 1970). Faced with the alarming prospect of their own pending consignment to irrelevance, their accusations are as predictable as they are pathetic.

As a fellow executive and former academic I implore you: Do not let the rancor of the academy or the vacuous protestations of modern day sophists dissuade you from your journey. Remember to whom you must give account. Your obligations begin and end with shareholders. You were not hired to curry the feckless praise of the self-righteous advocates of an obsolete management paradigm. If you persist in the judicious application of the principles contained in this book, you will surely reap what you have sown.

A Special Note About This Volume

Given the controversial nature of this book and its aforementioned potential to confuse and offend the non-managerial class, it is imperative that the reader exercise extreme caution when reading this book in the workplace. To that end, this edition has been equipped with a secondary dust jacket, a cover for a fictional book called *Ethics, Integrity, and Sacrifice in the Workplace*. For the sake of your company and perhaps your own safety, it is recommended that this cover be placed over the book immediately upon receipt of it. This will essentially render the book invisible to your employees, who have no interest in such subjects.

Contents

List of Illustrations   xi

DEMOTIVATION:
The Foundation For A Management Revolution   1

THE FRUIT OF YOUR LABOR:
Learning To Identify The Signs Of Demotivation   25

THE PRAGMATIC CHOICE:
Four Reasons Why Demotivation Is Superior   37

CORE VALUES:
Helping Your Employees Understand What Really Matters   53

ORGANIZATIONAL STORIES:
Teaching Your Employees Their Role In The Organization   65

SELF-NARRATIVE:
Forcing Your Employees To Think About Their Futures   77

ATTITUDES:
Helping Your Employees Cope with Challenges   101

THE POWER OF SHARING:
Making Sure Your Employees Know How Important They Are   121

COMPENSATION:
Making Pay Fair   151

TEAMS:
Making The Most of Your Employees   181

CONCLUDING THOUGHTS:
Getting Started   215

References   227

Index   235

List of Illustrations

CONSULTING	9
FAILURE	15
INDIVIDUALITY	23
AMBITION	29
MEDIOCRITY	40
MOTIVATION	48
DEMOTIVATION	64
RETIREMENT	66
ACHIEVEMENT	72
DELUSIONS	78
DYSFUNCTION	82
MISTAKES	83
BLAME	118
DISCOVERY	157
GET TO WORK	158
FLATTERY	170
MEETINGS	188

The Art of Demotivation™

DEMOTIVATION:

The Foundation for a Management Revolution

People think they can all be pop stars, high court judges . . .
or infinitely more competent heads of state without ever
putting in the necessary work or having natural ability.
This is the result of social utopianism which believes
humanity can be genetically and socially engineered to
contradict the lessons of history.
—CHARLES, PRINCE OF WALES

I t is generally believed that a company's employees are its most valuable assets. It has long been argued that executives should view their employees as "human capital" with the potential to provide a significant competitive advantage. As Stanford Business Professor Jeffery Pfeffer (1994) says, "People and how we manage them are becoming more important because many other sources of competitive success are less powerful than they once were" (p. 6). Even more important than the competitive advantage employees are said to provide is their impact on a company's market value. Compensation experts Richard W. Beatty and Craig Eric Schneier (2001) have argued that the intangible value of the intellectual and relational capital created by employees has a greater impact on stock price than do the book value, earnings, or cash flow of a company.

These beliefs and others like them create a moral imperative for executives to "take care" of their employees. Executives believe they are obligated to make their companies as motivating, rewarding and satisfying as possible in exchange for the value the employees provide. After all, the argument goes, if the employees are the primary reason a company is successful, it's only fair that they should benefit from the company's success. Apart from the moral dimension, however, there's a pragmatic one. If the employees provide unique forms of intellectual and relational capital that enable a company to differentiate itself, executives have a compelling strategic incentive to ensure that their employees are happy. To do otherwise would be to alienate their greatest strategic asset.

These beliefs have the unique quality of being both *obvious* and *obviously wrong*. They are obvious because we have for decades been propagandized by the arbiters of opinion to believe they are true. These arbiters have been so successful that most executives are unwilling to openly question their dogma; do so and one runs the risk of being labeled as unenlightened, irrational, greedy, or something equally stigmatic. These beliefs are obviously wrong, however, for both logical and empirical reasons. Logically, they can only be true for those companies that lead their respective industries. If one is generous with the definition of "leadership" and assumes it refers to the top 20% of companies in a given industry, that means that the remaining 80% of companies in that industry are not leaders, they are followers that are trying to become leaders. Moreover, if the employees provide the competitive advantage for some companies to be leaders, they are also the *source of competitive disadvantage* for average or substandard companies. It's this disadvantage that consigns the vast majority of companies to the undesirable status of non-leaders, and has led many to the brink of financial collapse. Empirically, executives realize that the noble picture of employees painted above does not square with their experience. They realize that their employees create just as many problems as they solve. They bring their personal problems to work, they immerse themselves in petty politics, they actively search for reasons to resist the company's initiatives, they complain about every minor difficulty, and yet they continue to demand more and more from the company.

This book is for the vast majority of executives who are not industry leaders, executives who have grown weary of spending ever-increasing sums of money on ineffective programs designed to coax their employees to do what they are already paid to do. In this chapter I intend to lay out a new approach to employee productivity that takes as a given the natural weaknesses, immaturity, and inertia of most employees, and uses the unique power disjuncture in the executive/employee relationship to confront employee weaknesses head on. This new approach is designed to disabuse employees of the narcissistic fantasies they cling to—fantasies which not only hinder their productivity, but also produce indignation at even the slightest recommendation for improvement.

Before I disclose the tenets of this new approach, it's important to understand why it's vastly superior to traditional approaches to employee productivity. To this end, I will begin with a brief discussion of the conventional approaches to solving the problems of employee motivation and productivity.

MOTIVATION: THE PHLOGISTON OF PRODUCTIVITY

The 19th century was an era of unprecedented scientific discovery and technological innovation. The successes in these areas produced a tremendous optimism in the ability of humankind to solve its most difficult problems—an optimism unseen since the planning stages of the Tower of Babel. The cornerstone of this optimism was the remarkable utility of the scientific method. At the same time, the industrial revolution and the emergence of the modern-day factory were creating new problems in the management of large groups of unskilled labor. Consequently, it was only a matter of time before scientifically trained researchers from a variety of disciplines began to tackle the most elusive, intractable problem of all: employee productivity. It did not take very long before productivity (p) was conceptualized as being a function of skill (s) and motivation (m), or: $(p = f(s)(m))$. Since the skill required to do a job was relatively easy to determine, the problem that became paramount was employee motivation.

For almost a century, motivation has served as the phlogiston of the management community. At one time physicists and chemists believed that phlogiston was the substance that made things combustible (Fisher, 1978). Highly combustible items such as wood and coal were believed to be high in phlogiston, whereas substances such as iron were believed to be low in phlogiston. With the discovery of oxygen, belief in phlogiston dissipated and eventually disappeared. In the same way that phlogiston served as an unenlightened but scientifically accepted explanation for combustibility, motivation has come to be accepted as the fuel of productivity. Productive employees are believed to be high in motivation, whereas their unproductive counterparts are believed to be low in motivation. Consequently, social scientists have spent decades trying to understand the nature of human motivation, the conditions under which it is developed, maintained, and extinguished, and its impact on employees and other organizational processes.

The quest to solve the riddle of employee motivation has led researchers in a variety of directions. Some researchers see motivation as a function of something internal to employees, such as needs or drives which prompt the employees to act; others see it as a function of something external, in the form of rewards and punishments; still others see it as a combination of both internal and external factors. Naturally, these different beliefs about motivation have produced competing approaches to solving the seemingly intractable problem of employee productivity. These can be divided into two broad categories. One seeks to reconfigure the organization by restructuring roles and relationships between management and employees, and by implementing programs to make the organization maximally motivating. The other seeks to reconfigure employees by providing "insights" into their behavior in the hope of unleashing their "hidden" potential.

Reconfiguring The Organization

When social scientists began to tackle the problem of employee motivation, they began with the assumption that employees were naturally motivated to do something, even if they weren't motivated to work.

Their observations of supposedly weary, overworked employees who enthusiastically made their ways to bars, betting tables, and billiard parlors at the end of the day led them to conclude that low employee motivation was primarily of function of the work environment. One of the first approaches to reconfiguring the organization with the hope of improving motivation was to *make the nature of the work easier for the employee.* In his illuminating treatise, *The Principles of Scientific Management,* industrial engineer Fredrick W. Taylor (1911) noted that most employees would work only hard enough to avoid being punished. He believed this sorry state of affairs was due to a combination of several factors, not the least of which were the inherent laziness of employees, their gross misunderstanding of their own economic self-interests, and poor task design. He also argued that one of the reasons that rank-and-file employees were so lazy was that they were in roles that were beyond them. Whether due to ignorance, aptitude, or rank stupidity, most employees were unable to figure out how to perform their jobs most efficiently. As a result, they were unnecessarily burdened by the defects in their own character and/or mental acuity. Despite all of this, Taylor optimistically believed that employees were rational, economically motivated beings whose natural laziness could be overcome (i.e., employees could be motivated) if a company developed the appropriate management systems to compensate for its employees' weaknesses. The key to his solution was to do for employees what they could not do for themselves: namely, to scientifically determine the most efficient way to perform a task. After this was done, employees were to be assigned tasks that were appropriately suited to their skills (or lack thereof) and aptitude. For example, Taylor noted that the type of steelworker most suited to handle pig iron should be "so stupid and so phlegmatic that he more nearly resembles in his mental make-up the ox than any other type" (Taylor, 1911, p. 58). Once employees were assigned to their well-defined, perfectly suited tasks, it was the responsibility of management to provide them with incentives, oversight, and corrective instruction to ensure that the employees performed as optimally as could be expected according to the principles of scientific management.

Despite Taylor's undeniable perspicacity into the problems posed by employees' limitations, he is often criticized for having a harsh, utilitarian view of employees, one in which they are seen as little more than cogs in a giant corporate machine. This critique, however, is rooted in a gross misunderstanding of both Taylor and scientific management. Taylor's biggest weakness was not that he was harsh, it was that he was seduced by his own altruism and compassion for the average employee into trying to create an environment that would enable them to succeed. Consequently, he failed to reckon with the fact that employees are *not* like rats, chickens, or oxen that can be trained to do highly routinized tasks. Instead, they are more like an infectious disease that constantly mutates in ways that make it resistant to ever more powerful antibiotics. In the same way, employees constantly adapt to the work environment by developing new reasons and methods to avoid work.

The criticisms of scientific management continued to mount and a new management paradigm eventually emerged, one that rejected Taylor's assumptions that employees were both rational and economically motivated. This new paradigm posited that employees were more likely to be influenced by human relationships and the need to belong to a group than they were by reason or money. Appropriately, this new paradigm eventually came to be known as the *human relations movement.* The underlying assumption of the human relations movement was that if a company met it employees' needs for security and belonging, the employees would reciprocate by meeting the company's need for productive labor. Therefore, the human relations movement attempted to motivate employees by reconfiguring the organization to *make it satisfying for its employees.* The forms of this reconfiguration were both many and varied. Human relations researchers generated theories about almost every facet of organizational life that affected the interpersonal relationships within it: leadership styles, group dynamics, decision-making processes, goal-setting, superior-subordinate interaction, employee feedback, and the list goes on. The goal in all of this was to find out how to implement these processes in a way that made employees feel like the company was their home.

Understandably, it didn't take long for criticisms to be levied at the human relations movement. Critics charged that the movement's assumptions about employees were inadequate and condescending. In some quarters, human relations programs were said to be an example of "cow sociology" because cows were also believed to be more productive when they were satisfied. The more important criticism of the human relations movement, however, was that the hypothesized relationship between employee satisfaction and productivity simply did not exist. Satisfied employees were *not* more productive employees (Eisenberg & Goodall, 1993), and attempting to meet their needs was both expensive and frustrating for executives. At one point, motivational pioneer Frederick Herzberg (1989) from the University of Utah offered this scathing indictment of the impact of human relations programs:

> Over 30 years of teaching and, in many instances, of practicing psychological approaches to handling people have resulted in costly human relations programs and, in the end, the same question: How do you motivate workers? Here, too, escalations have taken place. Thirty years ago it was necessary to request, "Please don't spit on the floor." Today the same admonition requires three "pleases" before the employee feels that a superior has demonstrated the psychologically proper attitude (p. 28).

The failure of the human relations movement naturally led researchers to look for a new model to help them figure out how to motivate employees. Rather than completely abandoning the human relations model, however, researchers simply augmented and extended it into what eventually came to be known as the human *resources* model of management. The chief difference between the two models is that the human resources approach assumes that employees have a much more comprehensive set of needs that must be met for them to be motivated. In addition to needs for security and belonging, employees also have needs for achievement, autonomy, empowerment, self-actualization, and a host of others. Consequently, the human resource approach sought to motivate employees by reconfiguring the organization to *meet the needs of its employees*. Several techniques were developed to help employees meet their needs, many of which are still widely used today. Examples include Management By Objectives (MBO), Total Quality Management (TQM) participatory decision-making, team based work groups, participatory goal-setting, leadership training, and empowerment programs (Argyris, 1998, Herzberg, 1989). Despite all of their great promise, these process also have failed have the impact they were expected to have. Even Harvard's Chris Argyris, one of the major figures in the human resources movement, lamented the lack of success of empowerment programs when he said, "Few executives would deny that there has been little growth in empowerment over the last 30 years. . . . The change programs and practices we employ are full of inner contradictions that cripple innovation, motivation, and drive" (1989, p. 98).

It is clear that the quest to motivate employees by reconfiguring the organization has been a boon for employees and a bust for executives. Employees have had their jobs made easier, their work environments made more satisfying, and an ever-expanding cornucopia of needs met by their employers. As the same time, executives have had to spend increasingly huge sums of money to build complex, well-defined bureaucracies that are designed to employee-proof their operations, while simultaneously spending additionally huge sums of money on programs and perks to make their employees happy. Despite all of this, employee motivation is still a problem in need of a solution.

One of the things most remarkable about this sad state of affairs is the degree to which failed solutions continue to be reintroduced as new insights. For decades, business books have been written that claimed to contain the secrets, laws, principles, or techniques that executives could use to motivate their employees. Many of these books are little more than a repackaging and reintroduction of old ideas that didn't work the first time around. One has to wonder why this is the case. I may be cynical, but it seems clear that if the answer to employee motivation really had been discovered, there would be no need for new books promising to do the same. Could it be that the "solutions" executives have been sold have really been the source of the problems that prompted them to buy even more books that contained more "solutions?" As you read *this* book, I'll let you draw your own conclusions.

CONSULTING

IF YOU'RE NOT A PART OF THE SOLUTION,
THERE'S GOOD MONEY TO BE MADE IN PROLONGING THE PROBLEM.

Reconfiguring The Employee

Many executives don't believe they need to reconfigure their organizations, but they are still plagued by a myriad of employee problems. As a result, they seek the help of consultants from the multi-billion dollar motivational industry. These consultants promise to transform their employees from "Whiners into Winners" in two days or less by offering programs on topics like listening, giving feedback, "visioneering," creating a high performance culture, leadership styles, managing excellence, excellent management, bringing out the best in people, and that perennial favorite, teambuilding. Many executives suppress their instincts when they hear the consultants' promises, willingly suspending their well-honed skepticism in the hope that the siren song of the motivational industry just may make a difference. After all, these consultants are able to produce glowing recommendations from past participants in their programs and these invariably include expressions like "life-changing" and "insightful." What the executives fail to realize is that the life-changing insights sold by the motivational industry are *the source of their problems rather than the solution to them.* The consultants in the motivational industry are like ice cream vendors at a fat farm, pimps at a treatment facility for sex addicts, or drug pushers at a methadone clinic. They pander to your employees' cravings, and in so doing they exacerbate they problems they are paid to solve.

Much of what passes for motivation in the motivational industry is little more than egoistic, short-term enthusiasm, or warm feelings generated by the creative packaging of the "principles" of the human potential movement, which itself is little more than a curious amalgam of common sense, humanistic religion, sophistry, and psychological snake-oil. The primary objective of the motivational industry is to *stoke the fires of your employees' narcissism* so that they fall in love with themselves all over again, just like they did when they saw their own beauty in the distorted reflection of their mother's adoring gaze, prior to their exposure to any of the objective, real-world criteria that would define them otherwise. The insights peddled to your employees revolve around the ideas that they are uniquely equipped to do something special, that they have a proprietary configuration of underappreciated skills that they have yet to discover (or show any evidence of), that their weaknesses are really strengths, and that they are winners who have simply not had the chance to win. They are regaled with stories about people like Thomas Edison who regarded failed experiments as stepping-stones on the path to scientific discovery, and they end up concluding that their own personal histories of failure and non-achievement are signs that they are bound for greatness. In this systematic distortion of reality, they learn to label their stubbornness as conviction; their bad attitudes as a passion for justice; their willful subversion of the company's goals as a unique, underappreciated perspective on how the company should proceed; and their general surliness as a natural response to a global lack of appreciation for their supremely valuable uniqueness.

You may wonder how it's possible for these charges to be reconciled with the incredible success of the multi-billion dollar industry itself. The reason why the motivational industry *appears* to be so successful is that it uses employee feedback rather than company performance as the criterion for success. At the completion of a motivational seminar the employees are in the throes of a long distance romance with the "real self" they believe they are destined to become. Given the blinding emotional rush of their infatuation, they naturally regard the babble of the motivational industry as life-changing insight.

THE ROOT OF THE PROBLEM: THE NOBLE EMPLOYEE MYTH

The problem with both approaches to the search for motivation— reconfiguring the organization and reconfiguring the employee—is that they are founded upon wrong beliefs about employees, and as such, are doomed to fail. These beliefs constitute a contemporary version of the French philosopher Jean-Jacques Rousseau's Noble Savage Myth. Rousseau believed that in their natural, uncivilized state humans were essentially good and free, and that they were corrupted by their participation in civil institutions. Similarly, most motivation experts believe that employees are essentially good, responsible, and hardworking, but their managers and the companies they work for affect them in ways that lead them to do things inconsistent with their nature. This belief is at the heart of what I call the *Noble Employee Myth.*

The Noble Employee Myth has never been articulated as such, but it is a subtext that is present in almost everything that has been written about management/employee relations in the last 75 years. It is the product of what I call the *Motivational Educational Industrial (ME-I) Complex,* a movement made up of a decentralized, constantly evolving coalition of institutions that are intent on replacing the values of the Protestant Work Ethic with a "culture of narcissism" (Lasch, 1979). The ME-I Complex ubiquitously reinforces the idea that "the good life" is fundamentally a matter of self-fulfillment and self-esteem, and that the attainment of these pursuits is predicated upon the constant acquisition of goods and the unconditional affirmation of self. In the pursuit of these goals, the ME-I Complex is constantly seeking to subjugate "the corporation" to the individual, and its primary tool for achieving this is the Noble Employee Myth. The following are a sampling of the propositions that are part of the Noble Employee Myth orthodoxy:

- Engaging in productive labor is as natural for employees as rest or play.
- Satisfied employees are productive employees.
- It is the responsibility of management to create circumstances that unleash employee motivation.
- Employees should be able to count on their employers to meet their needs.
- The pursuit of profits should not be at the expense of employee satisfaction.
- Poor performance is a function of poor management or insufficient organizational resources.
- Each employee is a unique, supremely valuable wellspring of insight and innovation. As such, managers have a responsibility to appreciate his distinct personhood.
- Managers should care for their employees as people, independent of their contribution or detriment to the organization.
- Employees' failures are only rarely a sign of incompetence.
- Employees are the victims of corporate failures.
- Employees thrive under conditions of autonomy and self-determination.
- Poor decisions made by employees are the result of insufficient guidance or organizational constraint.

The problem with these beliefs, apart from their being patently false, is that they naturally lead to misdiagnosis and mistreatment of employee problems. This was clearly illustrated in a recent article about the supervision of underperforming employees. The authors' thesis is that *managers create their own poor performers* through what they call The Set-Up-To-Fail Syndrome (Manzoni & Barsoux, 1998). According to the authors, The Set-Up-To-Fail Syndrome has eight basic steps that undermine employee confidence and performance:

1. The manager and employee have a good relationship.
2. The employee fails or performs poorly.
3. The manager concludes the employee needs additional supervision.
4. The employee interprets the additional supervision as a lack of confidence in the employee's ability. As a result, the employee begins to withdraw.
5. The manager notices the employee's withdrawal and steps up supervision even further.
6. In response to the increased supervision, the employee engages in passive/aggressive coping strategies.
7. As a result of the employee's passive/aggressiveness, the manager becomes increasingly convinced the employee cannot handle the responsibility of the role.
8. Eventually, the employee is exasperated and gives up.

The authors see the biggest problem in this scenario as the manager's expression of lack of confidence in the employee. This is because the manager's lack of confidence undermines the employee's self-confidence, thereby handicapping the employee's performance. They argue that when faced with a lack of managerial confidence, employees generally respond in one of two ways. Some attempt to impress their managers and win their confidence by doing things like setting excessively high goals, volunteering for extra duty on multiple projects, or refusing to seek help on large projects. As a result of their delusional hubris, they generally fail. In so doing, they demonstrate that their attempts to impress their manager were rooted in poor judgment and they end up reinforcing the very perceptions they were hoping to overcome. Some employees start the process all over again until repeated failure forces them to give up. Others adopt a more passive response. Rather than fighting to win their manager's confidence, they stop making decisions, stop taking initiative, and stop tackling problems out of fear that their decisions will simply be overruled. They begin to passively take orders and do what they are told. As the authors put it, "Subordinates simply stop giving their best. They grow tired of being overruled, and they lose the will to fight for their ideas" (Manzoni & Barsoux, 1998, p. 106).

The authors go on to note that it is possible for employees to break out of the Set-Up-To-Fail Syndrome by developing a track record of success, but they bemoan the fact that this is often difficult to do once a negative impression has already been created.

> It's hard for subordinates to impress their bosses when they must work on unchallenging tasks, with no autonomy and limited resources; it is also hard for them to persist and maintain high standards when they receive little encouragement from their bosses. (Manzoni & Barsoux, 1998, p. 108)

The authors are unclear as to *why* it is difficult for employees to maintain high standards on unchallenging tasks, just because they don't receive much encouragement. By definition, an unchallenging task *shouldn't* require any encouragement—it is too easy. My guess is that by postulating that employees need encouragement to perform unchallenging tasks, the authors are laying the groundwork for a rationale that blames managers when their employees fail to live up to even vastly-reduced expectations. As is the case with almost all Noble Employee Myth–inspired literature, finding a way to exonerate employees and blame managers is regarded as insightful and progressive. But it also requires almost a complete denial of that which is most obvious. Along that line, I have four brief observations about The Set-Up-To-Fail Syndrome that provide a more helpful reading of the situation.

First, *failure is clearly endemic to the employee.* This is obvious from the fact that the downward spiral begins with employee failure, even when a positive relationship exists with the manager. If the employee fails when the manager has confidence in the employee, and the employee fails when the manager lacks confidence in the employee, the employee's failure is not a function of the manager, it is a function of the employee *(see illustration).*

Second, *a lack of adequate supervision over employees who fail or make mistakes places the company at risk.* It is an odd bit of reasoning which concludes that employees who fail do not warrant additional scrutiny. This is a bit like arguing that a felon does not warrant any attention from law

enforcement officials. Employees with too much autonomy and a legacy of failure are likely to do things that can hurt the long term viability
of the company.

A third point worth noting is that *employees who fail* should *experience
a reduction in their self-confidence.* There is a good chance that their failure is a sign their self-confidence is unwarranted and that they need to
acquire more skill, focus, or discipline to warrant their pre-failure level
of self-confidence. In this case, not allowing the employee to experience the loss of self-confidence and the attendant descent into the pit

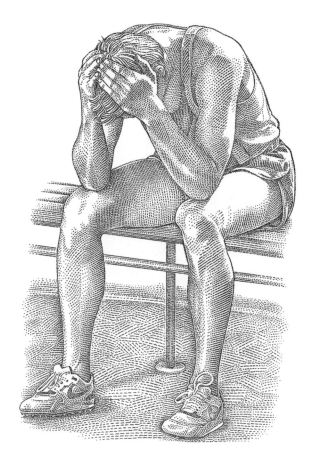

FAILURE

WHEN YOUR BEST JUST ISN'T GOOD ENOUGH.

of self-contempt robs the employee of the opportunity to be confronted with and disciplined by his limitations.

Finally, *it's okay if employees stop "giving their best" when confronted with a crisis of managerial confidence for the simple reason that it was "their best" which started the crisis.* Employees who cease to engage in ego-gratifying, autonomous failure, and instead submit to a soul-crushing, robotic compliance actually have a chance for redemption.

This much should be clear: The discernible goal of the proponents of the Noble Employee Myth is to disrupt the rational distribution and application of institutional power in modern organizations. They do this by invalidating accurate perceptions and rendering obvious courses of action obsolete. Their apparently irrational commitment to a subversive view of employees is most likely driven by a desire for a different kind of world, one they seem to believe can only be created by denying reality and pretending that their fantasy is true. This book is for executives who are tired of pretending—for those who want to understand the real source of their problems so that they can implement real solutions.

THE SOURCE OF THE PROBLEM: EMPLOYEES

Many executives are puzzled when I tell them that their employees are the source of their problems. Though they have known this intuitively and observed ample evidence of this fact, everything they have read and heard about management has taught them to look elsewhere—their culture, their business processes, their compensation systems, their job design, their training programs, and the like. Therefore, it is important to set the record straight. The following are six characteristics of employees that illustrate and clarify the risks they pose to the executives, shareholders, and customers of the companies they work for. The list could be much longer, but in the interest of space I have kept it short.

- **Employees make bad decisions.** For decades the proponents of the Noble Employee Myth have attempted to persuade, cajole, and browbeat executives into empowering their employees, then proceeded to shame them with charges of arrogance and elitism when executives expressed reservations about the wisdom of the idea. The truth of the matter, however, is that no matter how much executives would like to empower their employees, their employees possess a capacity for bad judgment that is beyond comprehension. A recent example of this occurred at a fast food restaurant in North Carolina. State law requires that food service employees keep their hands clean, therefore two of the restaurant employees concluded it would be a good idea to clean other parts of their bodies as well and converted the restaurant's industrial-sized sink into their own personal bubble bath. This unfortunate example of "out-of-the-box" employee decision-making left the restaurant manager in an unexpected struggle for survival. Not only did he have to convince the local health commissioner that the restaurant was sanitized well enough to reopen, he also had to convince his customers that their meals would not be prepared in a makeshift bathtub.

- **Employees make mistakes.** Even when employers do everything they can to make a job as clear-cut as possible, employees often make mistakes through negligence, mindlessness, or generalized incompetence. This was evidenced in a tragic case at a Florida hospital when a woman died after she was given a blood transfusion with the wrong type of blood. The accident was blamed on a mislabeled blood sample. Clearly, labeling a blood sample is a well-explicated procedure requiring no creativity or decision-making on the part of the employee, yet the employee failed at it nonetheless. In the same hospital a few months earlier, a heart catheterization was mistakenly performed on the wrong patient. The hospital provided a perfectly rational explanation for the error, saying that "No one compared the patient's wrist identification bracelet to the patient's chart." These are the kinds of routine errors made by employees that make attorneys and insurance companies wealthy, but create frustration and anxiety for executives, investors, and the consuming public.

- **Employees alienate customers.** This is so obvious that it hardly requires comment, but it deserves mention because customers are the source of revenue for any company. I suspect that all of us have been treated poorly by employees who could not care less about us as customers or about the reputation and revenue of the company they worked for. They were rude, arrogant, lazy, unresourceful, ill-mannered, and offensive. Now think for a moment: How many of your employees treat *your* customers the same? How many of your past customers are now ex-customers because of the way they were treated by the people you pay to help them? Moreover, how many of their friends and acquaintances did your ex-customers tell about the way they were treated by your employees? It is clear that your labor costs extend well beyond the salary and benefits you pay when you consider how much money you have to spend on marketing to attract new customers to replace those that your employees are driving away.

- **Employees lack maturity.** Despite all of the rhetoric about employee empowerment, competence, and value, even the proponents of the Noble Employee Myth do not seem to think very highly of employees, and rather than treating them like adults, they tend to treat them like children. This is clearly evidenced in the motivational bestseller, *Who Moved My Cheese?* The book (Johnson, 1998) tells a parable about two mice, Sniff and Scurry, and two "littlepeople," Hem and Haw. The mice and the little people both derive their happiness from cheese, which they both discover in large supply at Cheese Station C. Eventually, though, the cheese at Cheese Station C runs out and none of the four have any more cheese. When that happens, the mice immediately set out in a maze to find more cheese, but the little people—who represent employees—do not. Instead, they engage in all sorts of unproductive and ineffective rationalizations for why they should not do anything differently. Their responses include:

  - *They declare themselves "special"* and believe they should be exempt from the rigors of finding new cheese.

  - *They remind themselves that they are smarter* than the mice, though the mice have already found new cheese while Hem and Haw are waiting for the cheese to reappear at Cheese Station C.

  - *They blame one another* for not finding new cheese.

- *They avoid the effort* to find new cheese because they are comfortable at Cheese Station C, despite the fact that it no longer contains any cheese.

- *They do things that they know will not work* in the hope that one day cheese will reappear.

- *They attempt to deny the reality* that there is no cheese at Cheese Station C.

- *They fear change and avoid the risk* of potentially not finding any cheese by staying at a place that contains no cheese.

- *They confuse activity* with productivity.

The amazing popularity of the book suggests that employees identify with Hem and Haw and that they really do embody the traits mentioned above. As an executive, do you really want to give employees who identify with Hem and Haw more control in your organization? If the answer is yes, I suggest you stop reading at this moment, call the Chairman of the Board of Directors of your company, submit your resignation, and give this book to your successor.

- **Employees exploit their employer's generosity.** Executives often attempt to use incentive plans to get their employees to do what they were hired to do, but employees frequently engage in fraud and deception to exploit those programs and end up placing the company at risk. University of Wisconsin professor Barry Gerhart (2001) provides two poignant examples of employee fraud and deceit that should cause any executive to think twice before they decide to "reward" their employees for doing what they are hired to do.

In the first case, a major retailer was charged with fraud in both California and New Jersey for allegedly overcharging customers for auto repairs. The retailer had a compensation plan that paid employees based upon the amount of the repairs authorized by their customers. A California investigation found that in 34 out of 38 visits, "the shops gave unnecessary service and repair recommendations, with some of the unnecessary repair recommendations costing as much as $550" (Gerhart, 2001, p. 224). It is clear that what started out as an equitable plan to give employees who did more work more money, metastasized under the influence of the employees into an ugly, destructive case of consumer fraud.

In the second case, a premier insurance company ended up taking $2.05 billion in pretax charges to pay for the expected costs of the settlement of a class-action lawsuit brought by angry customers. Their agents were accused of "churning," whereby "customers with long-standing life insurance policies that had built up cash values were persuaded to take on new, larger policies with the assurance that the new policies would not cost any more" (Gerhart, 2001, p. 224). The agents were accused of tricking the customers into authorizing the liquidation of the cash value of their existing policies in order to pay for the new, higher-premium policies. Naturally, the executives at the company wanted to reward employees for selling new policies, but they did not intend for them to fleece the existing customer base in the process. It is clear that what started out as an attempt to acquire new clients became corrupted in the minds of the employees so that it became a plan to take advantage of their existing, loyal customers.

• **Employees steal from their employers.** Despite all of the fluff and bluster in the popular press about CEO pay being out of control, the real economic threat to corporations is employee theft. The US Chamber of Commerce estimates that employees steal over $50 billion annually from their employers. This is done through a combination of pilfering merchandise, cash larceny, inflated expense accounts, check tampering, filing false receipts and just about anything else they can get away with. A May 13, 2003 news release by the accounting firm Ernst & Young placed the annual price tag for employee theft in the retailing industry alone at over $21 billion, and their study found that "employee theft is the single biggest contributor to inventory shrinkage even though shoplifters far outpace dishonest employees. . . . Though employees accounted for only 1 out of every 10 apprehensions, the average value of merchandise recovered was nearly seven times that of the average shoplifter, $1,525 and $223 respectively" ("Ernst & Young Estimates," 2003; "Employee Theft," 1999; Klein, 2001). To make matters worse, the *Detroit Free Press* reports that 30% of all business failures are primarily due to employee theft.

It should be clear that employees are not the valiant icons of frustrated nobility the proponents of the Noble Employee Myth would have us believe. Instead, their self-interest, duplicity, and generalized lack of responsibility make them more of a liability to the company than an asset. Employees are a necessary evil. This is why management theories and programs based upon the Noble Employee Myth do not work; they simply frustrate executives and further expose the company to its greatest threat—the substandard, short-sighted, narcissistic performance of its employees. Tragically, despite the overwhelming evidence of widespread employee negligence and misbehavior, executives are the ones who are generally held accountable for poor corporate performance. It has become commonplace to hear about executives being fired by Boards of Directors for the aggregate failures of their employees. As a manager of flawed and fallen people yourself, you would rightly consider this misguided sacrifice of innocents to be both a tragedy and travesty. Yet these are barbaric and perilous times, and you must also allow that it could be *your* destiny as well, if you do not confront the problem head on. It is clear that executives need a management solution that is grounded in reality, in all of its unpleasant and disappointing detail, rather than in a fantasy world that represents the wish fulfillment of delusional employees and executive wannabes.

THE SOLUTION TO THE PROBLEM: RADICAL DEMOTIVATION™

At Despair, Inc. we have pioneered a radical new approach toward workplace productivity, one that goes way beyond the naïve dreams and unfulfilled promises of the motivational industry. It is an approach that is rooted in the reality of human weakness rather than the fantasies of human potential. It capitalizes on the emotional immaturity, irresponsibility, tendency to blame others, lack of self-discipline, willingness to take the path of least resistance, and general surliness of the average employee. It is designed to harness the dysfunction and toxicity inherent in your workforce and exploit it for your own financial gain.

We call this revolutionary new approach Radical Demotivation™. Simply put, Radical Demotivation™ is a relatively simple way of controlling your employees by manipulating their identities, their very senses of self and the hopes and dreams that shape the goals they pursue throughout the day. It is a way of striking at the very root of the problem—your employees' beliefs that they are entitled to more than you, in your judicious provision, have chosen to give them.

Radical Demotivation™ is based on the simple premise that your employees are also victims of the Noble Employee Myth, and as victims, they are tormented by a sense of self-worth that their skills, abilities, and achievements cannot support. As a result, their persistent failures regularly threaten their sense of self-worth and throw them off balance, prompting them to search for psychological props to help them restore a temporary measure of equilibrium. Rather than developing the skills and discipline necessary to succeed, and in so doing, forging an identity worthy of their self-respect, they look to you, their employer, to make them feel good about who they aren't. They do this by demanding that they be enabled to reap the fruits of success apart from their actually achieving success. They demand more income than they merit, more respect than they have earned, more autonomy than they can handle, and more leisure time than they need. All of these demands are designed to enflame the passions of an illicit love affair with themselves and seduce them into believing the lies of the Noble Employee Myth. The problem though, is that with every failure, with every year that passes, providing another milestone of non-achievement, the gulf between the person they are becoming and the person they claim to be grows wider. As a result, their angst grows more acute with each passing year, and with it, the temptation to blame you for the self-inflicted injury to their psyches.

Radical Demotivation™ capitalizes on this pathetic situation by systematically thwarting your employees' narcissistic impulse. It does this by recognizing that your employees are, first and foremost, units of labor that require optimization rather than appreciation. Moreover, to the degree that your employees' individual personalities are recognized, they are seen as sources of error and sub-optimization *(see illustration)*. Consequently, your employees eventually come to realize that

INDIVIDUALITY

ALWAYS REMEMBER YOU ARE UNIQUE. JUST LIKE EVERYBODY ELSE.

the uniqueness that the proponents of the Noble Employee Myth had taught them to cherish has been reduced and homogenized to little more than a source of "error variance" in the production process.

As time goes on, they eventually come to terms with the fact that the self which was the object of their egoistic obsession was nothing more than a fetishized doppelganger inspired by the Noble Employee Myth. As this phantom self begins to fade, the employee learns to embrace the real-self, the one that recognizes its legacy of failure and non-achievement and rationally concludes that it has no reason to demand anything of anyone. Instead, the employee lives with the constant recognition that he does not deserve to be employed, doubting that anyone else would ever be so foolish as to hire him, and becomes grateful for whatever he gets. This is the promise and pathology of Radical Demotivation™.

Very little learning is required to become a Radically Demotivating executive. In fact, many of you are probably unwittingly using some of these techniques on a daily basis, though without a comprehensive program you will not experience the full benefits. Still others of you have been using these techniques for years, experiencing the benefits of a radically demotivated workforce, but have never fully understood the reason for your success. In many cases, you probably felt guilty using some of these techniques because they fly in the face of the assumptions inherent in the Noble Employee Myth. Others of you have been afraid to use these techniques, even though they have seemed the most appropriate at different junctures. No matter your circumstance, I have good news. The more you learn, the more you will realize that the discovery of Radical Demotivation™ is a little like the discovery of a high fat, high sugar, no exercise diet: You always hoped it could be so, but doubted it was possible because all the "experts" said it was madness. Until now.

THE FRUIT OF YOUR LABOR:
Learning to Identify
the Signs of Demotivation

Men's faults do seldom to themselves appear.
—SHAKESPEARE, *The Rape of Lucrece*

When first exposed to the idea of Radical Demotivation™, many executives are a bit hesitant to embark on a comprehensive implementation of the program. This is because they misunderstand the nature of the Radically Demotivated employee. Many executives imagine that Radical Demotivation™ produces an unkempt, unskilled slacker who poses the very threat to the organization that the program promises to overcome. In this chapter I want to describe the true nature of the Radically Demotivated employee. My hope is to encourage those who mistakenly fear that the cure may be worse than the disease to confidently embark on a covert program of Radical Demotivation™ as soon as possible.

The goal of Radical Demotivation™ is to increase your control over your employees without resorting to the ineffective, cost-inflating techniques that naturally flow from the Noble Employee Myth. Radical Demotivation™ does this by reshaping the identities of your employees, yet leaving their skills intact for your continued use and exploitation.

Radical Demotivation™ targets your employees' identities because their self-concept is the locus of their hopes, dreams, goals, and desires. Employees who *believe they deserve more* than you are willing to give them are more likely to demand more and work less than those who *realize they are fortunate* to have whatever job you deign to give them, and who live with the constant, stimulating awareness of their absolute dispensability. Most employees initially resist the process of demotivation, but your persistence will eventually teach them that resistance is futile. You can be confident that over time Radically Demotivated employees will eventually give up the fight and accept that it is only in acquiescence to your goals and objectives that they will find peace. As one demotivated employee put it, "Rather than arguing with [my boss], I've ended up wanting to say, 'Come on, just tell me what you want me to do, and I'll go do it.' You become a robot" (Manzoni & Barsoux, 1998, p. 106).

This type of response is, of course, exactly what you're shooting for.

THE NATURE OF THE RADICALLY DEMOTIVATED™ EMPLOYEE

After it became clear that I could no longer trust the advice of the "experts" because of their commitment to the Noble Employee Myth, I realized I needed to a place where I could generate new knowledge. This led to the establishment of Despair Labs™, a state-of-the-art research and development facility that is unfettered by the typical constraints on human experimentation imposed by universities and professional organizations. Drawing its inspiration from Stanley Milgram's pioneering work on authority, the goal of Despair Labs is to develop a thorough understanding (i.e., epistêmê) of the nature of employee limitations and the means (i.e., technê) by which they can most effectively be overcome. The work done at this facility has helped me develop refine many of ideas presented throughout this book.

One of our consistent findings is that Radically Demotivated employees develop a clear set of attitudinal and behavioral characteristics that serve as tokens of their Radically Demotivated state. Though you should not expect *every* employee to manifest *every* characteristic, most

Radically Demotivated employees will manifest five or more of the following nine characteristics. It is important to note that our research also shows that employees with fewer than five of the identified demotivational characteristics are still clinging, however desperately, to the hope that their circumstances will improve, and though this may not appear troublesome at the time, we have found that nascent hope, however feeble, is always a cause for concern. Chronically motivated employees may require additional non-routine monitoring and intervention. Table 1 provides an overview of the nine characteristics and their corresponding benefits.

TABLE I. DEMOTIVATIONAL CHARACTERISTICS AND CORRESPONDING BENEFITS

Demotivational Characteristics	*Demotivational Benefit*
Feeling of powerlessness	Employee is satisfied with less
Sense of victimization by fate	Feels desperate loyalty to company
Low self-esteem	Loses need for employee recognition
Acute defensiveness	Does extra work as a means of ingratiation
Acute self-doubt	Works hard as a means of salvaging identity
Lack of emotional resilience	Works hard to avoid humiliation
Intense risk-aversion	Is satisfied being an extension of executive ambition
Chronic pessimism	Has better judgment; less money
Pervasive sullenness	Experiences accelerated acquiescence

THE 9 SIGNS OF THE DEMOTIVATED EMPLOYEE

1. Powerlessness

The most common feature of Radically Demotivated employees is that they *believe they are powerless to reach their most cherished goals.* Motivated employees get up and go to work every day because they believe that doing so is somehow instrumental in helping them achieve their hopes and dreams. Radically Demotivated employees, in contrast, believe all their efforts are futile in this regard, and going to work is simply a way of maintaining a largely unfulfilling—though occasionally comfortable—existence. This does not mean they are unable to accomplish tasks that require significant intelligence and skill, just that those accomplishments will not help them reach their most cherished goals. For example, an engineer in Albuquerque, New Mexico may dream of living in a Spanish hacienda along the Southern California coastline, but as the years tick by, despite his many accomplishments, he gradually becomes more and more convinced that he will never leave Albuquerque and that his most cherished dream is for someone more capable to live. Rather than being a means of achieving his goals, his job, like his mind, has become little more than a comfortable prison.

Employees who forfeit their dreams out of a sense of powerlessness learn to expect less out of life, and as a result, they are more apt to settle for whatever "crumbs" they can get. More importantly, their acquiescence to their "crumby" standard of existence leads them to make fewer demands on their employers. This has the important benefit of saving money on unnecessary programs designed to increase their job satisfaction, which they rightly come to regard as an oxymoron.

2. Victims Of A Hostile Fate

The second sign of Radically Demotivated employees is the *belief that they are victims of a hostile fate, and therefore they see no reason to engage in a program of self-improvement.* In other words, Radically Demotivated employees cynically believe the world is against them and nothing they do will change the way the world responds to them. When the job market turns south and unemployment is on the rise, many motivated workers attempt to improve their chances of future success by finishing a degree, working on an MBA, improving their resumé or acquiring a new skill. The Radically Demotivated employee sees little value in any of these activities and concludes that the likely payoff is not worth the effort. Instead, she believes the only thing that matters is being the unlikely and short-lived beneficiary of a shift in the political winds, and those winds are likely to reverse course and rise to gale force at any moment.

This cynicism regarding their ability to improve their situation also causes Radically Demotivated employees to be *amazingly loyal to the companies they work for.* As one might expect, this loyalty is not born out of any affection for the company or identification with its mission as much as it is born out of a paralyzing fear that any other company they might work

AMBITION

THE JOURNEY OF A THOUSAND MILES SOMETIMES ENDS VERY, VERY BADLY.

for would be even worse *(see illustration).* Given their experience with Radical Demotivation™, employees begin to fear that any change would be like jumping from the proverbial frying pan into the fire. They begin to fear change in and of itself. Like a drowning man who tightens his grip on a leaky life raft as he continues to float further away from shore, Radically Demotivated employees become increasingly committed to the companies they work for as their demotivation becomes increasingly radicalized. This dynamic makes Radical Demotivation™ a powerful technique for reducing turnover, which in turn reduces labor costs.

3. Acute Defensiveness

A third characteristic of Radically Demotivated employees is that they *become defensive very easily*. The most common defensive behaviors displayed include justifying and providing excuses for one's actions and opinions, attacking co-workers' actions and opinions, derogating others, blaming others for one's failures or shortcomings, and using hyperbole to describe one's achievements. For example, one warehouse employee being carefully monitored by Despair Labs boasted that he was able to eat 12 hot dogs in one sitting and then derogated a co-worker, calling him "pathetic" when the co-worker expressed an interest in eating healthy. Boasting about such dubious "talents" as hot dog consumption is commonplace and suggests that some employees still live with the hope of healing their wounded self-esteem by establishing a place at the top of an inconsequential pecking order. We encourage this behavior at Despair. Our research has shown that employees who reach the top of an inconsequential pecking order eventually realize that this is an achievement worthy only of an inconsequential person and gradually retreat, disappointed and ever more convinced of the futility of attempting to prop up their faltering self-esteem.

It is interesting to note that overtly defensive behaviors like those described above tend to be limited to interactions with peers and subordinates. While interacting with superiors, Radically Demotivated employees' defensiveness takes a much different form. Instead of being obnoxious, Radically Demotivated employees consistently engage in *compliant* behaviors. This appears to be an attempt at ingratiation, much like the behavior of a dog when it rolls onto its back in an attempt to get its master to scratch its belly. But unlike a dog that expects to be stroked by its master, Radically Demotivated employees are generally satisfied if they are simply able to avoid an overt expression of disapproval. Consequently, executives can generally ignore the ingratiating behavior without feeling any compulsion to affirm or stroke the employee.

Along this line, it is also worth noting that most Radically Demotivated employees eventually become acutely aware that the stature gap that exists between them and the executives they serve creates a hyper-dilution of the normal forms of currency used for ingratiation—fawning praise and slavish compliance. As a result of this dilution, ingratiating employees resort to the "hard currency" of longer hours and extra effort with no demand for increased compensation. This not only increases productivity and profits, it provides a strong repudiation of the destructive idea that job satisfaction and productivity are significantly correlated with one another.

4. Acute Self-Doubt

Fourth, Radically Demotivated employees *view the routine difficulties they encounter in the pursuit of challenging tasks as signs of their own failure or low skill.* Many successful people see challenging tasks as opportunities to learn. Despite the fact that he had over 1500 failed experiments, for example, Thomas Edison said he had never failed because he learned something from every failed experiment that got him closer to reaching his goal. In contrast, Radically Demotivated employees see every project as a *test of their current value* rather than as an opportunity to learn or grow. As a result, every difficulty is interpreted as an unspoken affirmation of their deepest fears: namely, that they are unskilled, unintelligent failures, and that their current lack of success is no mere temporary aberration—it is evidence that life really is fair and the "happy ending" they have frequently fantasized about may even be worse than their current "unhappy middle."

Given the constant challenge to their identity posed by difficult tasks, Radically Demotivated employees tend to *work very hard to try to convince themselves* of their own utility. Fortunately, this pathological need to prove the indeterminate has the unquestionable benefit of increasing productivity.

5. Lack Of Emotional Resilience

As might be expected from the fourth characteristic, Radically Demotivated employees have *very little emotional resilience in the face of difficulties.* As a result, when given challenging tasks, Radically

Demotivated employees tend to feel significant emotional distress. Every task is viewed as an assessment of their competence and value and difficult tasks produce acute feelings of incompetence and worthlessness. At first glance this may appear to be a weakness with the Radical Demotivation™ approach to employee relations, but it's important to keep in mind that conflicted, self-loathing emotional responses do not mean that an employee cannot adequately complete the assigned task. It just means that he will experience little or no job satisfaction in the process. But given the chronically low correlations between job satisfaction and productivity, any objections due to a lack of job satisfaction quickly become irrelevant. In fact, in most cases, the negative emotions will actually help accelerate the process of Radical Demotivation™. More important than that, however, is the impact these toxic emotions have on productivity. Employees who want to avoid the sting of uncontrolled, self-induced humiliation will work very hard, much harder than those who are possessed by arrogance and self-satisfaction.

6. Low Self-Esteem

Given the above characteristics, it should be no surprise that Radically Demotivated employees also have *low self-esteem in regard to their historic (non)achievements and their work life in general.* Given the pro-self-esteem propaganda that has dominated the cultural consciousness over the last three decades, this may sound like an undesirable side effect of Radical Demotivation™. In reality, however, low self-esteem is a rational response to the staggering realization that the investment of one's time, talent, and resources have produced little more than a life destined for acutely compounding disappointment. Indeed, the case can be made that the emergence of low self-esteem is one of the clearest signs that the employee has successfully dropped an anchor in the stormy harbor of accurate self-perception.

As the self-esteem of your employees gradually dissipates to an imperceptible level, the psychological vacuum this "cleansing" creates is correspondingly filled with a humility that is born of an acute recognition of their meager economic utility. For most employees, this produces a profound sense of shame when they are in the presence of the truly accomplished, such as yourself. This potent emotional cocktail eliminates any need for employee recognition programs; employees not only cease believing they merit any positive recognition, they fear that any attention given them will simply highlight the source of their shame. More importantly, though, the money you save through the elimination of such programs improves the bottom line, which is your mandate.

7. Intense Risk-Aversion

The negative emotions that Radically Demotivated employees experience when faced with challenging tasks cause them to be *very risk-averse*. This eliminates the irrational, peevish demands for "empowerment" and autonomy that are so common among the victims of the Noble Employee Myth. Instead, Radically Demotivated employees are focused on doing what *their superiors want them to do*. Rather than attempting to "make their mark" on the organization through innovation, initiative, or whatever euphemistic cliché they can come up with, Radically Demotivated employees are "satisfied" simply to let their labor be an extension of the ambition and initiative of the executives they serve.

I should note that a potential downside of the intense risk-aversion of Radically Demotivated employees is that they prefer simple, nonchallenging tasks that do not threaten their perceptions of competence. As a result, *it is essential that you constantly push them outside of their comfort zones.* In so doing, you will not only make them more productive, but you will cause them to live in a near-constant state of angst, uncertainty, and insecurity. These are three nutrients in the emotional fertilizer that can help Radical Demotivation™ take root and flourish in your employees' souls.

8. Chronic Pessimism

Eighth, *Radically Demotivated employees develop a deep and abiding pessimism.* They can suck the gall and wormwood out of the most objectively pleasant circumstances. Once your employees get to this stage of the Radical

Demotivation™ process, they develop very interesting interpretive patterns that hasten the development of the other characteristics. Specifically, Radically Demotivated employees develop two complementary patterns of interpreting their responsibility for their relative success or failure. First, they are quick to accept responsibility for failure when confronted by a superior, whether they were the cause of the failure or not. In the face of failure they naturally interpret their contribution as inadequate: They believe they either did the wrong thing or not enough of the right thing. In either case, they see their contribution as a major component of the failure event. The second interpretive pattern has to do with the way they interpret the causes for success. Rather than seeing themselves as major contributors to success, they discount their contribution and attribute their success to luck or a fluke (Seligman, 1998). These pessimistic interpretive patterns serve to reinforce their lowered self-esteem and hasten the Demotivational process.

One early beta-tester of Radical Demotivation, his own education steeped in Social Learning theory, has charged that the development of a deep and abiding pessimism is a shortcoming of the Radical Demotivational approach because the interpretive patterns that spring from that state are not necessarily true. In reality, however, this fostering of pessimism is one of the most robust strengths of Radical Demotivation™. The truth is that pessimistic employees not only make more accurate judgments than their optimistic counterparts (Seligman, 1998), they also grow to despise the naïveté and utterly unwarranted self-regard that characterizes their optimistic coworkers. In fact, many pessimistic employees will eventually engage in efforts to undermine the esteem of their assured brethren so as to achieve greater coherence among the elements of their social environment. Those who demonstrate an aptitude for this may justify consideration for a position of leadership in your Radically Demotivating organization.

9. Pervasive Sullenness

Finally, *Radically Demotivated employees tend to be chronically sullen.* Our research indicates that this is a pervasive attitude, but not a permanent one. The acuteness and duration of the sullenness stage varies greatly depending upon the employee's internal resistance to the Radical Demotivation™ process: The greater the resistance, the more protracted and more acute the sullenness. Over time employees learn that resistance is useless and they experience something analogous to the Stockholm Syndrome (the phenomenon experienced by hostages when they begin to bond with their captors and view their rescuers with suspicion and fear). At this point, your employees will have made peace with their destiny, will have convinced themselves that they enjoy working for you, and will begin to actively search for ways to make *you happy, even at their own expense.* When this happens, you will have successfully orchestrated a complete role-reversal of that prescribed by the Noble Employee Myth, and in so doing, you will restore equilibrium to the executive-employee relationship.

It should be clear that embarking upon a program of Radical Demotivation™ does not require filling your company with unskilled slackers who require more oversight than they are worth. Instead, it is an unobtrusive process of persistently changing the way your employees see themselves, their role in the company, and their sense of entitlement. Moreover, this process leaves your employees' skills intact and may even enhance them in some cases. It should also be clear that the "negative" emotions that most employees will experience in the process are not just natural, they are also instrumental in reinforcing the veracity of the path you are leading your employees down. In that regard, they are can be considered "positive" emotions. But the key benefit—above any organizational optimization and heightened self-knowledge of your employees—is financial. Radical Demotivation increases profitability by raising productivity and lowering costs. In so doing, it improves shareholder value and the incentive value of executive profit-sharing plans. As an executive who has been where you are, I can confidently say "there is hope." You can not only have it all, you can spend a lot less to get it. Progress begins when you boldly start a covert program of Radical Demotivation™.

THE PRAGMATIC CHOICE:
Four Reasons Why
Demotivation is Superior

To believe in one's dreams
is to spend all of one's life asleep.
—CHINESE PROVERB

A fter reading the first two chapters I am sure that some of you are a bit conflicted. In spite of your good intentions, you know that your varied attempts to motivate your employees have not produced the improvements to morale or productivity that you had been led to expect. Yet the intrinsic weaknesses of your employees move you to pity rather than disgust. They may remind you of your own pre-adolescent "awkward stage," or of a much pitied relative who is disproportionately afflicted by a different gene pool, or of the pathetic recipients of your charitable giving. Whatever the reason, you are so bound by the Noble Employee Myth that you're quicker to assume that your employees' redemption lies in some future self-improvement seminar rather than in a demotivating confrontation with reality. My goal in this chapter is to help those of you who waver; to replace your timidity with temerity by providing several compelling arguments for adopting Radical Demotivation™ as your management paradigm.

In my research I have identified four basic reasons why Radical Demotivation™ is superior to the various theories concocted by the purveyors of the Noble Employee Myth. This is not an exhaustive list by any means, but it should be sufficient to convince even the most skeptical among you of the pragmatic superiority of demotivation over the idealistic folly of motivation.

Before I get started, however, I feel the need to remind of your solemn duty as an executive. Though the architects of the Noble Employee Myth would have you believe otherwise, *you are a trustee of the capital of your shareholders, not a custodian of the malformed fantasies of your employees.* Your charge is to increase excess, discretionary capital, not subsidize the ego-gratifying delusions of your employees. Should you confuse your own purpose and subsume your goals to those of your employees, you may one day find yourself in the same unfortunate state as them, banished from the corridors of power by the decisions you have made.

RADICAL DEMOTIVATION™ ACKNOWLEDGES THE NATURAL WEAKNESSES OF YOUR EMPLOYEES

Unlike motivational programs that attempt to overcome your employees' weaknesses, Radical Demotivation™ capitalizes upon the natural weaknesses of your underachieving employees and enables *you* to overcome. Before you can do that, however, you have to eradicate the Noble Employee Myth from your subconscious and face the truth about your employees' condition. Have you ever considered all the time, money, and effort you've spent trying to get your employees to feel good about you, the company, their jobs, or themselves? Think about all the interactions you've had with employees when you tempered what you said to prevent them from feeling isolated or discouraged. Consider all of the money you've spent upon benefits, reward programs, or incentives. Now ask yourself: Have they worked? Do your employees really care about you and the company? Are they productive, optimistic, satisfied, and grateful? Of course not. Despite all you have done for them, most of your employees still have chips on their shoulders, still claim they are underappreciated, and still expect you to do more.

When confronted with the bitter harvest of your employees' entitlement inspired distemper, you've no doubt been tempted to ask yourself how and why you've failed. According the Noble Employee Myth, your employees should be happy and satisfied by now, but they aren't. This is because your employees are the embodiment of a psychological version of the entropy principle, a *mental* entropy that I call Mentropy™. According to the entropy principle, the natural world tends toward disorder and decay. In similar fashion, Mentropy™ states that your employees' psyches, their very selves, also tend toward disorder and decay. In other words, according to the Mentropy™ principle it is easier to be slow-witted than it is to be quick-witted; easier to be lazy than it is to be industrious; easier to be careless than it is to be disciplined. For this reason you shouldn't be surprised if your employees are obnoxious, indolent, and idiotic, and don't respond to your attempts to improve them.

As an executive, you need to realize that Mentropy™ will prevent most of your employees from reaching the goals they have set for themselves. No less an authority than Og Mandino, the optimist/motivational author *par excellence,* said the odds were 75 to 1 that an individual would not invest 10 minutes per workday in a simple task that would triple his income within a year (Mandino, 1972). Prophets and sages throughout the ages have realized that your employees are simply unwilling to do what it takes to succeed: to confront and overcome their weaknesses, to take the necessary risks, and to persevere in the face of difficulties. Instead, they will race through life seeking the path of least resistance. They will burrow their way deep into the comfort zone and ultimately, they will finish disappointed. This process was eloquently described by Mihaly Csikszentmihalyi, a psychologist who spent a portion of his career studying the psychology of optimal experiences and why people do or do not experience them. He notes that most people go through life ignoring the banality of their existence because they believe that one day their fortunes will change and life will be better. Nevertheless, by middle age they cannot avoid

MEDIOCRITY

IT TAKES A LOT LESS TIME
AND MOST PEOPLE WON'T NOTICE THE DIFFERENCE
UNTIL IT'S TOO LATE.

wondering whether their best days are behind them and whether the good life they always expected to live will ultimately elude them *(see illustration)*. He describes the normal adult's eventual confrontation with his lack of achievement as follows:

> But inevitably the bathroom mirror shows the first white hairs, and confirms the fact that those extra pounds are not about to leave; inevitably eyesight begins to fail and mysterious pains begin to

shoot through the body. Like waiters in a restaurant starting to place breakfast settings on the surrounding tables while one is still having dinner, these intimations of mortality plainly communicate the message: Your time is up, it's time to move on. When this happens, few people are ready. "Wait a minute, this can't be happening to me. I haven't even begun to live. Where's all that money I was suppose to have made? Where are all the good times I was going to have?" (Csikszentmihalyi, 1990, P. 12)

As you can see, you have no reason to feel guilty or responsible for your employees' inevitable failure. You are not preventing them from becoming all they can be, *you are simply forcing them to reckon with all that they already are.*

RADICAL DEMOTIVATION™ IS EASY TO LEARN

You have probably noticed that most motivational programs inspired by the Noble Employee Myth place at least part of the responsibility for poor employee performance on the shoulders of managers and executives. For example, executives are often told that defiant and unfocused employee behaviors are a function of their particular "leadership style," and that rather than expecting their employees to learn how to accommodate their style, they need to learn to use different styles to accommodate their employees. Similarly, they are given instructions on how to improve their listening, the feedback they provide, the way they resolve conflict, the goals they set, and so on. Yet any business leader who has jumped on the self-improvement treadmill in the hope of improving employee performance has learned that it is no more effective than using a treadmill as a means of transportation.

One of the chief benefits of Radical Demotivation™ is that it enables executives to be themselves. It does not constrain you or your managers by enrolling you in annoying, ineffective self-improvement programs designed to remove the burden of productivity from where it rightfully belongs—your employees. As a result, the skills required to implement a program of Radical Demotivation™ are very easy to learn and employ. In most cases, the process of acquiring these useful skills is simply one of unlearning the ineffective "skills" taught by the motivational industry. It's a bit like learning to eat dessert again after years on a low-sugar diet. Imagine *not* having to worry about whether your employees found their jobs "fulfilling," or whether they identified with your vision, or whether you had to get their "buy in" on your decisions. Imagine not having to choose your words carefully to avoid offending someone, or trying to be fair. This freedom is the promise of Radical Demotivation™.

We have a manager at Despair, Inc. who came to us after spending years in a huge, bureaucratic consulting firm. She quickly learned the power (and pleasure) of using Radical Demotivation™ to manage her warehouse employees. This manager joined our company after a months-long process of learning that she was not as marketable as she had been led to believe by her outplacement specialist. During the interview process she became intrigued by our vision of despair at Despair, Inc. But as can be expected, she was initially conflicted by our approach due to years of exposure to high doses of motivational propaganda. All of that changed one fateful day.

One morning, for a variety of reasons, she was in an unusually foul mood: Her fiancé had recently grown distant and that morning had recommended that she look into plastic surgery, traffic on the way to work had been a bear, and she accidentally hit a small stray dog as she took an opening and rushed toward the freeway exit. As a result of hitting the dog, she was followed off the freeway by several incensed drivers who hurled threats and obscenities at her. Frightened by the animal lovers, she called the police. When the police arrived the animal lovers were already gone, but they issued her a littering violation for leaving the slain animal in the road.

As a result of the morning's events she arrived to work about two hours late. Belatedly checking on the productivity of her group she found that surprisingly they were right on target for meeting their daily box-packing quota, even without her oversight. She reasoned that she had been too easy on them in the past and proceeded to raise the productivity goal by 10%.

As she walked back to her station, she overheard some of her employees grumble derogatory obscenities, one of which included the word "fat," but she was in too bad a mood to care and ignored them for the rest of day. After her team had left for the day, she found that they had increased their productivity by 7% and she experienced what she described as an epiphany. Not only had she increased productivity by 7%, she had a reason to chide her employees the following day for missing the new target by 3%. Moreover, she had not spent her day encouraging and coaching her employees, she simply expressed the raw emotion of a manager on the edge who was sick and tired of treating her employees like wayward adolescents in need of love and understanding.

From that day forward, she has continued to be one of our top performers. Over the past two years she has increased the productivity of her group several times without a corresponding increase in compensation for any of them. None of the employees on her team believes that they have any transferable skills and therefore none of them believes that they have a future outside of Despair, Inc. As a result of their fully-realized Radically Demotivated state, turnover is non-existent and absenteeism is limited to cases when an employee is severely ill with a contagious disease. When asked what she likes best about Despair, Inc., she offered, "It gives me the freedom to be myself."

RADICAL DEMOTIVATION™ SEPARATES
THE AUTHENTIC FROM THE ARTIFICIAL

One of the most important tasks for any executive is to identify those employees who are best suited to become the next generation of leaders (Bossidy & Charan, 2002). But executives who are duped by the Noble Employee Myth tend to have so much confidence in the average employee that they fail at this crucial task. If you asked them whether they were hiring, promoting, and developing the best candidates, they would naturally say that they were, but their naïve faith in the goodness and potential of their employees prevents them from making sound judgments about their employees.

Radical Demotivation™ aids executives in this task by winnowing the wheat from the chaff, separating the *authentically* motivated employees from those who are *artificially* motivated. Authentically motivated employees have several characteristics that make them potential candidates to take over the mantle of corporate leadership. They tend to be intelligent, articulate, and self-disciplined. They are resilient in the face of obstacles and prefer solving problems to assigning blame. They hate getting mired down in gossip and interpersonal politics and they treat others with respect. In contrast, the artificially motivated employees display many patterns of behavior that are frequently mistaken for signs of competence, but they lack the inner strength and discipline required to be effective executives. Artificially motivated employees love corporate pep rallies, office parties, and glad-handing with executives. They tend to demonstrate remarkable enthusiasm for whatever incentive plans the company rolls out, though they are rarely able to articulate the relevant details of those plans. They love to attend meetings so they try to sit on as many committees as possible. It is common to hear them talk about how hard they work, but they rarely talk about anything they have accomplished. They are very skilled at ingratiation and use flattery to build social relationships in the hope of deflecting attention from their lack of genuine achievement. They are generally well connected to different social networks. This gives the appearance of widespread respect, but in reality they just love gossiping about others. These behaviors are often interpreted as signs of commitment and initiative. In reality they are the unfocused activities of a group of posers who cravenly seek security and acceptance. These are not the type of people who are fit to be executives.

Most executives believe they can easily spot the difference between the authentically motivated and the artificially motivated in their ranks, but sadly, that is not true. Many artificially motivated employees advance well beyond what their skills and abilities should allow because their incompetence goes undetected. This is because motivational programs inspired by the Noble Employee Myth unintentionally produce false criteria for evaluating employees, and these criteria favor the artificially motivated over the authentically motivated. How? The artificially motivated thrive on motivational programs and *their enthusiastic, unproductive activity is seen as evidence that the motivational program is working*. In contrast, authentically motivated employees are generally uninspired by motivational programs, particularly those that appeal to narcissism rather than responsibility. Moreover, genuinely motivated employees are often critical of motivational programs—they regard them as condescending, unenlightened, and a waste of time and money. When faced with this contrast, executives who have had their judgment impaired by the Noble Employee Myth naturally assume that the artificially motivated employee is the true leader who is committed to the company's goals. When the time comes to promote someone they pass over the authentically motivated employee for her less competent counterpart.

Once an artificially motivated employee has budgetary authority, she continues spending money on unnecessary motivational programs. Since she rightfully attributes her own ascendancy to past motivational programs, she genuinely believes that such programs are a key to success. What she fails to realize is that personal success in the form of organizational ascendancy is not the same as productivity or competence. Consequently, the motivational programs this type of employee pays for do nothing more than create a system in which other artificially motivated employees are given preference over their authentically motivated cohorts. Over time, the organization ends up with several layers of ill-suited, artificially motivated middle managers who have no idea what they are doing. This is one of the reasons why so many organizations end up with redundant, unproductive, wasteful bureaucracies despite having invested huge sums of money in motivational programs to prevent that very thing from happening.

Radical Demotivation™ prevents this malignancy from taking root in an organization. It does this by transforming employees who are seeking to be artificially motivated into employees who are genuinely demotivated. How? By denying them the affirmation their narcissistic souls crave and by rendering meaningless the unproductive activity they are typically so proud of. Once employees realize they will not be rewarded for meaningless activity, they cease to volunteer for committees, their enthusiasm for pep rallies and incentive programs wanes, and they avoid confrontation with executives out of fear of inadvertently disclosing areas of incompetence they have successfully concealed. A program of Radical Demotivation™ also sets the stage for the authentically motivated to demonstrate why they are naturally suited to become the next generation of executives. Because they focus on accomplishment rather than activity, they humbly take comfort in the skills they have acquired and work hard to develop new ones along the way. They are impervious to Radical Demotivation™ because they do not begin from a point of baseless arrogance. They would rather hear justifiable criticism than be praised by those who don't know any better. They find recognition a cheap substitute for genuine accomplishment and place little value on pep rallies and plaques. Motivational programs obscure these important qualities, but Radical Demotivation™ allows them to shine.

RADICAL DEMOTIVATION™ PRODUCES THE SAME RESULTS FOR LESS MONEY

At this point, some of you may still prefer ineffective motivational programs over Radical Demotivation™ because you would rather have happy, enthusiastic employees than those who are sullen, introspective, and compliant. You do not mind spending more on wages and benefits, you believe escalating employee demands are an important part of organizational development, shareholder value is a tertiary concern, and you believe that the company has a responsibility to make its employees as happy as possible. You need to understand that this is a false choice. There is no way to create employees who are happy, enthusiastic, satisfied and productive. If there were, it would have happened a long time ago and the perpetual distrust, division, and unarticulated rancor that exists between executives and employees would cease to exist. Instead, over time, Radical Demotivation™ and ineffective motivational programs produce nearly the same results. The difference is that Radical Demotivation™ produces results that are exploitable, and it does it in a lot less time for a lot less money. Let me explain why this is so.

Motivational stimulation is best understood in the context of a broader, cyclical process of hope, disillusionment, and despair. As "The Motivation Cycle" *(Figure 1)* illustrates, most employees who are

FIGURE 1. THE MOTIVATION CYCLE

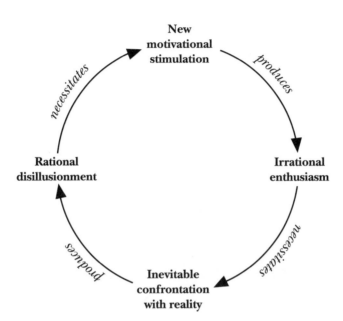

exposed to a motivational stimulus initially experience *irrational enthusiasm.* For a time after the stimulation, they believe that they are winners, that love is the answer, and that they are just one failure away from success. After a period of enthusiastic floundering, however, the employees are jarred back to reality by their inevitable confrontation with the coolly rational cause-and-effect relationships of an indifferent universe. In contrast to the way they felt after the motivational elation, their confrontation with reality leads them to conclude they *are* losers, that love hurts, and that they are just one success away from certain failure.

The pain inherent in this experience naturally produces rational disillusionment—the conviction that hope is little more than youthful folly and that one must accept and adapt to one's limitations. Over time, however, the disillusioned employee becomes "open" to new motivational stimuli, though it must be of a different type, quality, or dosage than what the employee has already experienced. This is because the Motivation Cycle inoculates the employee against the efficaciousness of any prior stimuli, thereby requiring increasingly seductive motivational propaganda to overcome the employee's self-protective emotional resistance.

MOTIVATION

IF A PRETTY POSTER AND A CUTE SAYING ARE ALL IT TAKES TO MOTIVATE YOU, YOU PROBABLY HAVE A VERY EASY JOB. THE KIND ROBOTS WILL BE DOING SOON.

The escalation of this dosage follows a rather predictable path. Employees often begin with a motivational poster, something as innocuous as a kitten hanging onto the branch of a tree with the caption "Hang in there, baby." When this loses its ability to inspire hope in employees' hearts, they will graduate to more focused messages targeted specifically at their achievement motivation, messages that address items like their attitude, persistence, or risk-taking. Posters, note cards, screensavers, mousepads, or coffee mugs that contain motivational aphorisms are all considered "low dosage" because they quickly decay into low-grade ambient stimuli. An employee can see a mousepad every day without thinking about the motivational message emblazoned upon it.

When quips and aphorisms no longer stimulate their delusions, employees will often begin listening to self-help tapes or reading self-help books to try to recover that magic feeling they had the first time they believed that success was a journey rather than a destination. These tapes or books will typically focus on something like the employee's attitude, sub-conscious, priorities, fears, or communication skills. Given the number of tapes and books available, an employee can stay at this stage for many years, always "learning" but never able to live the promise of the message.

Our research suggests that maxims, aphorisms, tapes and books are "gateway" motivational stimuli to other more addictive forms. Once books and tapes are no longer satisfying, employees will often begin attending one-day seminars with motivational speakers. At this point, they are often so addicted to the motivational high that they will travel for hours to listen to their favorite speakers. Inevitably, however, the excitement of the motivational seminar wears off, becomes commonplace, and is no longer stimulating. At that point, the employee is probably a full fledged "Motivational Junkie" and is at risk of getting mixed up in motivational retreats, "trust falls," ropes courses, and/or wilderness adventures. More often than not, when all of this has produced an acute level of confusion and despondency, the employee will take the final step and begin fire-walking. Once employees realize that they can walk through fire but are still terrified to call a prospect or confront a coworker, there is no place to go but to the psychological equivalent of the Hanoi Hilton that we call Radical Demotivation™.

When The Motivation Cycle is modeled graphically along with time along the **Y** axis, it reveals its true form with dreadful irony—it is nothing more than a downward spiral, or as we prefer to call it a "Demotivation Vortex" *(see Figure 2 on following page).* Those subjected to this vicious cycle eventually lose any ability to experience even the slightest stimulation when exposed to motivational stimuli. They are, in effect, Radically Demotivated.

It generally takes employees who are stuck in the downward spiral of the Motivation Cycle somewhere between five and twenty years to pass through the Demotivation Vortex, depending upon their degree of lucidity and/or natural optimism. But by implementing a program of

FIGURE 2. THE DEMOTIVATION VORTEX

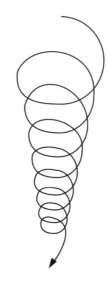

Singularity of Indignity

Radical Demotivation™ you can achieve the same result in 18 months or less. Furthermore, motivational speakers, seminars, and retreats are very expensive. An in-demand motivational speaker can command over $60,000 for a single presentation. In contrast, Radical Demotivation™ requires no additional out-of-pocket expenses. The money you save by eliminating such wasteful programs from your budget can be reinvested in those things that have a genuine and lasting ability to inspire you and your fellow executives, for whom success is both a journey *and* a destination.

I hope it is clear by now that Radical Demotivation™ is a superior approach to your human relations problems. It does not try to make your employees into something they are not, the techniques are easy to learn, and it separates the authentically motivated from the artificially motivated. More importantly, however, it is demonstrably superior to motivational industry solutions, achieving similar results in far less time, at no cost, and with several additional benefits which I will detail in subsequent chapters. Properly implemented, Radical Demotivation™ has the power to lower your costs of doing business, to decrease employee attrition, even while raising productivity and profitability. Put bluntly, it is both an executive dream and employee nightmare come true.

CORE VALUES:
Helping Your Employees Understand What Really Matters

It is a folly to expect men to do all
that they may reasonably be expected to do.
—RICHARD WHATELY

Over the past century, organizational theorists have used different metaphors to illuminate their understanding of the way organizations function (Bolman & Deal, 1991; Morgan, 1986). For the first three quarters of the century the *machine* and *biological* metaphors were the dominant ways of understanding organizations. The machine metaphor led researchers to focus on understanding how to create organizations that were precise, reliable, and efficient. (It is still part of our business vernacular to describe an organization's operation as a "well-oiled machine.") The biological metaphor, on the other hand, led researchers to focus on the systems that enabled an organization to learn, grow, adapt, and most importantly, survive. In the last quarter of a century, however, it has become very popular to view organizations as *cultures* (Deal & Kennedy,

1982; Smircich, 1983), and the analytical attention has shifted from efficiency and survival to patterns of meaning and value and how they are enacted in organizations (Weick, 1979).

One of the conclusions reached by analysts using the culture metaphor is that leaders who want to create an enduring, visionary company need to clarify their *core values* (Collins & Porras, 1994). These are the values that are most important to the direction of the organization and to the decision-making within it. As consultants Francis Gouillart and James Kelly (1995) put it:

> Values define the firm's nonnegotiable behaviors, as well as provide the guideposts for navigating through gray areas. They set forth the "do's" and the "don'ts," the "always, under any circumstances" and "the never, under any circumstances." They are the essence of the corporate culture. . . . They are expression of its "personality," determining its attractiveness to employees, customers, and all others who have a say in whether the firm will prosper. (p. 46)

Similarly, Collins and Porras (1994) define core values as "the organization's essential and enduring tenets—a small set of general guiding principles . . . not to be compromised for financial gain or short term expediency" (p. 73). The core values of visionary companies serve as the stakes in the ground and the degree of adherence to them is a measure of the company's integrity.

Some of you are probably wondering what this discussion of core values has to do with Radical Demotivation™. You've no doubt heard plenty of culture-talk about values, vision, rituals, myths, and other academic chimera, and despite the insights they supposedly provide, you have found that trying to use these ideas to build your organization is a bit like using balsa wood to build a house. I empathize with you and I have good news: The benefit to be gained by articulating your core values is not limited to those who want to create visionary companies. It is also useful for executives who want to implement a program of Radical Demotivation™. This is because, to be effective, core values have got to be authentically lived out within the organization. As Collins and

Porras (1994) emphasized in their discussion of the importance of developing a core ideology:

> When articulating and codifying core ideology, the key step is to capture what is authentically believed. . . . It's not what [visionary companies] believed as much as *how deeply they believed it* (and how consistently their organizations lived it). Again, the key word is *authenticity.* (pp. 75–76)

The requirement for authenticity is a huge lever for prying open the door of hope and introducing confusion, cynicism, and despair into the organization. When an executive violates the values that she (a) declares to be those of "the organization," (b) claims to be an adherent of, and (c) uses to judge the attitudes, decisions, and behaviors of her employees, she makes it clear that the values have different meanings for different people, and this inconsistency introduces an unsettling uncertainty into the organization. Moreover, *her* violation of the values suggests they are impractical, inconvenient, or overly constraining. When those same values continue to be used as part of the criteria for evaluating employees, they quickly learn that the constraining force of the values and the security they provide are dependent upon where they stand relative to the fault lines of power that run throughout the organization. The less power the employee has, the more they are required to exemplify the company's core values, and vice versa. This is what I call the Power/Values Differential™ (PVD).

Clearly, this is a lesson that must be learned by every employee, but it would be imprudent for executives to openly acknowledge that this is so. Therefore, Radical Demotivation™ is designed to maximize the impact of the PVD by denying its very existence. This is done by developing a *collusive* relationship with your employees; one that *systematically suppresses acknowledgment of the dynamics that violate the relationship in order to maintain the relationship.* To understand how this is accomplished as part of a comprehensive program of Radical Demotivation™, I first need to discuss the nature of collusion and its variants. After the discussion of collusion, I will give you some practical guidelines for articulating your core values, introducing them into the organization, and reinforcing them in routine interaction.

A WORD OR THREE ON COLLUSION

Collusion is a psychoanalytic term in the same family as *il*lusion and *de*lusion. All of them refer to a systemic misapprehension of reality, but collusion differs in that it requires two parties to participate in and reinforce the fiction. In most cases, collusive relationships entail complementary misapprehensions of the nature of the relationship, such that both parties derive different, unacknowledged benefits from maintaining their shared delusion (Laing, 1969). Historically, collusion has been seen as a feature of interpersonal relationships, but the results of our experiments at Despair Labs indicate that the psychological dynamics underlying the collusive relationship can be fruitfully applied at work. In our research, we have identified three types of collusion that employees experience.

Enlightened Collusion. Enlightened collusion takes place when at least one of the parties realizes that the identities they are affecting constitute a fiction, but due to the irrelevance of the issue at hand nobody cares. As a result, enlightened collusion tends to be playful rather than pathological. An example of enlightened collusion is a middle-aged man who still wants to see himself as athletic as he was in his twenties. He knows his tennis game is not what it used to be, but he still likes to see himself as a tough competitor. His wife is equally aware of his declining performance, but continues to tell him things like "You could have beat Andre Agassi today." They both know that barring divine intervention he would have been utterly humiliated by Agassi, but it makes him feel good to hear it and she enjoys supporting him. This is the most innocuous, and for our purposes, the least effective form of collusion.

Covert Collusion. Covert Collusion occurs when both parties derive so much from the relationship that neither of them is willing to entertain the idea that there is anything pathological about it. The paradigmatic example is the wealthy older man whose third marriage is to a twenty-something trophy wife. Their covert collusion magically transforms his money into wit, compassion, and charm, while her beauty psychologically transforms her into an intelligent, stimulating soul-mate. This type of collusion will naturally occur among your employees as they resort to progressively more futile ways to anchor their identities in something more stable and more tolerable than their own self-perception. As an executive, this is something you cannot control, though you can enjoy it when you see it.

Demotivated Collusion. Demotivated Collusion occurs when one of the parties to the relationship is completely engulfed and subjugated by an identity imposed upon him by the other party. Demotivated Collusion requires a substantial power differential on the key issues over which the relationship is defined, coupled with the willingness on the part of the more powerful party to impose his will on the other. In the process of engulfing an individual or group in a collusive relationship, the engulfed party will typically resist at a visceral, non-conscious level. This is an essential part of the process because the resistance is usually mixed with guilt, anxiety, anger, despair, and indifference (Laing, 1969). Over time, however, after the resistance is overcome and the collusion is in place, the subjugated party will vehemently deny collusion and any residual negative emotion. Instead, he will completely identify with the subjugated identity and claim it as his own.

Some of you may be wondering what this discussion of collusion, as interesting as it is, has to do with your company's core values. The answer is very simple: *A program of Radical Demotivation™ requires that you violate your core values and then subjugate your employees into a collusive relationship that leads them to deny the violation and reaffirm the values.* In so doing, your employees will learn to live with the disjuncture between their public profession and their private anguish. This disjuncture will contribute to the process of surrendering their identities to you and your executive team, and this will eventually lead to the state of Radical Demotivation™. As Psychotherapist R. D. Laing (1969) said, "A slave may collude with his master in being a slave to save his life, even to the point of carrying out orders that are self-destructive" (p. 90). This, clearly, is the promise of Radical Demotivation™.

GUIDELINES FOR DEVELOPING CORE VALUES

As mentioned earlier, a visionary organization's core values must be authentically believed and lived—particularly by the organization's leadership—if they are to provide their intended inspiration and guidance to the employees. Since Radical Demotivation™ replaces inspiration and guidance with collusion as the intended purpose for articulating the company's core values, authenticity is unnecessary, and in some cases, it may be an obstacle. It is far more important that the stated values be *acceptable* to the employees than that they be *believed* by the executives. This will not only lead the employees to accept them as being authentic, it will make it easy for executives to violate them. Along that line, I have developed a few guidelines for developing core values that accelerate the process of Radical Demotivation™. If you already have a set of core values, I recommend that you update them using the guidelines in Table 2.

TABLE 2. DEVELOPING CORE VALUES

Guidelines for developing Core Values
Outsource the development of core values to consultants.
Do not anchor core values to transcendent social values.
Values should be stated as ambiguously as possible.
Values should be inconsistent with the company's strategic market focus.
Values should be anchored to objectives over which the employee has little control.
At least one value should be employee-oriented.

Guideline 1: *The development of your company's core values should be outsourced to consultants.* Executives are often tempted to perform this task themselves, but when they do, the values they articulate tend to have too many references to "profitability" and "shareholder value"—things for which their employees unashamedly have no regard. Consequently, they diminish the values' collusive potential. In contrast, a good consulting company with a core competency in public relations can craft a set of values that the average wage-earner will find seductively appealing.

Guideline 2: *Core Values should not be anchored to any transcendent social values.* Some companies are part of industries which have the potential to fulfill values that virtually all of us hold. For example, pharmaceutical companies can serve the public good by helping to eradicate disease and relieve pain. Though it is tempting to refer to socially transcendent values in the statement of the company's core values, you run the risk of creating a vision for your employees that is larger than the company. Many employees are willing to invest their lives into activities designed to "reduce suffering," "help the helpless," or "prolong life," even if doing so is difficult and the rewards are largely intangible. The problem with this is that it makes employees feel good about themselves, and despite the apparent benefits, it has the unintended consequence of reinforcing their narcissism. Fortunately, most of you own or run companies with little, if any, redeeming social value; they exist primarily to make you wealthy and to provide access, for both you and your family, to the stature and respect that only money can buy. Therefore your value statements should be peppered with phrases like "quality products," "industry leader," "innovative," and "customer satisfaction." These expressions have the benefit of generating widespread assent, while at the same time being devoid of any concrete semantic content.

Guideline 3: *Core values should be stated as ambiguously as possible.* Stating your values ambiguously has two key benefits: (a) Employees will tend to infuse ambiguous statement with their own meanings, thereby generating widespread assent among people who hold significantly different understandings of the statements; and (b) the multiple meanings afforded to an ambiguous statement make it more difficult to hold you accountable for violating the value (Eisenberg, 1984). In other words, it gives you "wiggle room" to violate the value and then deny it if you are challenged.

Guideline 4: *Your values should be inconsistent with your strategic market focus.* In their book *The Discipline of Market Leaders,* Treacy and Wiersema (1995) argue that companies must choose among one of three basic value disciplines, which are the primary values companies brings to customers: innovation, customer intimacy, or operational efficiency. In a Radically Demotivating corporate culture you need to determine your value discipline and state core values that conflict with it. For example, if your value discipline is operational efficiency and you have a budget that requires that you be lean and efficient, include a core value statement that references customer intimacy—something like "We go the extra mile for our customers." If you do, your employees will always be conflicted between the company's stated value (customer intimacy) and its clear, omnipresent, unarticulated value (operational efficiency). This creates a lose/lose situation for the employee. If he resolves the conflict in favor of the customer he can be chided for being slow, wasteful, or inefficient. On the other hand, if he resolves the conflict by efficiently discounting the customer's input, he can be reproved for violating the company's core values. Simultaneously, the value conflict creates a win/win situation for executives because it gives them the freedom to be inconsistent—or even capricious—in their criticism of the way employees choose to resolve the conflict. Since any criticism can be rooted in the competing value, the conflict has the effect of taking any institutional power that would be conferred on the employees by acting consistently with one of the values and transferring that power to the executive who trumps them by pointing to the competing value.

Very few employees will actually be able to articulate the conflict. Since most of the employees will accept your core values without question, the conflict will manifest itself as an ill-defined sense of failure that they will learn to live with. Those that do identify and articulate the conflict are at risk of becoming troublemakers. If they begin to spread their theories about the value conflict, fire them before lucidity spreads throughout the organization like a staph infection.

Guideline 5: *One or more values should be anchored to objectives over which the employee has little control.* The most obvious example of this principle is to create a core value that targets customer satisfaction. This is obviously no problem if everything goes well, but in the case of service or product failures the employee is caught between trying to follow the company's policy for handling such matters and satisfying the customers. If the employee has enough failure experiences and is reproached accordingly for violating the core value, he will begin to resent the customers and hold them in contempt. This will make it harder for him to treat them well and the entire demotivating process will begin again.

Guideline 6: *At least one of your core values should be employee-oriented.* I recommend that you include words like "respect," "care," and "dignity" in the statement of the core value. One of the old standards that has been used in scores of companies is very simply: "We treat our employees with respect and dignity." Your employees will naturally buy into the value and hope that it is true, but with every conflict they encounter that resolves against them they will grow increasingly cynical.

These guidelines are very easy to understand and implement, but don't be misled into believing they're unimportant. If you put them into practice, you will lay the symbolic foundation for an organization that needs a collusive relationship to stabilize the tempestuous psychological conflicts that bedevil your employees.

INTRODUCING THE CORE VALUES TO THE ORGANIZATION

After your core values are developed, you need to introduce them to the organization. The introduction of the core values is typically the launch of the covert program of Radical Demotivation™, so it is important that it is done well. Table 3 shows a few suggestions for introducing your core values to the organization.

TABLE 3. INTRODUCING VALUES TO THE ORGANIZATION

Guidelines for Introducing Values to the Organization
Values must be introduced by senior leadership.
The introduction should be a large, defining event.
Leadership must pledge allegiance to the values.
Employees must publicly profess allegiance to the values.
Employees should be given a "gift" that includes the values.

1. The core values should be introduced to the organization by the Senior Leadership. Everybody needs to know they that are sanctioned by the top brass.

2. The unveiling of the core values should be a large, defining event in the history of the organization. As many employees as possible should be present for the unveiling, either in person or virtually.

3. The leadership needs to place a rhetorical stake in the ground and pledge their commitment to the values. The key is to substitute the fanfare of the declaration for the drudgery of the implementation.

4. Elicit a positive response from your employees after each value is revealed. Continue doing this until almost everyone is responding positively, even if their response is half-hearted and motivated by a desire for you to quit asking them to respond. To this end, don't be hesitant to use ridicule to humiliate employees who appear uninterested in the company's values. Many employees who are not motivated by the values *will* be motivated to avoid public humiliation. This process is very important because it is the first step in developing the collusive relationship with your employees.

5. Give each of your employees something with the core values emblazoned upon it and refer to it as a "gift." It does not matter if it is a coffee mug, t-shirt, mouse pad, or poster. The key is to begin their bonding with the core values. The fact that you

gave them a gift will cause them to evaluate the values more positively and assimilate them more quickly, whether they realize it or not.

REINFORCING THE CORE VALUES IN DAILY LIFE

After the core values have been introduced, they need to be reinforced and violated in the day-to-day course of events. You will have to determine the best way to transgress your values, but here are a few suggestions for their routine reinforcement.

1. Fill the organization with reminders of the core values so that your employees cannot avoid them, even if they try to ignore them. You can do this by having motivational banners made to hang in every key operations center and smaller posters that are displayed in customer service areas. The fact that your employees spend their days in an environment that reminds them of the core values will accelerate their cynicism and make them acutely aware of routine violations.

2. Begin to make references to core values as the rationale for the decisions that are made in the organization. For example, if you buy pizza for group of employees to eat during a working lunch, say "This is because we treat our employees with respect and dignity." This will begin to teach your employees that "respect and dignity" includes denying them a lunch break, but having been bought off with a slice or two of pizza, they will overlook the eradication of substantive meaning from the core value. As this pattern repeats itself in a variety of ways over the months, your employees will slowly begin to surrender their original understanding of the core values and the hope it generated.

3. Learn to begin public addresses with, "In keeping with our core values. . ." or "According to our core values. . ." After this, it does not really matter what you say. The introductory phrase will reinforce the idea that the core values are in force, and any conflict with the values that might occur after the introductory phrase will produce uncertainty and confusion, both of which are rest stops on the way to Radical Demotivation™.

4. Finally, fire, demote, or discipline employees who point out the conflict between the core values and your decision-making. Enough said!

DEMOTIVATION

SOMETIMES THE BEST SOLUTION TO MORALE PROBLEMS IS
JUST TO FIRE ALL OF THE UNHAPPY PEOPLE.

If you are serious about Radical Demotivation™, it should be clear that you need to develop a set of core values, present them to the organization, reinforce them to staff and begin a program of systematic violation. As you set out on your journey, it is important to begin with the end in mind (Covey, 1989). Imagine a workforce that is wholly committed to a set of values that simultaneously constrain their behavior and afford you the freedom to do as you please. Imagine a situation in which the employees who are typically the most obstinate and indignant are rendered mute by their hypocritical violation of the values they have publicly professed their allegiance to. Now imagine that you don't have to imagine anymore. This is the promise of Radical Demotivation™.

ORGANIZATIONAL STORIES:
Teaching Employees Their Role
in the Organization

One of the most ordinary weaknesses of the human
intellect is to seek to reconcile contrary principles, and
to purchase peace at the expense of logic.
—ALEXIS DE TOCQUEVILLE

Thomas Watson Jr., son of the founder of IBM, often told the parable of a nature lover who loved to watch ducks fly south for the winter. Out of compassion, he began to feed them in the nearby pond. Over time, they ceased to fly south at all because the food in the pond was so plentiful. After a few years they became so fat that many of them could barely fly at all. Watson was known to conclude the story with the following application: "You can make wild ducks tame, but you can never make tame ducks wild again. . . . the duck who is tamed will never go anywhere anymore. We are convinced that business needs its wild ducks. And in IBM we try not to tame them" (Deal & Kennedy, 1982, p. 88). Watson used the parable of the ducks to communicate an important value to his employees: He did not believe in making things too comfortable at IBM. To do so made employees weak, helpless, and unproductive.

For decades organizational researchers have studied stories like this in an effort to understand how they affect organizational culture and performance. The research indicates that stories serve multiple functions, such as clarifying the values, vision, and purpose of the leadership; facilitating organizational identification; generating organizational commitment; and institutionalizing patterns of authority and decision making (Bolman & Deal, 1991; Deal & Kennedy, 1982; Martin, Feldman, Hatch & Sitkin, 1983; Martin & Powers, 1983; Morgan, 1986; Schein, 1991). For our purposes, the most important role stories play is *as symbolic tools that enable executives to unobtrusively shape the way employees view the company and their role within it.* By circulating the right types of stories—stories which include the themes most conducive to a program of Radical Demotivation™—executives can reinforce a powerful idea: that left to their own devices employees are hapless failures, powerless to achieve their hopes and dreams, but, due to the goodwill of the company, they can gratefully look forward to a life of servile obedience until their labor is no longer needed.

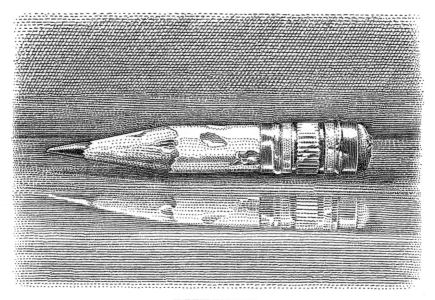

RETIREMENT

BECAUSE YOU'VE GIVEN SO MUCH OF YOURSELF TO THE COMPANY THAT
YOU DON'T HAVE ANYTHING LEFT WE CAN USE.

This type of unobtrusive control is achieved by manipulating what former Yale University professor Charles Perrow (1986) called the "cognitive premises" that prompt and guide action. He described the benefit of unobtrusive control as follows:

> The control of premises, while far more difficult to achieve, is even more effective [than other, more overt forms of control]. Here the subordinate voluntarily restricts the range of stimuli that will be attended to ("Those sorts of things are irrelevant," or "What has that got to do with the matter?") and the range of alternatives that would be considered ("It would never occur to me to do that"). (p. 129)

By manipulating employees' cognitive premises—i.e., their taken-for-granted assumptions, values, and patterns of cognition—executives can control those employees with less effort than is required by more direct methods, such as giving commands or developing policies. Moreover, once these cognitive premises are in place, compliance can be achieved without the conflict that often occurs with employees who believe they are "entitled" to greater respect or autonomy.

In this chapter I want to discuss the role of stories and storytelling in the organization as a specific type of symbolic management. Most executives are aware that employees share stories about what has happened in the organization, but in most cases they are painfully unaware of the content of those stories. Foolishly, they hope that their virtuous actions and intentions are understood and accurately disseminated throughout the organization, but if they actually heard what their employees said about them, how their motives and decisions are routinely maligned, they would realize that they have once again been duped by the Noble Employee Myth. Consequently, any comprehensive program of Radical Demotivation™ has to reclaim this symbolic territory from self-serving employees who fail to recognize their absolute dispensability and incorrectly believe themselves qualified to sit in judgment of their superiors.

In the discussion that follows, I'll begin by providing a brief description of the typical themes of organizational stories and the motives that drive them. It should come as no surprise that the myopic self-centeredness of your employees is revealed in the stories they tell. This will be followed by an overview of equity theory and how it bears upon organizational storytelling. Equity theory is a powerful framework for understanding the relationship between a company and its employees, and when used correctly, it can help you address many of the fundamental injustices that are characteristic of organizations plagued by the Noble Employee Myth. Finally, I'll discuss five principles for using stories to advance a program of Radical Demotivation™.

THE NARCISSISTIC IMPULSE OF EMPLOYEE STORYTELLING

In a surprisingly interesting examination of the types of stories that were told across several organizations, Stanford University Professor Joanne Martin and her colleagues found that employees tended to tell stories that helped them answer seven questions about what to expect from their companies in different situations (Martin, Feldman, Hatch, & Sitkin, 1983). The seven questions are:

1. What happens if I break the rules?
2. Is the big boss human?
3. Can the little person rise to the top?
4. Will I get fired?
5. Will the organization help me when I have to move?
6. How will the boss react to mistakes?
7. How will the organization deal with obstacles?

These questions are very revealing. All of them, in one way or another, focus on the needs and concerns of *the employees;* none of them focus on the needs of *the company.* Why don't employees tell stories that answer questions like, "How can I get more work done today?," "How can I get by on less?" or "How can I maximize shareholder value?" The reason why they don't is very simple: The stories they tell reflect a *fundamental narcissism* that is endemic to the average employee. This narcissism causes your employees to be preoccupied with their own "needs," dreams, and goals, often at the expense of you and/or the company. As part of a program of Radical Demotivation™, you have to dislodge their narcissistic reflex and create a selfless co-dependency that motivates your employees to seek the good of the company, independent of any personal benefit.

The Stanford study also found that organizational stories are often characterized by what can best be described as Accufession™, a communication pattern akin to psychological projection in which a speaker *accuses* one or more others of possessing the same motives, intentions, and characteristics that she embodies, though she typically denies possessing them, both to herself and to others. As such, Accufessions are often derogatory in nature, though they need not be. An executive who responds to an employee's failure with, "She tried her best but the odds were stacked against her" is as likely to be engaging in Accufession™ as an employee who says, "My boss is a greedy, selfish, dirtbag." The defining characteristic of the Accufession™ is that the *accusation* references the qualities of the *accuser* rather than the qualities of the *accused*. The Accufessional nature of the organizational stories employees told was evidenced by the fact that they included whiny, self-serving patterns of attribution that foolishly exonerated themselves from any responsibility for problems in the organization. Martin, et. al. (1983) described the *employees'* general pattern of attribution as follows:

> The top people are neither admirable nor approachable; status and competence are not matched; the organization shows few signs of caring about its people and their personal well-being; disruptions are neither minimized nor particularly justifiable; mistakes are not forgiven; and obstacles are problematic and difficult for the organization to overcome. (p. 447)

Clearly, this sort of brutish, self-serving misdiagnosis of the causality of organizational problems—which is so typical of employees—is a strong argument for the need for Radical Demotivation™. Left unchecked, employees who make these attributions can cause a whole host of problems, most of which will end up costing you money.

STORYTELLING AND EQUITY THEORY

Many executives are at a loss when I discuss this topic with them because they misunderstand the psychological principles involved in Radical Demotivation™. They say they have plenty of "bad stories" and "tales of oppression" circulating throughout their organizations, but their employees are still militant and demanding, they still waste the company's time and money without a hint of shame, and they are most productive when manufacturing excuses for their lack of achievement. They ask me where is the compliant sullenness, the loss of hope, and the self-loathing they had hoped for? It's clear that these executives have missed the nuance and subtlety of Radical Demotivation™. Unfortunately, stories of oppression tend to *support the belief that there is something wrong with the company rather than the employee,* thereby enabling employees to justify all sorts of antagonistic or spiteful behavior. Remember, Radical Demotivation™ is about changing your employees' perceptions of themselves, their role in the organization, and their expectations for the future. Therefore, you need to get them to fixate on their *real* failures, not your imagined ones.

One of the psychological principles I have found most useful in this regard is a component of Equity Theory (Adams, 1965; Walster, Walster, & Berscheid, 1978). According to Equity Theory, when an inequity exists in a relationship, the party who has benefited the most from the relationship (i.e., the exploiter) will be motivated to restore equity with the person who has under-benefited from the relationship (i.e., the victim). In general, equity can be restored in two ways: The exploiter can *compensate* the victim or the exploiter can *require less* from the victim. This opens a world of opportunities for the Radically Demotivating executive. As Walster, et. al., (1978) reported, exploiters apply these principles to restore equity in a variety of ways: "Uneasy transgressors may find relief by confessing their sins, in self-criticism, by apologizing and making reparation to their victim, or in promising to modify their future behavior" (p. 24). Clearly, this is in keeping with a vision of a Radically Demotivated workforce, but executives often get tripped up here because the Noble Employee Myth has taught them to see the employee as victim and the company as exploiter. But in the brave new world of Radical Demotivation™ those roles are reversed: The employee is the exploiter and the company is the victim. Therefore, Radically Demotivating executives have to find a way to affect a paradigm change that casts the employee as the exploiter and the company as the victim. One of the best ways to do that is through organizational stories.

Given this theoretical framework, it's easy to understand why stories of oppression do not have the Radically Demotivating effect one might expect. Instead, they cast the employee as a victim who has a "right" to expect redress from the company to restore equity to the relationship. It is important to use stories to create a contrary perception: that the company, despite repeated failures by its employees, patiently endures their incompetence and continues to employ them out of compassion, benevolence, or goodness. Once these cognitive premises are set, employees will unwittingly respond to their own failures with humiliation, confession, and a commitment to do a better job for the same pay in a hopeless attempt to restore equity to the relationship. With this in mind, there are several principles to keep in mind when sharing organizational stories.

PRINCIPLES OF STORYTELLING IN RADICALLY DEMOTIVATING ORGANIZATIONS

The veracity of a story is less important than its believability. As Bolman and Deal (1991) put it:

> The success of such stories is only partly related to their historical validity or empirical support. The central question is whether they are credible and persuasive to their audiences. A story, even a flawed story, will work if it speaks persuasively to the experience, values, and aspirations of the listeners. This is both the power and the danger of symbolic leadership. (p. 444)

Many executives are uncomfortable with this type of statement because they see it as an endorsement of lying. They reason that if they start to lie, they'll be no better than their employees. But the statement

ACHIEVEMENT

YOU CAN DO ANYTHING YOU SET YOUR MIND TO WHEN YOU HAVE VISION,
DETERMINATION, AND AN ENDLESS SUPPLY OF EXPENDABLE LABOR.

is not so much an endorsement of lying as it is an acknowledgment of the fact that every story is modified as it is told and re-told. Details are added or omitted, names are confused, hyperbole is introduced, motives hypothesized, and so on. Even if you tell a story with perfect accuracy, most of your employees remember it imperfectly. Moreover, post-modernism and deconstruction have un-tethered "the text" of a story from any traditional anchors to reality, thereby rendering believability the only salient quality of a story. Therefore, it is important to tell stories that make your case, even if the details are sketchy.

Success stories should portray the company and/or the executives as the protagonist(s), leaving non-executive contributions anonymous. The key here is to create a vision of the company as successful and victorious and its executives as heroes, while casting non-executives as nameless extras who are destined for obscurity *(see illustration)*. This teaches your employees to contribute to the common good without expecting any sort of special recognition. Moreover, most employees will feel lucky to be part of a successful organization and begin to admire you for virtues that you may not even possess. Once this begins to happen, they will tend to add resolution to their image of you-as-hero by naturally assuming you have additional character qualities not even referenced in the story (or stories). As this process progresses, your credibility will increase and your reality constraints will decrease; i.e., they will believe almost anything you say.

In failure stories, you should name individual employees as direct contributors to the failure and describe the company and/or its executives as victims of the malice, ingratitude, or incompetence of the employees. These stories will spread across your employees like a flu because of their gossipy quality, and also because they carry the prospect of public humiliation for one of their coworkers. You have probably noticed that insecure people with little purpose or vision in their lives can get very wrapped up in the lives of others and would rather gossip than eat. Consequently, these types of stories become food for their emaciated souls and give them a temporary reason to live. Moreover, as I mentioned in a previous chapter, many Radically Demotivated employees seek to reinforce their egos by establishing a place in an irrelevant pecking order. Stories that humiliate their coworkers give them an opportunity to mock those coworkers and "knock them down a peg or two," even when they are already right beside them on the bottom peg.

I recently witnessed the power of this principle at Despair, Inc. During a brainstorming session last year, Ng, a member of our "creative" team, suggested an idea for a particular product. Chad, another member of the team, said he did not find the idea particularly amusing and/or demotivating, and as a result, did not think it was worth pursuing. Nevertheless, the team adopted Ng's idea and turned it into a product. They discounted Chad's criticism because, as explained by Mandy, the Project Manager, "Chad always says that. He's an idiot. He hasn't got a creative bone in his body." Since Mandy and Chad were engaged at the time, her assessment seemed credible to the rest of the team.

As it turned out, Chad was right and the product did not sell well. In fact, the only demographic that purchased it in significant quantities was Ngs' family. When another "iffy" idea crossed my desk about a month ago, I said to somebody, "I want to avoid another Ng disaster.

That was one of the biggest failures in Despair's history and it cost me dearly. He's the reason there were no bonuses last year." About two hours later I heard some shouting and went to check out what was causing the commotion. Ng was in a shouting match with three other employees who had surrounded him like jackals. He kept saying things like "It was just an idea," "It was a team decision," "We were brainstorming, do you know what it means to brainstorm?!" Despite Ng's protestations, the other employees hurled epithets at him and called him an incompetent moron. As this story quickly spread throughout the rank-and-file, it even generated a new bit of jargon at Despair, Inc. Now, whenever somebody is the personal victim of somebody else's incompetence, they are said to have been "Nged." Ng keeps a pretty low profile these days.

Tell stories that articulate employee failures, but highlight corporate patience and benevolence. The goal here is to capitalize on the principles of equity theory. Your story should make it clear that employee failure warrants termination, but due to the goodwill of the company and/or executives, the offending employee was spared from termination. It is important that you do not create the impression of merely *overlooking* an employee's failure. It has to be clear that the full force of the failure has been felt but the employee has been forgiven. This clearly casts the employee as the exploiter and the company as the victim.

Tell stories that include unnamed employees who emulate Radically Demotivated qualities. One of the virtues we cultivate in non-executives at Despair, Inc. is a paranoid kind of self-erasure. As a means of dislodging their fundamental narcissism, we circulate stories that include unnamed employees who take pride in receiving no recognition for their efforts and who are willing to labor in obscurity to avoid the possibility of being blamed for a corporate failure. Given the anonymity of the characters, there are fewer constraints to use actual people as the protagonists of the story. In fact, if you do not have any employees who embody Radically Demotivated qualities, it is just as effective to use a hybrid of several employees to represent the archetypal ideal employee, someone I like to call the *Zero with a Thousand Faces*™. These types of stories are very effective in company-wide addresses because they generate a "buzz" which reinforces the point of the story. For example, I recently told the following story to a large group at Despair, Inc.

> We have an employee, who has chosen to remain anonymous, who symbolizes everything we stand for at Despair, Inc. He comes to work early and leaves late. He keeps to himself and is willing to do whatever his supervisor tells him to do. Not long ago, he was asked to work extra hours to finish a large scale project for a particularly ineffective branch of the government. As a result, he missed his daughter's ballet recital one evening and forgot to pick up his wife from the airport the next. When I heard about his sacrifice, I called him to my office along with the Director of Human Resources. I asked him what he thought I should do about his situation, and he simply said "Nothing, please don't fire me. I need the job." With that, I let him go back to work. Let's give him a big round of applause and the anonymity he deserves.

These types of stories teach our employees to value hard work and obscurity, and to see both of them as their own reward. They quickly learn that individuality is their enemy and uncompensated productivity is their best chance at job security.

I encourage you to experiment in your own organization with the principles described above. Organizational stories are more than just interesting accounts of organizational life. If used correctly, they can be an effective means of manipulating the cognitive premises your employees use to understand the nature of organizational reality and their role within it. Furthermore, by using equity theory as a psychological lever to dislodge your employees' fundamental narcissism, you can tap into the power of Radical Demotivation™ by casting the company as the victim in an employee-led project of exploitation. This will take some time, but when it is successful, you will reap the harvest of Radical Demotivation™.

SELF-NARRATIVE:
Forcing Your Employees
to Think about their Futures

The mass of men lead lives of quiet desperation.
—THOREAU

When we were growing up most of us were exposed to the story of Icarus, the naïve Greek youth who got so wrapped up in pursuing his dreams that he ignored his father's warning and flew too close to the sun. When Icarus eventually realized his error, "he fluttered his arms as fast as he could. . . . He cried out to his father, but it was too late" (Bennett, W. J. 1993, p. 213). As we all know, at that point his fate was as certain as the law of gravity. The story of Icarus is not just a light-hearted tale about the wisdom of obeying one's parents, it is also a cautionary tale about the folly of pursuing one's dreams.

Stories like this become part of the popular culture and are intended to teach us something important about life and how to live it. We are taught from a young age to interpret "the moral of the story," which represents the distilled wisdom the story is intended to communicate. In the previous chapter, I discussed the role of organizational stories in

DELUSIONS

THERE IS NO GREATER JOY THAN SOARING HIGH ON THE WINGS OF YOUR DREAMS,
EXCEPT MAYBE THE JOY OF WATCHING A DREAMER WHO HAS NOWHERE TO LAND
BUT IN THE OCEAN OF REALITY.

manipulating your employees' cognitive premises. The goal was to affect the culture as a whole in support of a covert program of Radical Demotivation™. In this chapter I will consider the role of stories again, but I want to take it to the next level; I want to make it personal. This time, I will consider the "stories" of your employees' lives and how you can help them become the main characters in their own self-scripted cautionary tales. More specifically, I want to discuss how to use failures in your employees' lives to induce them to author their own Radically Demotivating self-narratives.

Executives who are imprisoned by the Noble Employee Myth are always trying to get their employees to see themselves as winners. Motivational speakers often try to "unlock" a hypothesized power of positive thinking by teaching employees to visualize success sometime in the future. In essence, they are attempting to get employees to see themselves as the protagonists in their own personal Horatio Alger stories, stories with titles like "The Loser Who Won," or "The Idiot Who

Defied the Odds and Made a Fortune." I've learned something from these motivational speakers. With the discovery of Radical Demotivation™ I found that I could also use self-narrative to drive Radical Demotivation™ deeper; that through interaction with my employees *I could prompt them to use the failures in their own lives to author their own Radically Demotivating self-narratives.*

I quickly found that this approach was both more powerful and more seductive than I previously would have imagined. Rather than simply identifying with other failures, employees would come to see themselves as paradigmatic failures and therefore learn to face the future with the fear, loathing, and dread that are endemic to Radical Demotivation™. I realized that if implemented correctly, Icarus' *final moment* of dreadful awareness of his unavoidable destiny had the potential to become the *continual present* for Radically Demotivated employees everywhere. They would be haunted by the gnawing apprehension that their past and present failures were omens of an approaching, undeniable reality— that there would be no "happy ending" to their story, that their dreams of future success would taunt them like the mocking howl of a hyena as it celebrates the defeat of its prey, and that the only notoriety they would achieve would be as the protagonist in a self-scripted cautionary tale which would be told to future generations until their very existence faded into the obscurity and irrelevance they had earned. This was a vision I felt compelled to make available to fellow executives as part of a comprehensive program of Radical Demotivation™ *(see illustration)*.

This may sound too good to be true, but I can assure you that it isn't. The best part is that after a little practice, inducing employees to author their own Radically Demotivating self-narratives can become second nature; you will not even realize you are doing it. Before you get started, though, you need to understand a little bit about narrative theory.

Don't worry, this isn't going to degenerate into an English lesson. I only want to share those things that we have found most useful at Despair, Inc. I shared this information with the leadership team at Despair, Inc. and it had a transformational impact on our employees that was beyond my wildest imagination. Within two weeks, 37% of our employees walked up to me and spontaneously apologized, and I don't even know why—presumably out of a sense of shame for being who they are. The goal here is to emphasize the power and pathology of inducing your employees to construct their own Radically Demotivating self-narratives. There are three things you need to understand about narrative before you get started: (a) Its role in cognition and sense-making; (b) the essential components of a well-formed narrative; and (c) the uses of narrative form in Radical Demotivation™.

NARRATIVE AND COGNITION

Several theorists have argued that the narrative structure of stories is fundamental to the way we process information and interpret our experiences (Bennett, 1992; Fisher, 1987; Gergen, 1994). As Professor Walter Fisher (1987) from the University of Southern California put it:

> Symbols are created and communicated ultimately as stories meant to give order to human experience and to induce others to dwell in them in order to establish ways of living in common, in intellectual and spiritual communities in which there is *confirmation for the story that constitutes one's life.* (p. 67)

In other words, our identities and our experiences in the world only make sense if they are placed within the context of an evolving narrative that ultimately becomes the story of our lives. A similar idea was echoed by Kenneth Gergen (1994), social psychologist at Swarthmore College, when he said that "self-narratives function much like oral histories or morality tales within a society. They are cultural resources that serve such social purposes as self-identification, self-justification, self-criticism, and social solidification" (p. 188). For our purposes, it makes sense to add to Gergen's list "self-loathing" and "self-condemnation." The point to all of this is that your employees have a narrative impulse; they are always trying to create a coherent story out of the events in their lives, not just as a means of describing themselves to others, but *as a means of defining who they are to themselves as well.* Consequently, the story of their lives is naturally open to revision as the events of life unfold. Given that so much of their waking life is spent at work, you as their employer have absolute control over many of those life-shaping events. In light of this, consider the impact of being passed up for a promotion by a less competent co-worker, or another lateral move to a new department without a pay increase, or being "forgotten" again when the rest of the team goes to lunch together. I can tell you that from our experiments, even the most dogmatically self-confident employees begin to experience a level of self-doubt that is seldom experienced by the children of even the most distant and critical parents.

NARRATIVE COMPONENTS

Given the narrative impulse of your employees, you will be much more successful at inducing them to create Radically Demotivating self-narratives if you understand some of the components of a well-formed story (Gergen, 1994). We teach our managers to listen for inconsistencies and inadequacies in their employees' self-narratives and use them as an opportunity to introduce alternative narrative components. When used skillfully, these become a powerful means of subjecting your employees to your own version of revisionist history. Rather than discuss all the components of a well-formed narrative, I want to focus on the three that are most relevant to a program of Radical Demotivation™.

First, a well-formed narrative should have a *point that provides meaning and coherence* to the events that comprise the story. If there is no point to the story, the events that make up the story become irrelevant. Consequently, your goal is not simply to introduce chaos and confusion into the lives of your employees, it is to provide them with alternative, credible, interpretations of their lives up to the present, so that they will naturally construct a future filled with disappointment and despair.

During our initial internal experiments we saw the power of this theory in the case of Rose. Rose, a divorced woman who was "glad to be rid of her worthless husband," is a particularly abrasive person who until recently maintained a delusional belief that it was her job to "put others in their place." She prided herself on blurting out offensive, inap-

propriate comments to her family and coworkers because "they needed to hear it." She saw it as a sign of strength and integrity to say what
others dared not say, and oblivious to her own lack of achievement, she
seemed to believe that she would increase her stature by putting others
down. One day Rose was boasting to me about how she had put a few of
her coworkers in their places. She then began to complain about how
wearying it was dealing with losers at Despair all day, as if I was not acutely aware of the same burden, particularly in that very moment. I feigned
interest and handed her a Dysfunction poster and said, "Here, maybe
this will help." Mistakenly thinking we had something in common, she
enthusiastically opened it up and read the damning indictment, "The
only consistent feature of all your dissatisfying relationships is you."

DYSFUNCTION
THE ONLY CONSISTENT FEATURE OF ALL YOUR DISSATISFYING RELATIONSHIPS IS YOU.

Immediately her face turned beet red. Like a doctor who is forced to join
the leper colony after discovering that she too is a leper, Rose realized
that she was not just surrounded by losers, but that she was one of them.
The goal of her life changed from trying to straighten out everyone else's
life to straightening out her own life. Since that time Rose has sought rec-

onciliation with her husband and put a Dysfunction Desktopper on her desk. She now regards all of her previous "victories" as stigmatic recollections of her folly and is simply grateful to be employed.

Rose is an example of someone who misunderstood the point of her life because she had a mistaken self-perception. As you recall, the root of all your employee problems is that most of them think far too highly of themselves and therefore demand of you more than they deserve. In stark contrast to Rose and others like her, you probably have at least a few employees who have no point to their lives. They have no passion, drive, or direction. They just seem to bounce from one job to another like a pinball before it disappears into the gutter. Since these people have no real trajectory to their lives, you have an opportunity to supply them with one. We have several of these aimless waifs at Despair, Inc. I can always identify them because they seem to grumble about everything; they have no criteria for evaluating anything other than their immediate sensory experience. When I hear them mutter and complain about the (lack of) direction of their lives I often remind them of what our Mistakes poster says—it could be that the purpose of

MISTAKES

IT COULD BE THAT THE PURPOSE OF YOUR LIFE IS
ONLY TO SERVE AS A WARNING TO OTHERS.

their lives is only to serve as warning to others, that they are walking cautionary tales, and they should take comfort in the fact that their lives serve a broader purpose than their own satisfaction or fulfillment. Curiously, some of them demonstrate a new-found sense of pride in being an object of scorn. In such cases, it would seem that they are unable to distinguish between the deferential attention afforded to the truly accomplished and the contemptuous apprehension reserved for the truly obnoxious. Naturally, this self-serving lack of judgment consigns them to remain in their unfortunate but clearly deserved state.

In addition to having a point, a well-formed narrative must include *events relevant to the point to the story.* Every person's life includes many successes and failures of different magnitude and relevance. An individual may have scored well on an exam, struck out during the baseball game, helped a stranger with directions, or completely and finally alienated the only person who could have made her feel complete. Most of the "events" in our lives slip into history and are barely even accessible to our memories without external probing. The events we do tend to remember, however, are those that provide evidence for the stories of our lives. Consequently, understanding one's life is essentially an interpretive event, and as such, it can be reinterpreted by helping an employee remember or make salient the events in her life she would prefer to forget. Armed with this understanding, our managers are taught to ask their employees questions and listen for inconsistent, incomplete, or conflicting self-narratives. This not only creates the impression of "caring" for the employee, it provides a rich supply of information the manager can use to help construct new self-narratives that are consistent with our program of Radical Demotivation™.

Let me give you an example of how this works in practice. We hired a young man who had recently graduated with a degree in finance from an Ivy League university. He loved to talk about his early interest in finance, the capital structure of Despair, Inc., his interest in earning an MBA, and his desire to be the CFO of Despair, Inc. when it is a multi-billion dollar enterprise, blah, blah, blah. When I could endure his self-aggrandizing blather no longer, I decided to do a little experiment. I could tell from the way he dressed and carried himself that he was no "ladies' man," so I began to ask him questions about his personal life, whether he desired to get married, etc. After several revelations about failed romantic relationships that resulted in "friendships" (and/or restraining orders), I pointed out to him that his academic achievements seemed to improve with every romantic failure. Over the following weeks I made the same connection a few additional times during casual conversation. Finally he had what can best be described as an "Icarus moment," the moment he "realized" that he had always been a loser in love and that his academic achievements were an attempt to compensate for the pain of his romantic failures. He began to see his past achievements as little more than unsuccessful attempts to impress the growing list of women who had rejected him, and to realize that his dreams of being a CFO were a cheap substitute for what he really wanted out of life. After about a month of disillusionment he even concluded that he had no real interest in finance and was depressed because he was stuck in a boring career with no hope of success. Having felt somewhat responsible for his depression, I decided to help him out by moving him to the shipping department, where is flourishing. He is now responsible for monitoring a giant funnel and keeping it filled with packing peanuts throughout the day. He works for an attractive blind woman who thinks he's "cute." He finally feels at peace with himself. This is a clear example of the win/win results made possible by a program of Radical Demotivation™.

Finally, a well-formed narrative *specifies the causal linkages* between the events that comprise the story. To make sense, narrative has to explain how the protagonist moved from the beginning to the end of the story. Consider the following story of Hector: Hector was an academically poor college student who attended class infrequently and almost did not graduate. Now Hector is a wealthy investment banker who is worth several million dollars. This narrative about Hector does not make sense because it does not explain how he went from being a chronically underperforming college student to a successful investment banker. Consequently, it is not a very believable story. If I add to the story that Hector's father is the founding partner of an investment banking firm who mentored him and counseled him to invest in the IPO of a company that produces and manufactures revolutionary products designed for pessimists, losers, and the chronically unsuccessful, the story would suddenly make sense.

Similarly, if you choose to talk to your employees you will find that many of them have unrealistic dreams and plans for the future with no clear understanding of the causal linkages required to achieve them. They boldly and ignorantly talk about what they are going to buy or what they are going to do "someday," unaware that they have a better chance of being struck by lightning than buying or doing any of it. Their inability to detect the absolute disjuncture between their present achievements and their fantasized futures often creates an unwarranted optimism that cries out for redress. We teach our managers at Despair, Inc. that the narrative disjuncture revealed by these declarations is a subconscious plea for help—that they have an obligation (and opportunity) to help their employees create a narrative that eradicates misplaced hope and frees them up to face the future as tragically as it will likely unfold. In some ways the process is akin to a psychological enema; it's humiliating, but once hope is eliminated the employee will feel better (and bitter).

It should be clear that manipulating the components in an employee's self-narrative can have a dramatic, Radically Demotivating effect on the employee's view of himself and his future. Once an employee comes to believe that his life has been a series of mistakes, failures, and misjudgments, and further, that his best days are behind him, he will cease to believe that he is "entitled" to much of anything and begin to sheepishly hang his head in shame. Not surprisingly, some employees resist this process. Some do so by desperately reasserting their original self-narrative, hoping someone will affirm their delusion, while others slip into a fragile state of denial and are sometimes seen rocking back and forth, staring at the floor, or beating their heads against the wall. To help these employees acquiesce to their new self-narratives, it's important to make them as believable as possible. One way to increase their believability is to induce your employees to construct self-narratives that approximate prototypical, culturally accepted narrative forms.

NARRATIVE FORM

The form of a narrative refers to the historical trajectory of the protagonist. An infinite number of narrative forms are possible, but we have been culturally conditioned to find certain forms more believable. As Gergen (1994) says, "Certain forms of narrative are broadly shared within the culture; they are frequently used, easily identified, and highly functional. In a sense, they constitute the syllabary of possible selves" (p. 194). For example, a typical crime drama includes a fearless detective who overcomes several obstacles to eventually solve the crime. In this case the detective is the protagonist in a heroic narrative. This is the type of story your employees can easily identify, though rarely identify *with*. In contrast to the heroic narrative, imagine a crime drama with a detective who gives up at the end because he believes he doesn't have any good leads and decides to move on to the next crime that he won't solve. Though this happens all the time, most listeners would not find it an acceptable story. This is why it is important to induce your employees to see their lives in the context of a culturally salient narrative form; it makes the truth easier to accept.

It may seem that for a narrative to be acceptable it has to have a happy ending. Fortunately, that is not true. Executives have several options available to them to induce their employees to construct Radically Demotivating self-narratives. In the next section we will begin by covering three easy to identify structurally simple Radically Demotivating narrative forms. We'll then move on to a discussion of two self-narratives that are more structurally complex, but offer tremendous opportunities for rapid reinterpretation of an employee's self-narratives. Finally I will conclude the section with a brief word of caution.

All Radically Demotivating self-narratives are *regressive* in nature; they create a dreadful vision of the future that consists of reaping the bitter harvest of a life filled with failure, excuse-making, cowardice, missed opportunity, and risk avoidance. The first Radically Demotivating narrative form is the *Squandered Potential Narrative (Figure 3)*. Very simply, it refers to a life in which an individual has consistently taken the path of least resistance and therefore never achieved anything significant or satisfying. The Squandered Potential Narrative is depicted in the graphic below. The **Y** axis represents achievement valence, either positive or negative, while the **X** axis represents the chronological trajectory.

FIGURE 3. THE SQUANDERED POTENTIAL NARRATIVE

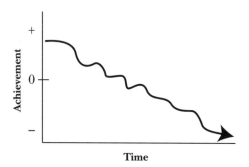

Any employee who did *not* begin life with a significant physical, economic, or cultural disadvantage is susceptible to the Squandered Potential Narrative. They may have started life wealthy or middle-class, be brilliant or of average intelligence, be beautiful or average-looking. None of this matters. The key is to get them to see themselves as having squandered whatever potential they had out of fear and/or indolence. When this occurs, some employees will feel ashamed at their lack of achievement and attempt to change course, but don't be alarmed; it's a normal part of the process. Inertia is on your side and will work like quicksand to drag them back into what John Bunyan called the "slough of despondency." From the moment of their decision to change the course of their lives, every failure, every unfinished task, every day wasted in front of the television, every criticism they encounter, and every pound they gain will serve as an indictment of their half-hearted attempt to change. Over time, the entire program of self-reformation will gradually be reduced to another chapter in their constantly unfolding story of failure, mediocrity, and squandered potential. When this happens they will be sufficiently inoculated against any future inducements to improve, thus sealing their

Radically Demotivated destinies and providing you with a surprisingly gratifying sense of accomplishment.

The second Radically Demotivating narrative form is the *Lost Opportunity Narrative (Figure 4)*. In this narrative, the individual realizes that out of fear and/or laziness, she has repeatedly passed up opportunities for success that would have enabled her to achieve dramatically more satisfaction out of life than she has achieved thus far, or will achieve in the future. One of the core features of the Lost Opportunity Narrative is the belief that opportunities for success cannot be created, they are something that one must be "lucky" enough to serendipitously encounter in life. Consequently, opportunities for success are rare and one has to be able to act upon them when they arise. Moreover, the discovery that one has passed on a great opportunity is like spending a fortune because you're expecting an inheritance only to discover you were written out of the will: You're not just in debt, but have already lost one of your only chances for financial independence. As you might expect, this has a perfectly rational compounding effect on the individual's sense of doom. The Lost Opportunity Narrative is illustrated in the graphic below.

FIGURE 4. THE LOST OPPORTUNITY NARRATIVE

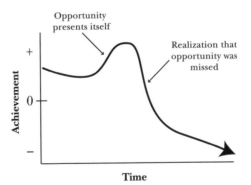

Not long ago I got to see the impact of the Lost Opportunity Narrative on Tom, a recently hired engineer at Despair, Inc. After Tom had made it through a series of interviews, I was prepared to make him an offer. As

I was explaining that part of our compensation was in stock options that vested over ten years, Tom got visibly excited. I asked him what was wrong and he said, "Nothing. I passed up a chance for stock options in 1994 and I promised myself I would not do it again." Then Tom told me that he was offered a job at Cisco Systems in 1994 that included 10,000 stock options but turned it down to work for a local utility because it was a "stable" company and they offered him $2,500 more in annual salary. Tom realized that if he had taken the job at Cisco Systems with the stock options, by 1999 he would have been worth several million dollars.

After hearing Tom's story, I had a feeling he was right (and ripe) for Despair, Inc. My hunch was confirmed at a recent Despair, Inc. "survivor party" (i.e., a potluck for employees who avoid being fired during the annual "spring cleaning"—a purge of those expected to provide the least utility in the upcoming year) when he saw Jean, the bubbly, strikingly attractive wife of the guy who parks and washes my car. It turns out that Tom and Jean knew each other in college. Moreover, Tom was hopelessly in love with Jean while they were in college but never said anything because he *feared* her rejection. Rather than reveal his feelings, he decided to *play it safe* and just be Jean's friend. Though it had been years since they last spoke, Tom was clearly flustered in her presence. Still, he managed to appear interested in her account of how she met and married the guy who parks and washes my car. It was amusing watching Tom sweat during the conversation, but the real drama started when Jean looked at Tom and said, "Gosh, why didn't you ask me out in college? I had such a crush on you. I did everything I could think of to attract you to me but you just wanted to be friends." Tom turned sheet white, mumbled something about being an idiot, and excused himself because he was feeling sick. Jean said it was great to see him again and, without a hint of irony, welcomed him to Despair. Since that time Tom has often made references to not feeling well, is quite subdued in his emotional displays, and tends to stare at the ground when he walks. Having lost in love and passed on a fortune, Tom says that Despair is his only hope. We'll see how that works out.

The third Radically Demotivating narrative form is the *Achilles Heel Narrative.* In this narrative, an individual experiences atypical success

FIGURE 5. THE ACHILLES HEEL NARRATIVE

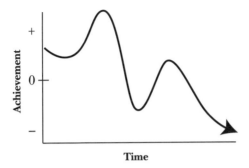

or good fortune, but due to one or more character weaknesses eventually loses it all. This is the paradigmatic narrative of child stars who spend their money on drugs, professional athletes who are thrown in jail for various forms of sexual or physical assault, and executives who engage in insider trading. In all of these cases the individuals are in a favored position, but lose everything due to their greed, immaturity, arrogance, or stupidity. Individuals who are prone to enact the Achilles Heel Narrative are different than those who live out the Squandered Potential or the Lost Opportunity Narratives in that they are likely to have several brushes with success; they are the same, though, in that they ultimately end up losing it all and living lives filled with shame and regret.

The Achilles Heel Narrative was wonderfully illustrated in a 2002 CNN/Money story about lottery winners and dot-com whiz kids who lost their fortunes almost as quickly as they had made them. The article featured the story of Peter Grandich, a high school dropout who became a stock broker and got lucky when he predicted the crash of 1987. He became known as the "dropout/whiz kid" and made a fortune. Grandich lived the good life: He had a mansion in New Jersey, owned race cars and race horses, and spent plenty of time playing golf. As can be expected, however, it didn't last. He eventually got involved with raising money for a gold mine that turned out to be a hoax. In commenting on the event, Grandich said: "I lost 75 percent of what I had in less than a year. . . . Some people get suckered by their own actions, their own greed—that was me" (Geary, 2002).

Stories like those of Peter Grandich do a good job of teaching your employees that even if they are successful, their weaknesses will creep up and knock them senseless like a suckerpunch to the back of the head. By the time they realize what has happened it will be too late to do anything about it. At that point most employees will simply give up, but others will repeat the cycle over and over until they are dizzied by their repeated losses and sick with unmitigated self-contempt.

NARRATIVE FORM AND THE ZONE OF OPPORTUNITY

As you and your leadership team listen to your employees drone on about their pathetic lives, you will find numerous opportunities to induce the Radically Demotivating narrative forms described above. In this process you will also find an interesting phenomenon that creates a special opportunity for the Radically Demotivating executive: namely, a clear disjuncture between the obvious course of an employee's life and his perception of that course. It is one thing to wrestle with and submit to the demotivating reality of the trajectory of one's life; it is another to completely misinterpret the warning signs and blithely construct naïvely optimistic self-narratives. This disjuncture, between the regressive nature of the course of one's life and an optimistic self-narrative, creates what I refer to as a *Zone of Opportunity (Figures 6 and 7)*. Very simply, the Zone of Opportunity is an explanatory defect in an employee's self-narrative. In our experiments we found the Zone of Opportunity in two types of narratives: (a) when the employee has no real understanding of their current situation, and (b) when an employee refers to dreams in the distant future but has no idea how to achieve them and is not on course to realize them.

The first of these narratives is the *Optimist Narrative*. As can be seen from the graphic, the optimist continues to expect a future filled with success and good fortune even as repeated failures and difficulties argue to the contrary. It should also be noted that the disjuncture between the optimist's trajectory of hope and trajectory of achievement becomes more acute over time, thus increasing the size of the Zone of

FIGURE 6. THE OPTIMIST NARRATIVE

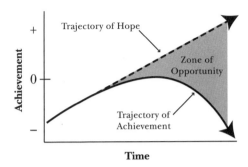

Opportunity. The story of Rose recounted earlier is a good example of an employee who was living under the delusion of an Optimist Narrative. Once she realized that she was just like the others she had criticized, her Trajectory of Hope immediately became congruent with her Trajectory of Achievement, thus transforming both of them into a Trajectory of Despair.

The second narrative that includes a significant Zone of Opportunity is the *Fantasy Narrative* represented below.

FIGURE 7. THE FANTASY NARRATIVE

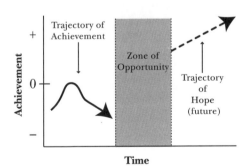

The Fantasy Narrative is easy to identify because the employee continues to refer to a fantasized "someday" when his life will be radically better than it is now. This someday is generally far enough in the future to remain unscathed by reality and is characterized by happiness, prosperity, satisfaction, and achievement. Employees deluded by a Fantasy Narrative will often refer to a time when they will "give back" to their family, the community, or some other group or institution, despite the fact that an objective assessment of their historic trajectory of achievement suggests a future filled with disillusionment and economic dependency upon the government, their families, and miscellaneous non-denominational religious institutions. Another telltale mark of the Fantasy Narrative is that that employees do not do anything that would actually create an opportunity that would enable them to reach their dreams: no self-improvement, no risks, no extra effort, nothing. All they do is continue to hope and dream, but it is a hope that is rooted in ignorance and compounded by stupidity.

As was the case with the Optimist Narrative, the Zone of Opportunity in the Fantasy Narrative becomes more acute over time. As time goes on and your employees come closer to the end of their lives, they have less time to achieve all of the things they fantasized they would achieve but have made no progress toward thus far. Because these people are so blinded by their fantasies, they fail to notice their continued lack of progress. As a result, simply pointing out their lack of progress to date and/or their absence of any understanding of how to achieve their goals is often enough to shatter the fantasy and kick them a long way down the path of Radical Demotivation™.

This was the case with William, an employee who left Despair, Inc. shortly after the collapse of his Fantasy Narrative. For reasons I never understood, William demanded that others call him "Stubby," a childhood nickname given to him at birth by his mother. Stubby was fiftysomething years old when he worked at Despair, Inc. and surprisingly incompetent for a man his age. He always used to wear Hawaiian print shirts to work and talk about buying a sailboat and sailing to exotic tropical locations. Nobody really cared much because they knew he was an idiot and that his declarations were no more meaningful than Shirley MacLaine's metaphysical blather. One day he returned late from his break, irritating his manager. When she asked him why he was late he apologized and said he had just gotten a new issue of *Boating*

Life and had lost track of time reading about the "new 50 footers." Fed up, she looked straight into his eyes and said, "Give me a break. What makes you think you're going to achieve in the next ten years what you couldn't achieve in the last 35? The bottom line is that your sun is setting. The closest you'll ever get to sailing to a tropical island is watching a 'Gilligan's Island' rerun." Shaken, Stubby returned to work and didn't say much. It seemed that he had never quite reckoned with his finitude, the reality that his years were racing past him and that all of his *hope for the future* had caused him to fail to reckon with the *reality of the present*. As a result, he had squandered the opportunities inherent in every waking moment on the false hope that one day "his ship would come in"—literally. He quit a few weeks later. The last I heard he was living at the local rescue mission and had decided to become a motivational speaker, giving lectures on goal setting and time management.

CONFRONTING A PROGRESSIVE ACHIEVEMENT NARRATIVE

As you can see, listening to your employees and inducing them to construct Radically Demotivating self-narratives can help you to make a genuine difference in their largely undifferentiated lives. Nevertheless, I don't want to give the impression that every Radically Demotivating transformation will be as rapid or pervasive as the examples mentioned above. I used those "best case scenarios" as illustrations of what is possible with practice. In fact, it is likely that you will encounter a few employees who have stable self-narratives that are resistant to change. If their self-narratives are already regressive you have nothing to worry about. But you may discover one or more employees with *Progressive Achievement Narratives (Figure 8)*. I raise this as a word of caution because these employees have the potential to subvert a robust program of Radical Demotivation™. Employees with Progressive Achievement Narratives have a great deal in common with executives, but they often have not yet come to grips with the fact that they are different than the run of the mill employees they work along side of. Consequently, they continue to spread hope where none should exist.

FIGURE 8. THE PROGRESSIVE ACHIEVEMENT NARRATIVE

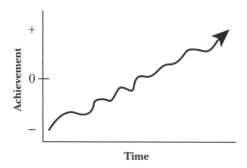

Employees with Progressive Achievement Narratives tend to be persistently optimistic because they have forged their self-narratives in the furnace of tribulation. They have learned to persist in the face of failure and found ways to compensate for their personal weaknesses. A striking example is Roger Crawford, who was born with Ectrodactylism, a rare birth defect that affects the digits on hands and feet. Crawford was born with no hands: just a thumb growing out of his right forearm and a thumb and finger growing out of his left forearm. Similarly, he only had 3 toes on a shrunken right foot and his left foot, which was eventually amputated, was withered and folded beneath him. Despite these severe disadvantages, Crawford earned a spot on his high school football team and eventually became a professional tennis player (Crawford & Bowker, 1989). As you can imagine, people like this are pretty impervious to Radical Demotivation™. Moreover, employees with Progressive Achievement Narratives must be handled very carefully. Left unchecked, they naturally tend to encourage others and inspire those around them. They reignite hope and teach others to create optimistic self-narratives. If they gain too much influence in the organization, they can become like your own personal Pied Piper, leading the rats out of the city. This can unravel everything you have worked for and put you back at square one.

Therefore, you need to take control of the situation and use such persons for your purposes. Our research suggests that you have three basic options. The first option, which is by far the least risky, is to find a reason to terminate their employment. This will send a message to the rest of your employees that an inspiring attitude is not tolerated in your organization, and it will put them on notice that they run the risk of the same fate if they're not careful. That message can be demotivating in and of itself. The downside of this approach is that employees with a Progressive Achievement Narrative tend to be competent and reliable and their departure will most likely be a genuine loss to the organization.

The second option is to promote them to an entry-level management position and make them responsible for their cohorts' performance. This is quite risky and should not be done willy-nilly. The only time this option should be tried is when the employee recognizes how different he is from his cohorts and has begun to disassociate himself from them. This disassociation is a sign of the formation of an executive mentality, and as such, it provides a measure of insurance against the likelihood that he will attempt to infect his employees with an irrational hope in their untapped potential.

The final approach is to use these employees as a foil in your dealings with other employees, especially those who might be affected by a Squandered Potential Narrative. When they are confronted with a visual reminder that they have not achieved near as much as their cohorts have, many employees will feel even more worthless than they normally do (Swann, Pelham & Krull, 1989). By keeping employees with a Progressive Achievement Narrative in the organization, the rank and file will repeatedly be forced to confront the fact that all of their excuses for their lack of achievement can be reduced to laziness, apathy, and squandered potential. This is also risky, however, due to the Progressive Achievement's potential to inspire others, as noted above. Therefore, I recommend that you give Progressive Achievement employees a role that minimizes their contact with others. This reduces the likelihood that they will have the opportunity to encourage others, but gives you an opportunity to use them as an object lesson whenever you deem it appropriate.

PUTTING IT INTO PRACTICE

Given the rather arcane nature of narrative theories of identity construction, I realize that it may not be clear how to access the power and pathology of Radically Demotivating self-narratives. In the remainder of this chapter I want to discuss six conversational tactics you can begin to use immediately with your employees. Over time you will discover that there are many ways to accomplish this, but these tactics will get you started until you get the hang of it. All of these tactics should be woven into routine conversation so they appear to be normal, routine observations. To the degree that the employee views these comments as genuine observations based upon his progressive self-disclosure, he will be convinced of the accuracy of the Radically Demotivating self-narrative he is being induced to construct. As a result, he will gradually acquiesce like the proverbial frog in water brought slowly to a boil.

1. **Minimize success.** Everybody experiences success to some degree or another, but people evaluate their successes differently. Your goal is to minimize the positive impact of an employee's success so he believes it is invalid to use the event as part of a progressive self-narrative. There are several ways you can do this:

   a. Compare the employee's achievement with an achievement warranting greater merit, thereby rendering the employee's achievement pale in comparison.

   b. Highlight others who have made a similar achievements but ultimately ended up failures.

   c. Attribute the employee's success to luck.

   d. Note that the achievement does not require any special skill or talent, just a willingness to do what most people are uninterested in doing.

   e. Question the value of the achievement.

   f. In cases where the success was contingent upon human judgment, suggest that the achievement was a political victory rather than skill or talent based victory.

2. **Accentuate failure.** In the same way that people evaluate their successes differently, they also attach different degrees of significance to their failures. Your goal here is to maximize the relevance of the failures in their lives so that they become convinced that the major themes are those of failure. Here are a few ways you can do this:

a. Express shock and surprise at the employee's failure. Communicate the idea that success in a particular area is so routine that her failure was a real shock.

b. Note that successful people typically do not fail in the way your employee failed.

c. If the failure was contingent upon the decision of others (e.g., a panel of judges), highlight the rigor and objectivity of the judges.

d. Highlight the importance of being successful in the area where your employee failed.

e. Attempt to help the employee understand why she failed by pointing out weakness in her skills, appearance, character, or demeanor. It is important to locate the cause for the failure in attributes that are both personal and stable.

3. **Make connections between past and present failures.** As you get to know your employees, listen for past failures that you can bring up in the future. When the employee does fail, bring up the past failures in order to establish a pattern of past failures that explains the current failure.

4. **Identify similarities with other failures.** Interestingly, people identify with others based upon the most cursory similarities (Cialdini, Finch & De Nicholas, 1990). Have you ever noticed that people will pay extra to wear clothing with an insignia that identifies them with a brand, sports team, or university? You can use this same power of cursory identification by highlighting similarities between your employees and other notable failures. For example, I recently pointed out to an employee that he went to the same college as a local high-profile criminal. When enough of these associations are made, the employee eventually comes to see that "people like me" tend to fail.

5. **Share statistics that suggest that people with characteristics similar to those of your employees tend to fail.** Most of us are familiar with the data that suggests that single women over forty years old who have never been married have less than a 20% chance of finding a mate. Naturally, this strikes fear in the hearts of 35-39 year-old women everywhere who are looking for Mr. Right. You can use a similar approach in conversation with your employees. If you are

unable to find suitable statistics, just make something up and reference the New York Times. If it turns out you were wrong, they'll just assume the story was written by Jayson Blair or one of his ilk.

6. **Reinforce the idea that success and failure are determined by fate or destiny.** In so doing, you will effectively reinforce the idea that the employee really has little or no control over his life. To the degree that he accepts this idea, he will be helpless to improve the trajectory of his self-narrative. Instead, he will tend to adopt a passive, self-neutered, *que sera sera* attitude toward life which will virtually ensure his eventual arrival at the state of Radical Demotivation™.

If you're tired of the encouragement treadmill, of trying to give hope to those who have none, of propping up the fragile egos of those who would benefit by a well-earned collapse, I hope it is clear that Radical Demotivation™ is the answer you have been looking for. By making the errors, failures, and unpleasant associations of your employees the most salient features of their social identities, you can help your employees co-author Radically Demotivating, realistic self-narratives that include appropriately stigmatic pasts and dreadful futures. In so doing, your employees will be self-cauterizing the infectious wound of self-respect that creates the pungent stench of entitlement that makes them so unpleasant.

ATTITUDES:
Helping Your Employees
Cope With Challenges

He that falls in love with himself will have no rivals.
—BENJAMIN FRANKLIN

I n my travels across the country, I've had the pleasure to speak about Radical Demotivation™ with executives in corporations large and small, progressive and stoic, profitable and penurious. With the exception of an irredeemably optimistic few, I find that most of them are utterly disillusioned with the "solutions" offered by the motivation industry.

As noted earlier, they have been led by a chorus of self-styled experts to believe that "investing in their employees" means affirming their egos and acquiescing to their demands, and that leaders who make such investments can expect to reap a harvest of gratitude, loyalty, and general goodwill. Instead, they find workers growing ever more self-centered, convinced by self-esteem building programs that they have unlimited potential and enormous value. Emboldened by delusions of grandeur, they grow avaricious and petulant, their allegiance to the company replaced by loyalty to self. Not surprisingly, when their unrealistic demands remain unsatisfied, the workplace becomes an incubator for cynicism and rancor as attrition begins to climb.

Understandably, the executives I've spoken with find this state of affairs troubling and rightly feel they must do something about it. The motivation industry remedy for such symptoms is clear: if employees are unhappy, spend more on motivational programs and incentives. But like a weak parent who responds to a child's misbehavior with lavish praise rather than corrective punishment, executives who persist in such ego-inflating practices are abdicating their disciplinary responsibility and are even complicit in the personality malformation of the little people in their care.

When made aware of this disconnect—of the inverse relationship between their motivational investments and company morale—executives become intrigued by the possibilities of Radical Demotivation™. Some are quick to comprehend and zealous to implement. These "beta-testers" are already beginning to experience the tangible benefits—many of which have been mentioned illustratively (if anonymously) in this very book.

Yet others are cautious and express hesitation, just as I suspect many of you might. Perhaps you fear, as the aforementioned do, that this approach will make their employees even less happy than they already are. This may be true, but it's not relevant to a program of Radical Demotivation™. It's important to understand that any concern you may feel is a vestigial response that stems from the remaining influence of the Noble Employee Myth doctrine that employee attitudes are a "symptom" of the health of the organization. That doctrine leads one to injudiciously interpret "bad attitudes" as a sign that the employee works for a "bad company" with "bad management." But nothing could be further from the truth. As your demotivating worldview evolves, you find that your "concern reflex" will grow weaker and weaker.

In this chapter I want to help executives understand how to think about employees attitudes in the context of a comprehensive program of Radical Demotivation™. To properly understand why your employees maintain the attitudes they do, it is helpful to understand a little bit about the way they live and what drives them. I'm not suggesting that you waste your time in tedious, unproductive, personal conversations with them, but there is value in studying them as a particular social group, in much the same way that sociologists attempt to understand panhandlers or street gangs. To that end, I'll begin by briefly reviewing a few macro-level trends endemic to the employee culture that will help you understand the average life of an employee. These trends are important to understand because they represent the bitter harvest of those who are the "beneficiaries" of the Noble Employee Myth. When the fruit of these trends is combined with their native impulses, both the nature of their attitudes and the need for Radical Demotivation™ become clear.

Many executives, even those who have become convinced of the wisdom and prudence of Radical Demotivation™, are tempted to turn to the motivational industry to seek relief from the virulence of their employees' attitudes. This is because the motivational industry promises to train employees how to maintain a Positive Mental Attitude (PMA) in the face of challenging circumstances. Not surprisingly, most of these programs meet with only limited, short-term, overpriced success because they lack the reality-based understanding of human nature required to make a lasting difference. Having said that, the motivational industry is not uniform in their teaching about attitudes. There is an emerging strain of teaching that *is* consistent with a comprehensive program of Radical Demotivation™ and executives may want to avail themselves of it. To help executives sort the wheat from the chaff, I'll spend a few pages describing and critiquing both approaches to attitudes, and then conclude the chapter with a few practical guidelines you can use to manipulate employees' attitudes as part of a comprehensive program of Radical Demotivation™.

UNSURPRISING TRENDS IN EMPLOYEES' PERSONAL LIVES

According to an October 2003 report by the United States Federal Reserve System, non-mortgage consumer debt had risen to a record $1.98 trillion. This translates into an average debt of $18,700 per household. That may not seem like much, but it is a staggering amount of debt for the average employee. According to the U.S. Bureau of Labor Statistics, the average income of a private sector employee is approximately $37,500. This means that the average employee has non-mortgage debt that is 50% of his annual income. It is no surprise, therefore, that the American Bankruptcy Institute reports that over 1.6 million people filed for bankruptcy in 2003.

These data are interesting because they provide several insights into the personal lives of the average employee. It is clear that many—if not *most*—employees are *attempting to live lifestyles they have not earned,* and rather than exercise wisdom and restraint in managing their financial affairs, they would rather saddle their lives with debt in order to experience the *benefits of being someone other than who they are.* Not surprisingly, this behavior is consistent with the narcissistic fantasy encoded in the Noble Employee Myth. The data on consumer debt are especially interesting, though, because they provide a uniquely clear measure of the gulf between employees' aspirations and their achievements: the greater the debt, the greater the gulf. It may be difficult for an employee to know with certainty whether he is smart, likeable, competent, or respected, but it is quite easy to determine whether he can afford to buy something.

The fact that so many employees are willing to act imprudently when the consequences of their behavior are so disastrous leads one to wonder: What must the rest of their lives be like? There is good reason to believe that the same recklessness they show in managing their finances is evidenced in the rest of their lives as well. For example, despite the fact that there is more nutritional information available than at any time in history, the United States Surgeon General recently declared that the rate of obesity in the population had become a crisis. This is partly due to the fact that employees tend to forgo exercise in lieu of mind-numbing activities such as watching television. Similarly, recent data indicate that the divorce rate is hovering at about 50%, alcohol abuse is on the rise, and Americans are increasingly turning to antidepressants to make it through the day. All of these data, when taken together, paint a picture of the average employee as an overweight, unproductive, self-medicating couch potato who is burdened by both unhappy relationships and crushing debt. Though it's tempting to view this predicament as nothing more than a self-inflicted wound, it is also part of the devastation wrought by the culture of narcissism.

FAILURE BEGETS BEWILDERMENT BEGETS RAGE

I realize that the image of the average employee described above is an archetype, and that individual employees approximate the archetype in greater or lesser degrees depending upon the stage of Mentropy™ they find themselves in. Nevertheless, the Mentropic Principle states that over time employees will tend toward the archetype—a principle that routinely receives anecdotal confirmation in organizations throughout the world. As a result of this Mentropic descent, most employees eventually feel a sense of confusion and bewilderment as they gradually become aware of, and begin to acknowledge to themselves, the widening gulf between their aspirations and their achievement. Having fully appropriated the Noble Employee Myth doctrine that they were "unique" and "special," they had come to believe that there were bound for greatness. Instead, they find themselves struck by how pathetically unimpressive, difficult, and ordinary their lives really are. As one disillusioned employee put it, "I feel like a warm near beer at Oktoberfest."

To their credit, most employees eventually have at least some form of an existential crisis and begin to ask themselves, "What went wrong?" Privately, they wonder how they ended up stuck in such a quagmire of mediocrity. Though they were told they could "be anything" or "do anything" they wanted when they grew up, many of them begin to wonder if there might be genuine differences between them and people like Andrew Carnegie, Henry Ford, Bill Gates, Neil Armstrong, or even you. Despite the obvious answer to that question, most employees are all too eager to sacrifice the truth on the altar of self-esteem, and in so doing, they trade the banquet of lucidity the crisis has prepared for the warm gruel of self-delusion served up by the Noble Employee Myth. Rather than using the crisis to help them discover the manifold ways in which they have been their own saboteurs, they inevitably search for *reasons external to themselves to explain their failures* (Jones & Harris, 1967; Weiner, 1992). They see successful people as having a variety of "unfair advantages," ranging from more robust parental affection to better connections to the ill-defined, utilitarian explanation that successful people have "better opportunities." Naturally, these beliefs produce an irrational feeling of injustice, and this sense of injustice becomes the prism through which they view the world. As a result, your employees see themselves as unfortunate victims of an unjust "system" that fails to recognize "the unique value" they bring to the team, and as a result, leaves them benched on the sidelines as they watch others receive the rewards and accolades they so desperately crave.

Despite the fact that your employees will point to a host of external factors to justify their surliness, it's clear that their circumstances do not determine their attitudes. Many people are able to face seemingly insurmountable challenges with both vigor and aplomb. Granted, these people are generally executives, but the fact that they are able to rise above their circumstances illustrates the point nonetheless. The truth of the matter is that *the bad attitudes your employees bring to work stem from a single root of narcissistic presumptuousness that influences the way they think and feel about everything they encounter.* Much of what they do and say is guided by an unconscious drive to realize their narcissistic fantasies. When that desire is thwarted or otherwise left unfulfilled, they respond in a ways that are reminiscent of the earliest stages of infantile development, when the inability to satiate their desires was met with emotional outbursts designed to ensure that their caretakers were well aware of their displeasure. In other words, *bad attitudes among your employees are little more than an adult form of infantile rage.* As your employees have gotten older they have developed more sophisticated and socially acceptable ways of expressing their childish reactions, but they have never actually dealt with the narcissistic roots of their dissatisfaction. As a result, they spend most of their lives being unhappy and expressing their dissatisfaction to anyone who will listen. They do this because they have never learned to take control of and be responsible for their lives, and they hope that their current caretakers—you, the executives they work for—will be as responsive to their self-absorbed infantile rage as their parents were so many years ago.

This is why it's so important that you ignore their complaints and refuse their demands. In so doing, you are forcing them to grow up and become at least a part of who they claim to be. Listening to them will only seem to legitimize their demands and reinforce the foul source of their toxic attitudes. I won't pretend that this process is either pleasant or easy. As you might expect, when you refuse to succumb to their demands, they will blame *you* as the source of their problems. Not surprisingly, this produces bitterness, cynicism, and a baseless sense of victimization, all of which make them even less pleasant or useful than in their natural state of inutility.

It is out of this cesspool of compounded failure and emotional toxicity that the motivational industry promises to rescue employees by teaching them the "secrets of success." One of the secrets they teach is that an individual's attitude and the way he responds to different circumstances plays a role in his success. Despite the pedestrian nature of this proposition, employees often respond to it as though they have been made privy to the hidden oracles of the Secret Society of the Super Successful, and that having acquired this wisdom they now have what it takes to "join the club." Consequently, they develop a cult-like attachment to different motivational teachers or "schools of thought." Executives are often fooled by the apparent change they see in their employees, and they get duped into spending huge sums of money for what end up being cliché-driven pep rallies that produce little more than short-term enthusiasm and bold declarations of "new beginnings." In the next section I'll explain why most of the motivational industry's teaching about attitudes is unable to produce the long-term change it promises, followed by an approach to attitudes consistent with Radical Demotivation™.

ATTITUDES AS ALCHEMY

Modern day alchemists find their home in the motivational industry. Having reckoned with the impossibility of transforming base metals into gold, they have now set their sights on the equally futile goal of transforming the unremarkable everyman (i.e., an employee) into the incomparable superman (i.e., an executive). The promise of being transformed from the average into the extraordinary is seductive, and those who are desperate or gullible are susceptible to that promise. Naturally, this makes your employees easy targets.

As I mentioned earlier, at some point in their lives most of your employees will experience an existential crisis. Having spurned or mocked prior encounters with wisdom, choosing instead to adopt a "herd mentality" that produced little more than a slavish conformity to people who no longer matter, the crisis makes your employees open to new ways of thinking and acting. Motivational speakers respond to this crisis by offering your employees a salvific message of new life and personal transformation that in some ways mimics the Christian Gospel. It is a message, however, that is driven by materialism and self-adulation rather than by virtue and self-discipline. Your employees will tend to respond enthusiastically to the message because it feeds their narcissism and reinforces their battered self-esteem, but the transformation is doomed to fail because it is rooted in fantasy rather than reality.

The motivational industry's formula for personal transformation generally begins with the assertion that an individual must have faith in himself. This step is so important that Norman Vincent Peale, one of the motivational industry's most influential spokesmen, emphasized it at the very beginning of his motivational classic, *The Power of Positive Thinking*:

> BELIEVE IN YOURSELF! Have faith in your abilities! Without a humble but reasonable confidence in your own powers you cannot be successful or happy. . . . A sense of inferiority and inadequacy interferes with the attainment of your hopes, but self-confidence leads to self-realization and successful achievement. . . . This book will help you believe in yourself and release your inner powers. (Peale, 1996, p. 1)

One would expect Peale's prescription to be predicated upon the nature of the self being considered or the market value of their abilities, but that is not the case. It is the *belief in self* that is the key to success, not the *self in which one believes*. This is because the motivational industry takes as an article of faith that the self is a source of unlimited power and potential, and that success is simply a matter of nurturing the latent seeds of greatness that lie buried deep within the soul of *every person*.

Despite a chronic awareness of their own powerlessness, squandered potential, and diminished capacities, your employees tend to find these groundless assertions quite compelling. In response, they will gladly take a leap of faith and assert their own hidden greatness. When they do, the leap will fill them with youthful exuberance and impetuous feelings of benevolence toward themselves and one another. They will then interpret these powerful emotions as incontrovertible evidence of the validity of the "insight" they have just been taught. Incredibly, your employees conclude that the reason for their unimpressive banality is not that they expect too much and produce too little, but that they expect too little and doubt themselves too much.

After rekindling this long-discredited, counterfactual faith in themselves, the next step in the transformation is to "walk by faith" in their newly idolized selves by adopting a positive attitude. Motivational guru John Maxwell (1993, p. 34) describes the centrality of one's attitude to his eventual success with the following two propositions:

Resources - Right Attitude = Defeat
Right Attitude - Resources = Victory

If you take Maxwell's formula literally, "resources" such as talent, intelligence, discipline, financing, and time are less important to success than having the right attitude. This idea is consistent with similarly rigorous motivational axioms such as "attitude determines altitude," and that one has got to "believe to achieve." Employees are drawn to this teaching because it seems to "play to their strengths" in a way that talent, intelligence, and discipline do not.

Armed with their newfound faith and positive attitudes, employees will believe that they truly are transformed and that the success that has eluded them thus far will now be magically drawn to them. Not surprisingly, these beliefs are quickly challenged by an oppressive, ego-threatening reality that provides compelling evidence that they are really are not much different than they were before they took the leap of faith into their untenable fantasy of unlimited potential. To combat this intrusion of reality, the motivational industry has developed several techniques designed to help employees maintain their belief in themselves. These techniques have various names, such as self-hypnosis (Maltz, 1960), autosuggestion (Hill, 1960), Neuro-linguistic Programming (Robbins, 1986), and Neuro-Associative Conditioning™ (Robbins, 1991), but they all have a common goal: to "trick" the mind into believing something is true and real, irrespective of the truth or reality of the belief. This "magic formula" was clearly articulated by Napoleon Hill (1960) in his classic treatise on motivation and success, *Think and Grow Rich*: "It is a well-known fact that one comes, finally, to believe whatever one repeats to oneself, *whether the statement be true or false*. If a man repeats a lie over and over, he will eventually accept the lie as truth. Moreover, he will believe it to be the truth" (p. 35, emphasis in original). Repetition is not the only means of self-deception that Hill prescribes. He also advocates that a person *pretend* that she has already acquired whatever she demands and then act accordingly. This is because authentically living a lie makes a lie seem more authentic. In brief, your employees are taught to believe that a positive attitude rooted in an imaginary self that is untethered to the past, present, or any realistic scenario for the future is the primary engine of personal transformation and a necessary precursor to inevitable success. Not surprisingly, employees often demonstrate tremendous facility at applying this technique because it makes them feel the way they did when they were younger, prior to their brushes with lucidity and the onset of their existential crises.

These techniques may make your employees feel better, but they come at a high price. As noted earlier, research indicates that positive thinkers not only distort their self-perceptions, they also perceive the rest of the world less accurately than their pessimistic counterparts (Seligman, 1998). In fact, employees who are most successful at applying the teaching of the motivational industry have a lot in common with gambling addicts: They have a legacy of failure and the odds are stacked against them, but they have deluded themselves into believing that this time they will win. Naturally, all this solipsistic self-affirmation doesn't change the external facts of the situation; it just changes your employees' ability to grasp them.

A colleague of mine was recently the victim of a positive thinker named Ty. Ty was a project manager who wanted to improve his leadership skills so he could advance in the organization. Unfortunately, he got wrapped up in the teaching of a motivational speaker who convinced him he needed to be more of an optimist. Ty was responsible for a very complex systems integration project that was fraught with hazards and difficulties. When Ty was told about problems with various parts of the project, he resolved not to let them get to him and to look at them positively, in a way that was empowering. He reasoned that a problem was nothing more than a hidden opportunity that included the seeds of its own solution. As a result, Ty was able to maintain his cheerful disposition even as problems began to mount and compound. When he gave status updates to his boss about the project, his optimism was refreshing. He repeatedly reported that he was confident the project would be delivered on time and under-budget—a belief that he had sent to his subconscious mind via autosuggestion. Unfortunately, Ty could not achieve what his disciplined denial of reality had convinced him to believe. The project ended six months late and significantly over budget. As it turned out, *Ty was the problem that contained its own solution:* He was fired and a pessimist was hired in his place.

Ty's experience is sadly typical. It should be clear that a spurious faith in a narcissistic fantasy is not the path to the genuine growth and maturity required to transform an employee into an executive. Like the alchemists of yesteryear who produced iron pyrite (fool's gold) in their futile attempt to create gold, today's motivational speakers teach employees to *pretend they are something they are not* in the hope of convincing themselves and others that they are. Clearly, this strategy is antithetical to the reality-based program of Radical Demotivation™.

ATTITUDES AS ACQUIESCENCE

A significantly smaller segment of the motivational industry has taken a different approach to employee attitudes. Rather than arguing that attitudes are the means of personal transformation that enable employees to succeed, they see attitudes as a means of deliberate acquiescence that enable the employee to cope. This is a position at least partly consistent with a comprehensive program of Radical Demotivation™.

This contingent draws its inspiration from psychologist and concentration camp survivor Viktor Frankl. In his classic text, *Man's Search For Meaning*, Frankl chronicled his concentration camp experiences and the key psychological lessons he learned from them. The lesson most often invoked by the motivational industry is that every person ultimately has control over their own attitude, independent of their circumstances, however unpleasant they may be. Consequently, employees should not blame their circumstances for their attitudes—their attitudes are their own fault. Frankl described his discovery as follows:

> Even conditions such as lack of sleep, insufficient food and various mental stress may suggest that the inmates were bound to react in certain ways. In the final analysis it becomes clear that the sort of person the prisoner became was the result of an inner decision, and not the result of camp influences alone. Fundamentally, therefore, any man can, even under such circumstances, decide what shall become of him—mentally and spiritually. He may retain his human dignity even in a concentration camp. Dostoevsky said once, "There is only one thing that I dread: not to be worthy of my sufferings." (1963, p. 104–105)

Frankl's comments contain the type of reality-based insight that is endemic to Radical Demotivation™. To most executives the truth of his comments are self-evident, but to the proponents of the Noble Employee Myth they are anathema.

One of the most popular recent implementations of Frankl's insight is what has come to be known as "The Fish! Philosophy." The "philosophy" is articulated in the bestselling book *Fish!* (Ludin, Paul, and Christensen, 2000), which includes the fictional account of a manager who is put in charge of a department that is considered the "toxic energy dump" of the company. The words used to describe the group of employees who worked in the toxic energy dump were "unresponsive, entitlement, zombie, unpleasant, slow, wasteland, and negative" (p. 18). In other words, they were average employees.

After several weeks, the manager placed in charge of the group was frustrated with her inability to make a difference. She had received a warning that she could be fired if she couldn't fix the department, but she was at a loss as to what she should do. Serendipitously, one day she took a walk past the "world famous" Pike Place Fish market where she met a fishmonger named Lonnie who taught her the four principles of the Fish! Philosophy:

- Choose your attitude—Everybody chooses their attitude, whether they realize it or not.
- Play—Everybody should try to have fun at work.
- Make their day—Include customers, whether internal or external, in the fun.
- Be present—Listen to and be considerate of others.

The fictional manager was skeptical as to whether the principles would really work in her pretend organization, but she decided to try them anyway. As is so often the case with change agents, the theoretical manager initially met with resistance when she introduced the principles of the Fish! Philosophy to her hypothetical employees. But then, a make-believe breakthrough happened. An imaginary long-time employee spoke up and said that she hated coming to work because the company seemed like a morgue. She admitted that she was looking for another job, but threatened to stay if they could breathe some life back into the place. The others fictively chimed in and pledged to try the Fish! Philosophy. Not surprisingly, the group was transformed from a toxic energy dump into an office that functioned, in many ways, like a fish market. Moreover, the fictional manager was even awarded the "Chairman's Award" for her feat, which probably would have been well deserved if it were real.

Despite the fictional articulation of the Fish! Philosophy, there are several features about it that are consistent with a program of Radical Demotivation™. First, it's clear that the imaginary employees were dealing with the reality of their fictional situation rather than trying to deny it. As I mentioned before, Radical Demotivation™ is a reality-based approach to dealing with poor employee attitudes. Second, the employees were clearly identified as the locus of the problem. The toxic energy dump was created by an entitlement mentality among the employees who believed they deserved more than they had earned. Despite their initial grumbling and complaining about their jobs, there was nothing substantive about their jobs that changed. Once the individual employees changed their attitudes, the department changed. Third, the change in the employees did not include any groundless assertions of greatness or other signs of conversion to the cult of self. The change stemmed from the employees' honest appraisal of the situation they had created, a humble acquiescence to the limits of their capacity, and the satisfaction that comes from living within the parameters of their utility. Finally, nobody got a raise.

Though it is generally considered a motivational strategy, the Fish! Philosophy is a suitable complement to a comprehensive program of Radical Demotivation™. Its recognition that employees are the source of their own discontent and that job satisfaction is best achieved when employees acquiesce and adapt to their limitations is consistent with a demotivational strategy. Having said that, it's best to introduce it in the latter stages of a demotivational program when the employees are ready to accept the fact they have no realistic alternatives. Moreover, it is important that you first gut the Fish! by removing principles two and three before serving it to your organization. To the Radically Demotivating organization, unnecessary play and fun are as foul and unpalatable as the half-digested matter in the intestinal tract of the fish that inspired the program itself.

To executives who are busy building and managing the engines of prosperity, who have neither the time nor the inclination to parse sophistry, the motivational industry's teaching about attitudes can be a bit confusing. Much of what they say sounds right to the casual listener. Executives detect a measure of truth in the oft-recycled slogans and aphorisms that are a ubiquitous feature of the motivational milieu, and they identify with the inspiring stories of people who have used wit and determination to beat the odds and overcome adversity. Moreover, they know that attitudes are important and that successful people respond to crises differently than unsuccessfully people. Consequently, executives frequently assume that the motivational industry's teaching about attitudes will help their employees adapt more effectively to difficulties at work. Instead, it fosters a spurious sense of identification with their superiors and a mistaken belief in their own indispensability. As a result, employees not only fail to adapt to difficulties more effectively, they become more adept at being difficulties.

When one listens closely, however, it's clear that the vast majority of the motivational industry's teaching about attitudes is built on the erroneous foundation of the Noble Employee Myth. The idea that every employee has unlimited potential simply reinforces the self-adulating narcissism that is at the root of employees' sense of entitlement, and with it, their attitude problems. Even worse, the assertion that employees need greater confidence in themselves, apart from requiring a legacy of noteworthy achievement, also requires a willful retreat from reality. This is why the slogans, the pep rallies, and the bold claims of future success that are endemic to the motivational industry are unable to equip employees with the types of attitudes that might one day help them become executives. Consequently, this teaching is incompatible with a program of Radical Demotivation™.

PRINCIPLES OF A RADICALLY DEMOTIVATING APPROACH TO ATTITUDES

When people talk about a "negative attitude," they are generally referring to a state of mind that expresses itself in social interactions that are unpleasant for one or more of the participants. Consequently, many executives uncritically assume that negative attitudes are necessarily "bad" attitudes. In some cases this is correct, like when an employee is surly with a customer. In other cases they're not, like when an employee is surly with a co-worker who deserves it.

This social-interaction approach is a valid conceptualization of negative attitudes, but it's also incomplete. A negative attitude also refers to a state of mind that provides at least a modicum of torment for the person with the attitude, apart from any social interaction. In this sense, negative attitudes are best thought of as the self-inflicted wounds of the emotionally immature. This is an important distinction because an effective program of Radical Demotivation™ is likely to increase negative attitudes among your employees, especially during the early stages of the program. By stimulating the festering wounds of emotional immaturity, Radical Demotivation™ brings to the surface your employees' negative attitudes and accelerates the emergence of hopelessness and self-recrimination in order to facilitate their eventual acquiescence to your objectives. Therefore, don't lose heart if your employees appear to be getting worse rather than better as you implement the Radically Demotivating principles outlined below. That just means the process is working.

Before I get to the strategies for confronting employee attitudes, I need to point out that it is not uncommon for employees with negative attitudes to be rude or abrasive to whoever they come in contact with, including customers and vendors. This is little more than a childish, passive/aggressive form of acting out in the hope of hurting you by hurting the business. Therefore, it is important that you develop comprehensive policies governing your employees' interactions with customers and vendors that include severe penalties, including immediate termination for any unprofessional behavior[1]. Such policies will not only prevent your customers and vendors from being the victims of your employees' churlishness, it will also provide you with the legal documentation that you need to respond to an infraction in whatever way you see fit.

Make Employees Continually Prove Their Worth To The Organization By Completing Challenging Tasks

In an interesting program of research, Columbia University psychologist Carol Dweck and her colleagues (Dweck, Goetz, & Strauss, 1980; Dweck & Leggett, 1988; Elliott & Dweck, 1988) found that people who tried to *prove their worth* had a significantly more difficult time performing challenging tasks than those who tried to *add to their skill* by completing the same tasks. Those who attempted to prove their worth

---

[1] This recommendation is void where prohibited by law.

responded to the challenge with anxiety. They tried to discredit the value of the task, put themselves down, and became defensive. In contrast, those who attempted to add to their skill enjoyed the challenge of the task, stayed focused on discovering a solution, and experimented with various approaches to accomplishing the task. When the task was easy, the two groups responded the same way.

Executives often let their employees off the hook by giving them tasks that are too easy or by fostering a learning environment. By continually forcing their employees to prove their value to the organization, executives can strip away the façade of untested mettle that affords their employees the luxury of conceit. When implemented correctly, every difficulty, setback, and unanticipated challenge will chip away at an employee's security and self-confidence until they increasingly seem to portend impending doom. Naturally, this produces anxiety. The chronic sense of anxiety that stems from anticipating what feels like inevitable defeat is a potent weapon in the battle against employee narcissism.

Create A Diminished Feeling Of Choice

Choice is inherently self-indulgent. Any time someone exercises *their choice* they are indulging their self. Consequently, executives need to be careful not to provide their employees with too much autonomy; to do so simply bolsters their own unruly egos. Instead, they should apply the insights developed by Viktor Frankl who learned about the liberating dignity of controlling his own attitude in a circumstance of minimal choice. This is a lesson your employees need to learn, and Radical Demotivation™ is designed to create the circumstances to help them learn it.

As an aside, this is consistent with the ideas emerging in the exciting new field of *nanomanagement*. Drawing upon the nanotechnological principles of physics, engineering, and materials science, nanomanagers are working to determine the smallest degree of freedom necessary for their employees do their jobs. It's clear that excessive freedom creates more problems than it solves, including feelings of empowerment and self-worth. In contrast, lack of choice is inherently demotivating (Deci, 1980; Seligman, 1998). As such, it attacks the vanity that flourishes in your employees' souls.

Develop A Culture Of Blame

A culture of blame intensifies the anxiety and uncertainty of continually needing to prove oneself by multiplying the number of judges the employee must satisfy. This is important because longer projects may allow an employee to go an extended period of time without feeling the sting of evaluation from those who really matter. But a culture of blame can turn even the most mundane organizational phenomena into a hotbed of political activity. The constantly evolving political alliances that form around petty political issues, combined with the duplicity and subterfuge they inspire, create the real possibility that one could become her co-workers' sacrificial lamb for the most inconsequential infraction.

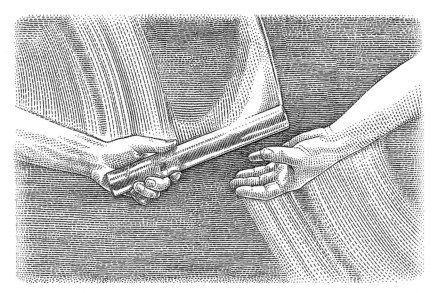

BLAME

THE SECRET TO SUCCESS IS KNOWING WHO TO BLAME FOR YOUR FAILURES.

Implement An *It Could Be Worse*™ Program

Your employees are like the proverbial Chicken Little: They like to exaggerate their problems and misfortune and claim that "the sky is falling." They will continue to do this as long as two conditions exist: (1) They believe they have a legitimate complaint, and (2) they believe someone will listen. The purpose of the It Could Be Worse™ program is to undermine the legitimacy of your employees' complaints. This is done, very simply, by proving to your employees that no matter how bad they think it is, It Could Be Worse™. There are a couple of ways this can be done very effectively. First, leverage your employees' inherent love for scandal and gossip by surreptitiously spreading rumors of impending difficulties—layoffs, cutbacks in perks, reorganization, office relocations and the like. Once they realize their jobs may cease to exist, or they may have to move, or work might get more difficult, their current situation will seem less dire. Second, start a newsletter that features a combination of current events and company news and make sure it includes plenty of stories of people who are in more difficult straits than your employees. It is difficult for even the most self-absorbed wage earner to remain ungrateful and demanding when other people, especially those with relevant similarities to your employees, are in appreciably less advantageous circumstances.

Practice Disciplined Apathy

Despite the normal human reflex to express interest in those who are hurting or troubled, you have to communicate to your employees that you *do not care* about their "problems" or their "suffering." As soon as they believe you care, they will immediately resume their complaints in the hope of eliciting your interest or compassion. Therefore, you must refuse; you must ignore them. Your employees have to believe that their complaints, moodiness and sullenness will never matter, and therefore they may as well grow up and deal with life.

If you've been burned by programs that were supposed to generate positive attitudes and goodwill among your employees, only to find them more demanding and petulant than you could have imagined, I hope it's clear that Radical Demotivation™ is the answer you've been looking for. By striking at the narcissistic roots of your employees' attitudes you have the opportunity to get them to reckon with the reality of their own banality. This reckoning should force them to abandon their fantasies of being more than they can be and the demands that come with it. Instead, the message should constantly be reinforced that their lives could not only be worse, there is a good chance that one day they will be. As a result, they should learn to be grateful for whatever they have, because one day it will be gone.

THE POWER OF SHARING:
Making Sure Your
Employees Know How
Important They Are

No man is pleased with a companion who does not
increase, in some respect, his fondness for himself.
—SAMUEL JOHNSON

One of the most important aspects of any organization is the communication that occurs within it. As Organizational Communication theorist Gerald Goldhaber (1993) has pointed out, communication has been called the "life blood" of an organization, the "glue" that binds it together, and the "force" that permeates the organization. Organizational communication is the means by which work activity is coordinated, information is disseminated, and the social needs of the participants are met (Coffee, Cook, & Hunsaker, 1994). It's clear that absent some form of communication it would be impossible for people to organize their activity, and without some measure of organized activity, for all practical purposes, an "organization" cannot exist.

The interpersonal interaction that takes place between executives and employees is clearly one of the most pervasive and strategic types of organizational communication. According to the late Fredric Jablin (1985) formerly of the University of Richmond's School of Leadership, from one third to two thirds of managers' time is spent communicating with subordinates, and the primary mode of that communication is oral, face-to-face interaction. Interpersonal interaction is the principal means by which relationships are developed and social identities are forged. Recognizing the increased complexity and often inadequate allocation of power in non-hierarchical organizations, Harvard Business School's Rosabeth Moss Kanter and Linda Hill have also highlighted the importance of developing interpersonal relationships to get things done. Hill (1996) has noted that as a person ascends in rank and responsibility in an organization, his success will increasingly depend upon his adeptness at developing effective work relationships with people who can help him reach his goals. Kanter (1989) agrees and has called the ability to leverage interpersonal relationships to accomplish one's goals the "new managerial work" of modern organizations.

SUPERIOR/SUBORDINATE COMMUNICATION AND THE NOBLE EMPLOYEE MYTH

For executives committed to a program of Radical Demotivation™, the academic literature on superior/subordinate interaction is of little use. As can be expected, most of that literature has been written by proponents of the Noble Employee Myth, and therefore it includes an acute pro-employee bias. For example, according to Jablin (1985), research into managerial communication indicates that employees' satisfaction with the supervision they receive increases as their managers' communication style becomes more "employee-centered." It should be obvious that this "finding" could have just as easily been stated, "employee satisfaction with supervision increases as executives find new ways to accommodate their employees' narcissism."

In spite of the absurdity of such employee-worshipping nonsense, it remains important for executives to ask: What exactly *is* employee-centered communication? The question is critical for the obvious reason that if you aren't careful, you may find that you yourself have inadvertently adopted an employee-centered communication style that is working against you. Those who persist in such folly might as well begin prostrating themselves before workers and offering animal sacrifices in appeasement.

It is hard to zero in on the real nature of "employee-centered" communication since most employees have no "center," just a hollow void where substance might have gone had more been demanded of them during the formative years. With a black hole occupying the space where their soul might've been, they house a swirling vortex of "unmet needs" in a constant state of implosion. Nevertheless, we can get an idea of what the term means by reviewing Charles Redding's summary of decades of research into superior/subordinate interaction. According to Redding (1972) "better supervisors" display the following five communication characteristics:

1. The better supervisors tend to be more "communication-minded"; they enjoy talking and speaking up in meetings; they are able to explain instructions and policies; they enjoy conversing with subordinates.
2. The better supervisors tend to be willing, empathic listeners; they respond understandingly to so-called "silly" questions from employees; they are approachable; they will listen to suggestions and complaints with an attitude of fair consideration and willingness to take appropriate action.
3. The better supervisors tend (with some notable exceptions) to "ask" or "persuade" in preference to "telling" or "demanding."
4. The better supervisors tend to be sensitive to the feelings and ego-defensive needs of their subordinates; e.g., they are careful to reprimand in private rather than in public.
5. The better supervisors tend to be more open in their passing along of information; they are in favor of giving advance notice of impending changes, and of explaining the "reasons why" behind policies and regulations. (p. 443)

As you read this list, it is worthwhile to notice that decades of research have *not* found that the so-called better supervisors do any-

thing like "highlight employee failures," "express appropriate indignation toward substandard work," or "ignore employee complaints." Is
that because these communication behaviors are not important? No,
it's because they do not fit within the orthodoxy of the Noble Employee
Myth. Instead, "better supervisors" have to endure "silly questions,"
they have to "ask" their employees to do what they are paid to do rather
than "tell" them to do it, and they have "be sensitive" to their employees' egos. It should be clear that rather than being a roadmap to
improved superior/subordinate relationships, these "findings" are little more than executive shackles forged in the minds of unproductive
employees and their academic apologists. As such, they are inapplica-
ble to a program of Radical Demotivation™.

THE PITFALL OF INDIGNATION

Once they choose liberation and start down the path of Radical
Demotivation™, many executives take a misstep or two that causes
them to stall. In their understandable zeal to eradicate the different
forms of employee pandering that have taken root in their organizations, they sometimes feel hamstrung labor laws and begin to wonder
if Radical Demotivation™ is a viable, legal alternative to managing their
employees. This apparent quandary is due to a gross misunderstanding of Radical Demotivation™ and what it entails. It is surprisingly
common for executives to make the mistake of assuming that Radical
Demotivation™ is a warrant for expressing the indignation they feel
toward their employees after enduring years of their unrelenting
exploitation. They believe that it entails being mean, rude, or abusive
in a vengeful effort to demean or humiliate their employees. Frankly,
nothing could be further from the truth. Those are the types of tactics
your employees resort to, and to be quite honest, they're beneath
you. Radical Demotivation™ is designed to dislodge your employees'
sense of entitlement in the most covert, unobtrusive way possible.
In fact, overt displays of rudeness and hostility are more likely to hinder the success of a covert program of Radical Demotivation™ than
to help it.

For those of you who find this assertion counterintuitive, let me explain. There are two fundamental reasons why treating your employees harshly, no matter how viscerally justified it may seem, is really not in your best interest. First, you have to realize that your employees are also the victims of the Noble Employee Myth, and as victims, they have no rational context for understanding your rebuke. They have been led to believe that they can be more than they are if only you would create the Eden-like environment they need to grow and achieve—that is, one which is supportive, affirming and motivating. They do not realize that they have grounded their identities in the intersection of a thoroughly discredited, simple-minded behaviorism and a self-worshiping humanism, both of which work together to foment their narcissism and exonerate them from taking responsibility for their lives. Blaming you and citing your unwillingness to acquiesce to their demands as an explanation for their lack of achievement is one of the few defense mechanisms they have against being inexorably compelled to face the fact that they have repeatedly squandered the opportunities presented to them out of a craven fear of confronting their weaknesses. Consequently, your employees have no rational or ethical context for understanding and benefiting from whatever interpersonal invective you may use, no matter how incisive or instructive it may be. As the Biblical proverb says, "A rebuke makes a greater impression on a discerning person than a hundred blows on a fool" (Pr. 17:10). Hence, a "hundred blows" levied against your employees will do no good. The scales may have fallen from *your* eyes, but I can guarantee you that they will have to be surgically removed from your employees' eyes. Fortunately, Radical Demotivation™ is a surgical instrument designed to do just that.

The second reason why it is unwise to be rude or harsh to your employees is this: Until they are completely disabused of the mesmerizing error of the Noble Employee Myth, they will continue to be animated by a sense of entitlement that influences everything they think, say, and do. This sense of entitlement leads them to believe that they have a *right* to be treated with respect, and that if you communicate with them in a way that is harsh or condescending, they will interpret your behavior as a violation of that right. If this happens, you've effectively shot yourself in the foot. As twisted as it may sound, your employees will use such an event to justify the belief that *you are the exploiter* and they *are the victims,* and as you undoubtedly recognize by now, this belief is one of the key canons of Noble Employee Myth orthodoxy. Consequently, rather than "teaching them a lesson" or "putting them in their place" (as many executives believe they are doing when they attempt to humiliate or deride their employees), being harsh simply serves to justify the employee attitudes and beliefs you are covertly endeavoring to overcome. Moreover, you will suffer a significant loss of credibility among employees who still feel a residual sense of entitlement. These employees will assume that the use of invective and vitriol are signs of a *character defect of yours* rather than a reasonable response to them and their behavior. It is only *after* your employees have been completely demotivated that harsh comments can be used without the risk of having them signify a moral or character weakness of yours. At that stage of the process you will simply be echoing the comments your employees tell themselves in the soliloquy of their own internal dialog, and at that point your employees will find even the harshest comments psychologically confirming. This, of course, is one of the unanticipated "soft" benefits of Radical Demotivation™.

SOCIAL NEEDS: THE FULCRUM OF RADICAL DEMOTIVATION™

So what are you supposed to do? If you can't be harsh, how do you exploit the tremendous potential inherent in the superior/subordinate relationship? Are you supposed to encourage your employees? Hardly. Are you supposed to treat them with the respect they demand? Of course not. These types of behaviors will only increase their self-confidence and make them even more demanding. To understand how you can appear to be both winsome and respectful, while at the same time relentlessly pursuing a covert agenda of Radical Demotivation™, you have to understand something about the psychological needs of your employees. I am not talking about the phantom needs of the organizational behaviorist—needs such as "self-actualization," "achievement" or "goal attainment." It's clear that scores of people who work in sweatshops, government bureaucracies, labor camps, and retail stores are able to survive their entire careers without experiencing anything like "achievement" or "self-actualization." I am talking about real psychological needs like recognition, understanding, and acceptance (Gordon, 1977, Laing, 1969). These are the types of needs that are rooted in our very nature as social beings, and when they are left unmet they tend to produce increasingly acute levels of insecurity, self-doubt, and self-loathing. These needs are like the soft, fleshy underbelly of the human soul, and when assaulted, they have the potential to render even the most self-absorbed narcissists vulnerable to a disorienting level of self-examination.

Radical Demotivation™ entails learning to communicate with your employees in ways that frustrate their attempts to meet those needs. In so doing you are engaging in a systematic process of psychological starvation. That may sound extreme, but let's face it; your employees' egos have become morbidly obese and nothing counteracts obesity like starvation. For years you have served as both butler and benefactor as they have feasted on the rich psychological delicacies of the Noble Employee Myth, but now it's time for you to serve them their just desserts.

Your employees have a cluster of needs that can only be met by another person. These needs are essential to the development and maintenance of their perceptions of themselves and the attendant self-acceptance and self-esteem they will feel as a result of those perceptions. This is because their identities are not immutable, isolated, psychological phenomena; they are socially negotiated, contextualized, value-driven social psychological accomplishments that are constantly renegotiated and re-contextualized throughout their lives. In other words, an employee cannot reasonably believe she is a particular type of person unless she can convince one or more others that she is that type of person. For example, how does one of your employees know whether she is bright, witty, competent, attractive, or likeable? It is only by getting feedback from others that either confirms or refutes her self-perceptions that she can answer those questions. If she receives feedback from others that she is competent, she has a good reason to think of herself as competent. By the same token, if she receives feedback from others that she is not competent, she cannot reasonably maintain the self-perception that she is competent. If she finds that some people find her competent while others do not, she would have to conclude that she is competent in some contexts but not in others, or that one of the competing groups does not yet know the "real" her.

Unless your employees are schizoid or psychotic, their need to achieve a measure of agreement between themselves and others about who they are is very strong. That is why *your employees are dependent upon you* and their coworkers to establish and maintain their understanding of who they are. That dependency is like a fulcrum buried deep within their souls. It enables you to dislodge years of narcissistic self-perceptions in all but the most psychologically detached.

DISCONFIRMATION AND CONFIRMATION: LEVERS OF PSYCHOLOGICAL TRANSFORMATION

In order to address your employees' narcissism head-on, you need to become skilled in the use of the psychological levers called *disconfirmation* and *confirmation* (Cissna & Sieburg, 1990; Laing; 1969, Sieburg; 1976). Disconfirmation is the process of providing signals or cues to employees which let them know that you see them differently than the way they see themselves, thereby giving them reason to doubt or question their self-perceptions. Conversely, confirmation is the process of signaling to employees that you see them the way they see themselves, thus confirming their self-perceptions.

Disconfirmation is the primary interpersonal strategy you must learn if you really want to fight employee motivation and the effects of the Noble Employee Myth. If you learn how to do this well, you will become the personification of Radical Demotivation™ in your organization. Interpersonal disconfirmation is the one conversational lever large enough to enable you to dislodge the foundations of your employees' sense of self-worth and entitlement.

Having said that, do not expect miracles overnight. Disconfirmation is effective but it takes time to drain the swamp of employee self-respect. Our experiments at Despair Labs indicate that employees often go through a phase of resistance that one executive dubbed "Custer's Bluster™," named after General George Armstrong Custer for his declarations of certain victory immediately prior to his decisive and final defeat. In a similar fashion, approximately 33% of your employees will make an indignant "last stand," but let not your heart be troubled: This is one situation in which persistence really does pay off.

To a lesser degree, you will need to learn how to confirm your employees as well, but this is only *after* your employees are well along the path toward Radical Demotivation™. Over time, your employees will begin to verbalize expressions of self-doubt and self-contempt. Those are the only times you should confirm your employees, and even then confirmation should be used sparingly. We've seen cases when confirming an employee's self-contempt actually gave rise to a brief episode of Custer's Bluster™. As strange as it may seem, the employees actually took pride in accurately diagnosing the sources of their shame. Is there any better example of the perversity of the Noble Employee Myth?

SHOOTING BLANKS?

At this point, I'm sure some of you are a bit confused. You believe that using confirmation and disconfirmation in the ways I've described sounds impotent, as though I am advocating that you pull your punches just when you have your employees on the ropes. Nothing could be further from the truth. Persistent disconfirmation has been associated with severe psychological trauma. According to the late British psychiatrist R. D. Laing (1969), disconfirmation can lead to guilt, shame, anxiety, and despair—the emotional jackhammers you need to break up the adamant, self-worshipping psyches of your employees.

To understand how this is so, consider the rather common experience of parents and offspring who understand the nature of their relationship differently. The paradigmatic disjuncture in relational definitions generally occurs in the offspring's early teen years as he attempts to assert more freedom and independence than the parents are willing to grant. When the parents ask the teen questions about his activities or whereabouts, the teen will often fly off into a rage, claiming that the parents are treating him "like a child." In other words, the parents are *disconfirming* the teen's self-perceptions of how much autonomy should be afforded to one as wise and omniscient as he.

The power of disconfirmation was wonderfully illustrated in a series of exercises conducted by UCLA sociology pioneer Harold Garfinkel. He sent his students home and had them act like boarders among their family members for between 15 minutes and one hour. As boarders, the students could no longer rely on knowledge of how their own families worked, and as a result, they were overtly polite and respectful, behaving as though they were trying to make a good impression on someone they had only recently met. Garfinkel (1967) summarized the findings from his students as follows:

> Reports were filled with accounts of *astonishment, bewilderment, shock, anxiety, embarrassment, and anger,* and with charges by various family members that the student was *mean, inconsiderate, selfish, nasty, or impolite.* Family members demanded explanations: What's the matter? What's gotten into you? . . . One mother, infuriated when her daughter spoke to her only when she was spoken to, began to shriek in angry denunciation of the daughter for her disrespect and insubordination and refused to be calmed by the student's sister. . . .
>
> Occasionally family members would first treat the student's action as a cue for a joint comedy routine which was soon replaced by irritation and exasperated anger at the student for not knowing when enough was enough. *Family members mocked the "politeness" of the students*—"Certainly Mr. Herzberg!"—or charged the student with acting like a wise guy and generally reproved the "politeness" with sarcasm. . . .
>
> Many accounts reported a version of the following confrontation. A father followed his son into the bedroom. "Your mother is right. You don't look well and you're not talking sense. You had better get another job that doesn't require such late hours." To this *the student replied that he appreciated the consideration, but that he felt fine and only*

wanted a little privacy. The father responded in a high rage, "I don't want any more of *that* out of you and if you can't treat your mother decently you'd better move out!" (p. 47–48, emphasis added)

Though Garfinkel's interest was not in the effects of interpersonal disconfirmation, his exercise was a good example of the process nonetheless. The students' interactions were disconfirming because their behavior *denied* the preexisting nature of the relationships they had established between themselves and their family members. Whereas the families expected a more intimate, casual relationship with the students, the students behaved in ways that suggested their relationships were more distant and formal. Consequently, the intimate relationships were disconfirmed by the students. The most striking feature of Garfinkel's results is that they show, in a rather dramatic fashion, how traumatic interpersonally disconfirming messages can be, *even when the messages are polite and respectful.* One might expect the families to respond as they did if the students were rude and obnoxious, but the fact that they were unusually polite and deferential highlights the intimidating influence of interpersonal disconfirmation.

Studies like these provide compelling evidence that using an interpersonal strategy designed to politely but persistently disconfirm your employees is not emasculating, as some have feared. You need to keep in mind that unwarranted politeness is disarming and will prompt your employees to want to believe what you have to say. As the same time, interpersonal disconfirmation is disheartening and will lead your employees to question, doubt, and eventually dislike themselves. When used in combination, these two communication strategies will function like an interpersonal sucker-punch that will leave your glass-jawed employees reeling with self-contempt but too stupefied to understand why.

To get good at this, you need to know how to identify the psychological targets of disconfirmation and the types of messages that are most effective. To that end, I will provide a brief review of the four elements of disconfirmation, followed by several tactics that you can begin to use in your organization.

THE ELEMENTS OF DISCONFIRMATION

Because the nature of human identity is both complex and opaque, it is often difficult to pin down the types of interactions that are either confirming or disconfirming. To make our understanding of disconfirmation more useful, Cissna and Sieburg (1990) identified four "elements" of our social identities that can become the targets of disconfirming interaction. The four elements are:

1. **The element of existence.** This refers to the fundamental belief that a person exists in space and time as a particular type of person with a unique, identifiable identity. The most intense forms of disconfirmation are being treated as though you do not physically exist, or as if you are a dramatically different person than who you believe yourself to be.

2. **The element of relating.** This dimension is based upon the recognition that significant portions of our identities are a function of being in certain types of relationships with other people and institutions. For example, you may be *the spouse* of a specific person, *an executive* in a specific company, or *a friend* of someone. To deny those relationships and the rights and responsibilities they entail would be to deny a portion of who you believe yourself to be.

3. **The element of significance or worth.** Very simply, this dimension refers to the idea that everybody likes to feel valuable, that others regard them as important enough to try to understand them, and to judge them positively when they are understood.

4. **The element of validity of experience.** This dimension refers to the need to have others to judge your experience of the world as valid enough that you be regarded as sane. The converse, of course, would be for others to express such doubt in your experience of the world that you have no idea what is real and what is false.

MAKING DISCONFIRMATION WORK FOR YOU

Building upon these elements, Cissna and Sieburg (1990) also identified several disconfirming patterns of interaction and three general patterns of confirming interaction. Using their taxonomy, I want to provide you with several concrete examples of how you can use interpersonal disconfirmation as part of a covert program of Radical Demotivation™.

The examples I have provided below are intended to be suggestive rather than exhaustive. My hope is that as you read them you will not only see how you can work them into your daily routine, but you will also think of new, equally disconfirming patterns of interaction that fit your own personal style. Unlike some of the other strategies required to implement a program of Radical Demotivation™, interpersonal disconfirmation provides you and the other executives in your company with an opportunity to imbue the demotivational process with your own idiosyncratic styles, or as the vacuously trendy pseudo-Zen aficionados would say, it gives you chance to *be* Radical Demotivation™.

I should also point out that many of these tactics need to be used selectively on specific individuals or groups that you have targeted, and even then, tactics will have to be varied according to situation. For example, you may have decided to ignore one of your employees, but then find you need the employee to carry some boxes for you. Naturally, you cannot ignore the employee when you are telling her where to put the boxes. As you gain facility in using these different tactics, you will find it easy to substitute one for the other as the need arises.

STRATEGY 1: DISCONFIRMATION BY INDIFFERENCE

These messages are intended to deny the existence or significance of an individual's physical, psychological, or relational presence. As such, they communicate to the person that as far as you are concerned he does not exist, and even if he did exist, he wouldn't matter. Expressing indifference is one of the most disconfirming types of messages you can send. As philosopher and psychology pioneer William James is reported to have said, "No more fiendish punishment could be devised, even were such a thing physically possible, than that one should be turned loose in society and remain absolutely unnoticed by all the members thereof" (Laing, 1969, p. 82). Though James' vision is not possible, you can approximate the experience through a variety of means. Cissna and Sieburg identified three primary types of disconfirmation by indifference: denial of presence, avoiding involvement, and rejecting communication.

Expressing Indifference By Denying Another's Presence

According to Cissna and Sieburg (1990), the persistent failure to secure the recognition and acknowledgement of one's physical or psychological existence has been associated with a host of psychological pathologies, including alienation, self-destructiveness, violence, and psychosis. As an executive, your vastly superior level of social power makes it very easy for you to leverage this dynamic in the lives of your employees. There are several ways this can be accomplished.

1. **Ignore employees in passing.** Throughout the day you will have several opportunities to come into contact with your employees, whether you pass them in the hallways or walk through their "work areas." Many executives make the mistake of glancing around and looking to see if people are working. Sometimes they smile, wave, or stop and talk to employees as they pass through a room. This is what Peters and Waterman (1982) called MBWA, or Management By Wandering Around, and it is incompatible with a successful program of Radical Demotivation™. I have talked to some executives who foolishly believe staring at employees as they walk by is intimidating and sends the message that the employees had better be productive. Nothing could be further from the truth. Making contact with your employees, no matter how casual or inconsequential, sends the message that they matter to you in some way, and that message is at least minimally confirming. Moreover, when you walk through a room the employees may look productive, but as soon as you leave they go back to alienating your customers, your vendors, and one another.

2. **"Forget" to include employees in notable events.** Can you imagine how you would feel if your spouse forgot your birthday? Naturally, you would feel like you didn't matter very much. You can use the same principle with select employees. Say I have a rising star who seems to be growing in self-importance. I'll begin to exclude him from key events such as business meetings, conference calls, lunches, and social activities. Once he discovers that all his cohorts are involved, he immediately feels a profound sense of alienation. He may inquire as to why he wasn't included. He wonders if I'm angry with him or if he did something wrong. At that

point I calmly and unapologetically explain that I am not angry and he is not being punished; I just didn't think to include him. I explain that when I was putting the list of attendees together, he never even crossed my mind. As you can imagine, an employee so filled with self-importance would much rather find out that I was angry or disappointed with him and that I had deliberately chosen not to include him, than discover that he mattered too little to warrant consideration one way or the other.

3. **"Forget" to include employees in the flow of information.** The dissemination of information is essential to the survival of any organization and employees want to be "in the loop" as much as possible. Informal networks emerge in every organization and one of their functions is to provide those who are "outside the loop" access to insider information. Given this dynamic, you can choose one or more employees and begin to exclude them from the distribution lists for memos and email. They will eventually get the information through the informal network, but they will also get the message that they are out of the loop. As with the tactic above, your rationale for not including them has to be that you did not think about it or that you simply forgot. As this continues, it will become increasingly obvious to others in the company that you regard the targets as both outsiders and inconsequential. As this recognition spreads, the informal sources of information will begin to dry up because the informants will fear being stigmatized through their association with the targets. The targets will eventually realize they are mere institutional ciphers, unnecessary to the success and well-being of the company, and that they are employed to *add* value to the company, not because they *are* a value to the company.

4. **"Forget" the names of certain employees.** This tactic was passed on to me by a golfing buddy who was an early tester of Radical Demotivation™. He is the founder and CEO of a financial services firm that employs about 135 people. Just after he started the program the company hired a hot-shot Wharton grad named Walker to be a securities analyst. Walker had dreams of being an institutional money manager and was sure he would impress everyone in the firm as much as he had impressed his profes-

sors. My golfing buddy, who himself was a financial prodigy in college, saw in Walker far more bravado than his talent warranted, and took the opportunity to put his own twist on interpersonal disconfirmation.

My buddy met Walker not long after he was hired. Coincidentally, my friend had also attended Wharton, and in "relating," discovered they had even been in the same fraternity. Walker spoke constantly about his lofty ambitions, his enormous popularity with peers and professors at Wharton, and of his certainty that he was destined to become the youngest partner in my friend's firm. My buddy welcomed him and sent him on his way.

Because they worked in different offices he didn't see Walker again for about four months. Then one day Walker was walking down the hallway of the executive offices and saw my friend walking toward him. Walker got a big grin on his face, stuck out his hand and said, "It's nice to see you again, sir." My friend stopped, looked him in the eyes and said, "Hello, thank you. I'm sorry. Have we met?" Walker was dumbfounded. He couldn't believe my friend had completely forgotten him. Walker reminded my friend of the initial conversation, his goals, his awards at their shared fraternity, Wharton, etc. My friend said he told Walker he vaguely remembered the event, that he hoped Walker was doing a good job, and welcomed him to the company again.

The next time he saw Walker was about three months later, at the company picnic. Walker was standing under a tree talking with another analyst who had been with the company about two months. My friend started walking in their direction, and when Walker noticed that he was coming to talk with them he straightened up and began to smile. Once he reached them, my friend introduced himself and asked Walker if he was the guest of one of the employees. The smile disappeared from Walker's face as he explained that he had been with the company for about seven months. My friend welcomed Walker again and told him that if he worked hard and impressed people in the company, he could really do well. Walker appeared immune to the pep talk.

The next move was, I believe, a stroke of genius on my friend's part. He realized he was at risk of looking like a premature victim of senility and would thereby mitigate the demotivational impact of his exchange with Walker. Therefore, he turned to the newer employee who had just witnessed the exchange with Walker and said, "Hello Paul, it's great to see you again. I hear you're doing a great job." At that point, it was clear that Walker psychologically "gave up the ghost" as any hope of "being somebody" left his soul. As my golfing buddy walked away, he quietly whispered to himself, "Mission accomplished," as it was clear to him that Walker was now entering the stage of Radical Demotivation™.

When he first told me the story we both laughed until we cried. Walker still works for him, does a great job, and has not asked for a raise in two years. Moreover, his security recommendations have been right on the mark and the firm has made millions off him. Now that Walker's competence has been established and presumptuousness diffused, my buddy is considering promoting him. It looks like Walker may be executive material after all. The important point to this story, though, is that you need to be willing to experiment with your own personal styles of disconfirmation. Remember, nothing ventured, nothing gained.

5. **Take credit for your employees' good ideas.** We all know that good ideas emerge from different places and that you cannot have all of them. You have probably noticed that every once in awhile one of your employees will stumble upon an idea that you wish you had come up with. Those occasions are good opportunities to disconfirm the employee by taking credit for the idea and leaving him anonymous. To the degree that the employee is psychologically invested in the idea, he will feel robbed or violated for not being given credit. As this process repeats itself many times with different employees, it will reinforce the reality that *it is employees' contributions that are important, not the employees who make them.*

6. **Disregard employee contributions.** Though it is true that an employee will occasionally have a good idea, the vast majority of their ideas are worthless. Nevertheless, we have all been taught to "encourage dialogue" between executives and employees and to

endure their "silly" ideas so as to not discourage them from "trying." This pattern has done nothing in the modern organization except to normalize mediocrity in the service of making the mediocre feel special. As you increasingly learn to embody the soul of Radical Demotivation™, you have to learn to ignore your employees' input as overtly as possible.

This can be done in many different ways. For example, I had an "employee suggestion box" installed in the Despair, Inc. call center and then made sure it was not opened for months. It eventually got so full that that the employees couldn't stuff any more recommendations into it. I thought that would be disconfirming enough, but I was wrong. The sign was too opaque for my employees to decode. I know this because after the suggestions were finally emptied and thrown away the suggestion box filled up again. This created the inspiration for the "Employee Suggestion Box" shredder decal[1], which I ordered to be applied to all of the shredders in the call center. That eventually did the trick. My employees finally got the message I was hoping to send: It isn't that I disagree with their suggestions, it's that I simply don't care about their suggestions. As a result, nobody has submitted one in months. They finally realize that their input will not make a difference.

Expressing Indifference By Avoiding Involvement

This next set of tactics will generally not be as disconfirming as the Denial of Presence tactics described before, but they still have the potential to create a variety of demotivating responses, including alienation, frustration, and a diminished sense of worth (Cissna and Sieburg, 1990). The goal with these strategies is to increase the social distance between executives and employees and to rebuild the social barriers that used to work so well at keeping the two groups distinct. Proletariat fantasies that "We all just put our pants on one leg at a time" fail to recognize that *your* pants are made out of pure virgin high twist wool and cost several hundred dollars a pair, while *their* pants are made out of a cotton/poly blend and can generally be picked up for about twenty

---

[1] Order yours today at www.despair.com.

bucks. Along this line, executives have to resist the siren call of their own vain desires to be "men of the people" and diligently reinforce the fact *they are different.* It is only by being different that you warrant a different level of respect, a different level of admiration, and a vastly different level of compensation. Executives and employees occupy vastly different roles in a legally sanctioned hierarchy, and in a Radically Demotivated organization they relate to one another in accordance with those roles. The apostles of the Noble Employee Myth have attempted to "re-humanize" the workplace. Your goal is to de-humanize the workplace.

1. **Never share personal information with your employees.** Some executives make the mistake of sharing information about their family, hobbies, notable experiences, or other things that reveal something about themselves as persons. Every time they do this they run the risk of inadvertently "connecting" with one of their employees.[1] If an employee finds out that you like the same sports team or movies, went to the same university, or were raised in the same state, they will take that opportunity to fantasize that they are "like you" in some meaningful way. Like a dark, aimless asteroid that is pulled into orbit around a brilliant star, they will attempt to bask in your reflected glory (Cialdini, Finch, & DeNicholas 1990) in the hope of convincing themselves that they, like you, are the sources of the light and direction in their own lives, and as such, are deserving of self-respect. You can prevent this by keeping details of your private life private. In so doing you will increasingly become an enigmatic icon of what your employees will never be; you will become for them a symbol of the hopes they dare not hope for and the dreams they dare not dream.

2. **Ignore the personal disclosures of your employees.** Employees are crafty. It is not uncommon for an employee to share something personal with you in the hope that you will do the same in return. The "norm of reciprocity" is very strong, and employees know that if they share something difficult, personal, or embarrassing,

---

[1] My aforementioned golfing buddy admittedly revealed his alma mater with Walker, but redeemed his mistake by forgetting not only the connection, but Walker himself.

you will feel constrained to share something about yourself. They think their disclosures are endearing, like when a puppy lies on its back, exposes its belly, and wags its tail. But you have to convince them otherwise! You have to convince them that their self-disclosures are no more endearing than a dog that vomits in bed. The way you do this is by completely avoiding the topic raised by the disclosure. For example, if an employee said, "I'm sorry I don't have that report done yet. I had to rush my wife to the hospital yesterday afternoon and our first child was born at two o'clock this morning. I didn't get a chance to finish it yesterday and I'm really wiped out today," the temptation would be to ask about his wife, the baby, whether everything went okay, etc. This is exactly what they are trying to do; they want to suck you into their world, to make you more "employee centered." These situations are tough but you need to be strong. The appropriate, Radically Demotivating response would be to ignore the fluff and simply ask, "When will the report be finished?" This will send the clear message that any attempt to humanize the workplace is misplaced, and that employees should attend to their needs on their time, not your time.

3. **Use impersonal references when talking with your employees.** This is similar to the point above, but a bit more subtle. Employees will often attempt to read a non-existent connection with you simply because you use first person pronouns like "I" or "me" or "my." It is much more effective to use third person pronouns such as "one" or to omit pronoun usage as much as possible. For example, you can substitute "I think this is a good idea" with "This appears to be a good idea." Instead of "Let me welcome you to the company," use "The company welcomes you." This may take a little practice, but the emotional distance that you will create will be worth it.

4. **Avoid eye contact and emotional displays.** Too much eye contact creates the impression that you are listening and that you care. Similarly, appropriate emotional responses, whether it be a grin, a grimace, or a groan, send the message that you understand the import of what they are saying. It is important to avoid any appearance of empathy or sympathy. Instead, you should remain

silent as long as possible whenever the employee is sharing something personal. The absence of what are called "backchannel" cues, the nonverbal signals that let a speaker know you're listening, will cause your employees to speak more quickly and omit unnecessary details as they begin to perceive that your patience is wearing thin. If remaining silent does not feel comfortable, provide muted, intermittent responses that are inappropriate to the emotional content of whatever your employees are attempting to tell you.

No matter what types of backchannel cues you use, be sure to avoid eye contact as your employees are speaking. Whether you have to look at your watch, stare out the window, sort through a stack of papers, or glance around the room in an effort to find something to fix your attention upon, do not stare at your employees. There are few things more subtly disconfirming than having someone from whom you are seeking understanding and empathy look as though they don't care about what you are saying. That is what makes this tactic so effective.

5. **Visibly "cleanse" yourself after contact with your employees.** This requires that you begin to see your employees as a source of contamination that requires you to take steps to counteract your contact with them. It is inevitable that at times you will shake the hands of certain employees, open the same doors they open, or use one of their pieces of work-related equipment. Whenever you do, you should publicly though unobtrusively engage in a symbolic cleansing ritual. For example, I try to keep a small bottle of antibacterial liquid in my pocket, and whenever an employee shakes my hands I pull out the liquid and disinfect my hands while he or she is talking. If you don't want to be as dramatic as the antibacterial cleanser, you can still make the point by wiping your hands on a tissue or even on your clothing. The key is to make it clear that the cleansing is a result of the contact.

It is really quite funny once your employees realize that you are cleansing yourself from your contact with them. At the moment of recognition, their speech becomes labored as they sort through the significance of the event and begin to wonder if they really are as vile as your behavior suggests. Some of them eventually conclude, yes, they are that vile. I know of one executive who didn't want to use the antibacterial liquid because he was scared it would leak in his pocket and ruin his pants. Instead, he opted to wear latex gloves whenever he came in contact with his employees. His tactic was so effective that over time the employees began to wear latex gloves themselves to protect themselves from one another.

Expressing Indifference By Rejecting Communication

These tactics disconfirm because they explicitly fail to respond to the *content* of one of your employee's messages. They subtly and perspicuously say to your employees, "I'm not listening," or "I don't care about what you're saying."

1. **Respond with irrelevant comments.** Very simply, this tactic involves responding to an employee's comment with a comment of your own that explicitly fails to take into account whatever the employee said. I find this tactic easiest to use in a meeting with a group of people. For example, if one of my senior staff makes an impassioned plea for something that I think is ego-driven, I'll simply change the subject by turning to another staff member and asking a question. This amounts to ignoring the employee by leaving their impassioned plea unanswered.

    With vain employees, I respond with an irrelevant *compliment* that I know they are likely to deny. For example, if an employee has put on a few pounds I'll ask, "Did you lose weight?"; if their hair is a mess, I'll say, "It looks like you're having a good hair day." The key is to find a way not to respond meaningfully to the content of their message, and the more unobtrusively irrelevant the better.

2. **Talk over your employees' comments.** One of the most frustrating conversational experiences is when someone thinks they know what you are going to say so they simply start talking before you finish. Because this is so frustrating, do it often. It communicates to your employees that in functional terms they are completely knowable and predictable, and therefore, their actual presence and the articulation of their ideas are unnecessary. Let's face it,

no matter how valuable your employees may be, this is a message they cannot hear often enough.

STRATEGY 2: DISCONFIRMATION BY IMPERVIOUSNESS

The second type of disconfirmation identified by Cissna and Seiburg is disconfirmation by Imperviousness. Impervious responses are designed to deny or distort the self-expression of another. They send the message that you see the person as different than they see themselves. These messages are not as disconfirming as Indifference messages, but they still have the potential to foster dehumanized relationships and self-doubt (Cissna and Sieburg, 1990).

1. **Deny your employees' self-understanding.** Your employees like to believe that no matter how ignorant or mistaken they are about the trivium, current affairs, history, or their cars, they at least know themselves. They regard themselves as experts in the sub-optimized subjectivity of their very souls—until, of course, they do something they know they should not have, and then they become impenetrable mysteries who are driven by the fictional forces of "the environment." The truth of the matter, though, is that your employees don't really know much about themselves. They have imperfectly remembered a relatively few historical details that, as we discussed in a previous chapter, they have strung into a somewhat coherent story that portrays them as a particular type of person.

   The simplest way to implement this tactic is to say to the employee things like "You don't really mean that," "You shouldn't feel that way," or "You only feel that way because. . ." As hard as it may be to believe, simple, persistent denial of the nature or valid-ity of an employee's self-experience, even without any supporting evidence for the denial other than the force of your own rival persona, is enough to thrust the employee into the quagmire of self-doubt.

2. **Impose your understanding on the employee's self-experience.** This tactic often follows the one above as the logical next step in a con-versation, though the previous tactic is not a prerequisite for this one. To implement this tactic you simply have to ignore the

employee's declarations and tell him what he's feeling. Employees find this disconfirming because, despite your indifference, you implicitly claim to understand them better than they understand themselves. In extreme cases this can have a tyrannizing or engulfing affect on an employee. For these reasons and because it is so easy to do, I use this tactic often. I recently had an employee tell me that she was feeling sick just before an important presentation. I ignored her self-experience and very politely said, "Don't be silly. You're not sick; you're just scared. I didn't hire you to be a coward who would fail me at the moment of truth. You've got five minutes to get it together and you better not screw up." She did a fine job on the presentation, apologized, and ran out of the room and vomited. As a result of our little "pep talk," she says her hesitancy was "just nerves" and has ceased talking about her feelings altogether.

3. **Assign them unimportant, demeaning tasks.** As employees ascend the great pyramid of the organizational hierarchy, they increasingly expect to be exonerated from performing less important, or menial tasks. It is for this very reason that I like to give employees tasks that they believe are beneath them. During meetings I like to ask managers to get me a cup of coffee or hang up my sport coat. In those moments they are transformed from supervisors with a measure of authority to prop up their egos, into my personal valets who are asked to do things that are unnecessary and unimportant. This reinforces the idea that in my eyes they are not as important as they think they are, and that any status they may have achieved in their groups or departments is meaningless when I am in the room.

4. **Exploit the symbols of rank and power.** Many of your employees invest significant portions of their self-worth in amazingly meaningless symbols of rank and power within the organization. You need to find out what those symbols are and exploit them to your advantage. I know an executive who found that several employees of her company had invested tremendous significance in the way email messages were addressed. If an employee's name was on the "cc:" line rather than the "To:" line, it was interpreted as a sign that the employee had lower rank. In a similarly obsessive fashion,

the order in which names were listed on either line was interpreted as an indication of how important the employee was at that time: The names that were added to the address list first were seen as more important than those who were added last. After discovering that her employees viewed email this way, this executive began to manipulate that way emails were addressed. As a result, she could create anxiety in an employee simply by making his name the last one to appear in the "cc:" list.

5. **Give your employees embarrassing nicknames.** This is the type of thing the bullies used to do in grade school, and surprisingly enough, it still works. Nicknames are generally a sign of intimacy, but if they are used right they can be humiliatingly stigmatic. For example, I have an employee who bent over to pick something up and the seam in her pants split. As a result, she was given the name "Flash" because of the unintended immodesty of her revelation. Given her normal sense of propriety and decorum, this event was especially humiliating. Creating the nickname Flash has memorialized the event and forced her to explain it to others many times over. She frequently has to explain that the flash was not intentional, that she is not a "lowlife," that she does not sell pictures over the Internet, that she has never been an exotic dancer, and that no, she will not flash for them. Despite her attempts to set the record straight and explain that Flash is an unfortunate nickname rather than adjective, whenever she wears a trench coat to work at least a few people stare at her to see if she's wearing anything underneath it. She hates the way other people see her and finds it emotionally draining that she has to explain herself so frequently. That, of course, is the goal.

6. **Make fun of your employees.** Use humor to poke fun at your employees' foibles, insecurities, and mistakes. This is a great way to have a good time and at the same time discover what really gets under their skins. One of the best things about humor is that you can say things that are inappropriately harsh or humiliating and then magically make it appropriate by saying "Just kidding." The best part is that the employee knows that even if you take it all back, there is at least a kernel of truth to what you said or it would

not have been funny. It's like "forgetting" to pull your punches while you are practicing for a fight scene in a school play: It wasn't a "real punch," but it felt like one.

7. **Use Pseudo-Confirmation.** One way to disconfirm an employee's "real self" is to confirm a false self. The nice thing about this strategy is that it makes you look like you are actually conforming to the standards of the Noble Employee Myth while you are actively working to overcome its influence. Moreover, employees will be so surprised to hear you praise them that they will want to hear what you have to say, but once they realize the praise has nothing to do with who they really are they will be unable to derive any benefit from it. Some of the ways this can be done are as follows:

a. *Praise the irrelevant.* The fact that you would praise the employee for something irrelevant tells the employee that in your mind, he or she is associated with irrelevance. This obviously robs the praise of its significance.

b. *Praise them for things they have not done.* Most of your employees will accept the praise even though they know they don't deserve it. As a result, they will feel guilty for accepting credit for someone else's work.

c. *Give great praise for small accomplishments.* This sends the clear message that you see the employee as so unskilled or incompetent that she needs praise and encouragement for minimal accomplishments. Any employee with a shred of dignity will find this demeaning.

STRATEGY 3: DISCONFIRMATION BY DISQUALIFICATION

These last few tactics are probably the most obvious to recognize and easiest to implement. Having said that, they are less disconfirming than the Indifference or Imperviousness responses because they imply at least moderate recognition and acknowledgment of the other person, both of which provide an element of confirmation. Very simply, disqualification messages are designed to attack the credibility, authority, integrity, or stature of the employee. They recognize the meaning of what an employee has said or done and then attempt to disqualify the meaning by disqualifying the employee.

1. **Indirect verbal attacks.** This occurs when you attack something that is clearly associated with the employee, such as an idea, a performance, or a work product. Describing an employee's idea as "stupid" or "juvenile," or a project they led as a "complete waste of money," is not a direct attack on the employee, but their association and identification with the idea or the project causes them to feel the sting of the denunciation.

2. **Direct verbal attacks.** This tactic attributes poor performance to relatively stable traits within the employee. Unlike the indirect tactics, which allow for the possibility that a poor performance is atypical for the employee, direct verbal attacks explicitly declare that it is a defect in the employee that is the cause of the poor performance. Instead of telling the employee that he had a "stupid idea," you directly tell the employee that he is "an idiot." This locates the source of the bad idea in the employee himself. Similarly, a failed project is not something that just happened, but the employee "is a poor project manager." Given the direct, potentially offensive nature of direct verbal attacks, they are best used only at or near the end of the demotivational process. Otherwise, as I explained above, your employees may respond with indignation and rebellion.

As you can see, the number of ways you can disconfirm your employees is legion. I have no doubt that some of these disconfirming conversational tactics are already part of your conversational repertoire, while others are not. The most disconfirming tactics are those that communicate indifference, but they are also the least common in routine conversation. Therefore, I recommend that you begin to practice them until you gain facility with them and are able to work them seamlessly into your routine executive/employee interaction.

THE CAUTIOUS USE OF CONFIRMATION

Considerably less research has been done into patterns of confirmation than into those of disconfirmation. This may be because interaction that is not explicitly disconfirming is often regarded as confirming, at least to some degree. Nevertheless, Cissna and Sieburg (1990) have argued that confirming messages have one or more of the following characteristics: (1) They express recognition of the individual, (2) they acknowledge the validity of the experience or self-understanding of the individual, and/or (3) they endorse the experience of the individual. As I mentioned above, the only place for confirmation in a program of Radical Demotivation™ is when an employee expresses a self-understanding consistent with your objectives, such as self-doubt, self-contempt, or the like. I also mentioned that some employees will take pride in the accurate diagnosis of the sources of their shame. As a result of this pathological possibility, confirmation has to be used both cautiously and sparingly.

TABLE 4. TYPES OF CONFIRMATION

Confirmation by Recognition	
Employee Comments	**Executive Response**
I don't think I did very well on that report.	*I understand what you mean.*
I suck.	*Okay.*
Confirmation by Acknowledgement	
Employee Comments	**Executive Response**
I feel like such an idiot.	*Don't deny your feelings.*
I have a problem making friends.	*Many of us share that same perception.*
I can't believe I made this mistake.	*We're all shocked by your failure.*
I feel empty inside.	*You know yourself better than anyone.*
Confirmation by Endorsement	
Employee Comments	**Executive Response**
Sometimes I hate myself.	*You are a good judge of character.*
I'm such a loser.	*I commend you for your honesty.*

In Table 4 on the opposite page I have provided examples of confirming responses that are consistent with a program of Radical Demotivation™. They are divided into the three types of confirmation with the employee comments on the left and the appropriate confirming yet demotivating responses on the right. As you review the responses, note that they serve to confirm the employee's emerging, radically demotivated view of self.

For those of you who had come to believe that interaction with your employees was limited to insincere expressions of gratitude and encouragement, or indignant, bitter tirades against sloth and incompetence, I hope you realize that you can make so much more of your time together. The time you spend engaged in direct interaction with your employees is one of the best opportunities you have to impart your own personal vision of Radical Demotivation™, and the most effective way to do this is through focused, persistent, interpersonal disconfirmation. Interpersonal disconfirmation allows you to be polite to your employees, while that same time using your institutional authority to strip them of their very sense of self and their attendant sense of entitlement. This, of course, is the primary objective of a program of Radical Demotivation™.

COMPENSATION:
Making Pay Fair

The reward of a thing well done is to have done it.
—EMERSON

One of the most important variables in the long-term health and vitality of an organization is the way it spends its money. Poorly negotiated agreements with suppliers, wasteful expenditures, unnecessary luxuries, and lavish perks can doom an otherwise viable company to the ash heap of mismanaged capital. It is in this context that you have to consider a sobering reality: The single highest operating cost for any business is typically the amount of money it spends on wages, benefits, and perks for its employees. The amount of money expended for employees in manufacturing industries can be as high as 33% of total operating costs, while in service industries the amount can rise to a staggering 89% (Carey, 1994). To make matters worse, recent data published by the Bureau of Labor Statistics shows that wages in the manufacturing sector rose by an average of 4.5% for the years ending March 2003 and March 2004, while wages in the service sector rose approximately 3.5% for the same periods. At the same time, many executives saw their incomes and net worth plummet as stock prices fell and their compensation was held flat. Even the executive-hating, neo-Marxist United for a Fair Economy group reports that CEO pay dropped by nearly 50% between 2000 and 2002. Surely this is not the way it's supposed to be.

THE UNACKNOWLEDGED PROBLEM
WITH EMPLOYEE COMPENSATION

Given the level of labor costs relative to other operational costs, over-paying for labor is arguably the most egregious form of fiscal irrespon-sibility executives can engage in. We all pay people to work hard to get the best prices on the technology, machinery, office space and real estate that we purchase, but at the same time we have been hood-winked into believing that it is somehow noble to overpay for labor. Despite the fact that such wanton disregard for shareholder value should be a source of shame, many executives actually take pride in making their companies "employee friendly" or "a good place to work."

The folly of this tendency is compounded when you realize that cap-ital investments become cheaper over time, whereas labor just gets more and more expensive. Given the time value of money and the fact that most capital investments continue to provide utility after they are paid off, the utility extracted from capital investments becomes an increasingly better value as time goes on. In contrast, most employees have a self-imposed upper limit on what they are willing to learn, there-by placing a ceiling on the quality of the work they can produce. There is also an upper limit to the amount of work they can accomplish in any given period of time, and that limit peaks and then gradually decreas-es as the employee ages. Consequently, once those limits are reached, assuming the employee continues to receive annual "merit" raises, the cost of the utility extracted from employee labor becomes an increas-ingly poor value.

It is clear that companies need a sound compensation plan if they are going to thrive, but most executives are unclear what criteria they should use to develop one. The number of compensation plans has grown so vast, and the neological inventions that support them so arcane, that executives have been led to believe they need consultants and commit-tees just to figure out how to pay someone to do a job. This is largely due to the tremendous confusion sown by proponents of the Noble Employee Myth who have spent decades selling "solutions" driven by dogma rather than data. Undaunted by successive real-world failures, each permutation of the myth has been euphemistically deemed even more "progressive" than the last, not because it affected the organization and its employees in any way approximating what it was supposed to, but because it resulted in increasingly bloated payrolls, militant employees, and frustrated executives. Unlike true leaders such as Teddy Roosevelt who used to "speak softly and carry a big stick," modern day executives have been assailed, maligned, and browbeaten into believing that they need to "praise frequently and write a big check."

Naturally, a comprehensive program of Radical Demotivation™ offers a way out of this costly, "progressive" quagmire. In this chapter I want to cut through the confusion and offer a few principles that you can use to develop a compensation plan that will not only work in your organization, but is also consistent with a program of Radical Demotivation™ . Before I do that, however, I think it is worthwhile to spend a few pages discussing the goals of a Radically Demotivating compensation plan and how they differ from those built on the foundations of the Noble Employee Myth. In so doing, I hope to illuminate the dogma that has hindered executives from maximizing the economic potential of their organizations.

THE ASSAULT ON FAIRNESS

There was a time when compensation was seen as the fair exchange of money for labor. Granted, executives and employees often disagreed over what was considered "fair," but they agreed upon the basic principles of the exchange. Moreover, as long as there was a large supply of unemployed people willing to offer their services at a better value than their already-employed friends, neighbors, and fellow citizens, executives were able to buy labor at fair market rates and everyone was relatively happy. All of this changed, though, with rise of the labor unions and the emergence of the social sciences near the beginning of the twentieth century.

The role of labor unions throughout this period is less interesting to me than that of social scientists. Most of you are already well aware of unions' roles as institutionalized labor cartels designed to extort profits from executives, shareholders, and their progeny. But given their waning memberships and the emergence of increasingly sophisticated robots, labor cartels pose much less of a problem to executives today than they used to.

In contrast, the pernicious influence of social scientists has seen a steady rise in the past century. Social scientists have declared themselves experts on almost every facet of social life, and they have spent enormous sums of both public and private money in their attempts to develop a thorough understanding of the obvious and the mundane. Over the last century they have produced an enormous body of conflicting and indeterminate evidence to support whatever ideological commitment they hope to package and sell. Cloaked with the same stature and institutional affiliations as the physicist, the chemist, and the engineer, they have been very successful at convincing executives that they can help them solve the seemingly insoluble problems of lackluster productivity, quality, and morale.

Social scientists have transformed employee compensation from a simple idea (the fair exchange of money for labor) into a complex web of marginally predictive theories that simultaneously excuse employees for poor performance and promise to provide executives with the psychological levers they need to coax their employees to do what they are paid to do. Executives have been propagandized to believe that paying employees adequate salaries and benefits is an "old recipe" that is insufficient to motivate employees to do their jobs (Pritchard, Watson, & Alcock, 2001), and that "compensation" should be thought of as a general term for a constantly expanding cornucopia of material, social, and psychological benefits. As reward and recognition expert Jerry L. McAdams (2000) put it, compensation is now considered the "total reward opportunity."

Executives have failed to mount an adequate resistance to this capital-intensive transformation for two basic reasons: First, their desire to be fair to their employees has made them an easy target of employee advocates who are unfettered by the constraints of reason, morality, or fair play; and second, they have mistakenly allowed the proponents of the Noble Employee Myth to define the nature of capitalist institutions and their relationship to their employees. In so doing, they have allowed themselves to be backed into a corner by bands of economic jackals who seek to destroy the corporation as we know it by confusing its purpose and stripping it of its resources. In the next section I will describe how executives have been duped into accepting too much responsibility for their employees' lives, and how this mistake has led to a confusion of purpose and an unwarranted transfer of wealth.

RESPONSIBILITY DISPLACEMENT

There was a time when the responsibility for an employee's performance was laid squarely where it belonged—at the feet of the employee. If an employee packed a box with the wrong items, installed a part incorrectly, or finished a project late and over budget, it was reasonably inferred that it was the employee who was to blame for his performance. That seemingly obvious conclusion, however, is no longer quite so obvious. It has become increasingly passé to hold employees accountable for their failures or lack of productivity, and instead, has become favorable to find culpability in one or more organizational variables that supposedly cause, encourage, motivate, or fail to prevent poor performance. It is more common to blame the system, the corporate culture, business processes, inadequate training, insufficient incentives, or almost anything other than the employee. This is because executives have increasingly become the victims of what I call *Responsibility Displacement*—the tendency to make the organization and/or its leaders responsible for employee failures, productivity, and morale. In essence, the organization is reified as a super-agent that absorbs the responsibility for its employees, while the employees are excused from the burdens of responsibility and accountability. This is a core principle of Noble Employee Myth orthodoxy and it has cost executives, shareholders, and consumers incalculable fortunes over the years. Executives who have been victimized by Responsibility Displacement naturally conclude that they have to do whatever it takes to create the conditions necessary for their employees to be happy and motivated.

In stark contrast, a comprehensive program of Radical Demotivation™ restores dignity, prudence, and judgment to the workplace by forthrightly laying blame at the feet of employees for their failures and holding them accountable for their weaknesses. In so doing, it introduces two powerful cost-free motivators that have been virtually eliminated by the Noble Employee Myth—shame and the fear of loss. Executives have been taught that blaming employees for their failures will lead to feelings of shame and a loss of self-esteem, both of which have been portrayed as undesirable. Avoiding these powerful emotions has robbed employees of the dignity inherent in being moral and economic agents with the right to experience the consequences of their actions. It is only by being allowed to feel shame for their failures that employees will develop the judgment necessary to censure themselves and forego demanding costly training and incentives as a precursor to doing the right thing.

Moreover, shame is a potent reminder of the limits to one's personal and economic utility. It imbues employees with a lucidity that compels them to question their relative value to the organization. The deeper their sense of shame, the more likely they are to invert their prior self-assessment and ultimately conclude that they cost the company much more than they benefit the company. This informal cost/benefit analysis not it not only resurrects the real fear that they might be fired, it also provides a compelling argument for the oft maligned decisions to automate and/or outsource the operation. As pathetic as it may sound, over-incentivized employees who are no longer motivated by additional, unnecessary rewards will usually be motivated by the fear of losing their jobs. As I am sure you are well aware, employees who live with the constant fear of losing their jobs and the economic insecurity that loss would entail are more likely to work hard and less likely to complain than their economically secure, overly confident counterparts.

DISCOVERY

A COMPANY THAT WILL GO TO THE ENDS OF THE EARTH FOR ITS PEOPLE
WILL FIND IT CAN HIRE THEM FOR ABOUT 10% OF THE COST OF AMERICANS.

MISSION CREEP

The institutionalization of Responsibility Displacement has led to the further fleecing of executives and shareholders via the largely unrecognized problem of Mission Creep. Compensation plans are no longer designed simply to buy labor, they are now designed to purchase a variety of psychological phenomena such as "satisfaction" or "motivation" as well. Consider, for example, the advice of compensation consultant James F. Carey, who argues that "Employee *satisfaction* is more important than any other objective in pay management. Pay must satisfy employees or the company has bought nothing" (1994, p. 9, emphasis added). Similarly, reward and performance design expert Michael Thompson says that,

> Compensation professionals have searched in earnest for the Holy
> Grail—the new panacea of compensation that will . . . deal with the

many challenges of fixing performance management. . . . The "right pay design" was to be the magic bullet to deal with performance and motivation. (2001, p. 111)

The architects of the Noble Employee Myth have been so successful at selling their agenda that the folly of this type of thinking typically goes unnoticed by the average executive. Perhaps this is the reason why the "many challenges of fixing performance management" persist despite the huge sums of money that have been thrown at them.

It is obvious that satisfaction and motivation are supposed to be proxy variables for productivity, and for that reason many executives believe they are acting wisely when they decide to enact programs designed to increase them. Unfortunately, nothing could be further from the truth. Paying to improve your employees' psychological states instead of simply paying for their labor is a bad idea for several reasons. First, it provides tacit acceptance of the Noble Employee Myth proposi-

GET TO WORK

YOU AREN'T BEING PAID TO BELIEVE IN THE POWER OF YOUR DREAMS.

tion that the personhood of employees can be separated from the util-ity they provide to the organization. This may make sense in a social context, but it is patent hubris in a work relationship. Employees love to believe that they are hired because there is something special about *them*. Most of them either do not understand or are unwilling to come to terms with the fact that it is not *them* that the company is interested in, it is the utility they provide to the company as a function of their engaging in a certain type of labor *(see illustration)*. As a result of this misunderstanding, employees believe they are fulfilling the conditions of their employment agreements simply by showing up to work, inde-pendent of what they produce, and that employers should pay extra for them to be productive. This is clearly both wrong and immoral, but executives who spend money on perks and incentives to make their employees happy and motivated reinforce their employees' sense of entitlement, and in so doing, simply increase the size of the "fix" required to support their egoistic habit.

The second reason why executives should not pay to satisfy their employees' psychological states is that it legitimizes an abusive, unjust employer/employee relationship. It allows employees to violate their portion of the employment agreement as a way of extorting additional compensation out of the company. Too many executives have come to accept mediocre performance from their employees as normal and understandable. When employees justify their lack of productivity because they find the work uninteresting or because the company is "not motivating," the apostles of the Noble Employee Myth argue that executives should listen to their employees and try to understand them. Though many people refuse to see the situation for what it is, the injus-tice and moral bankruptcy of the relationship would be immediately obvious if the tables were turned. What if an employer decided to pay its employees 30% less than they agreed upon unless the employee worked an additional 20% for free, and then justified their decision by saying that they were not "motivated" to pay their employees what they had agreed to? In addition to the legal action that would immediately ensue, the employer would be regarded as dishonest and unjust—and rightly so. The same, however, is true of employees who use these types of passive-aggressive strategies to extort more money out of their employers. Nevertheless, it happens every single day.

A final reason why executives should not pay to satisfy their employees' psychological states is that it sets a bad precedent, and in so doing it opens a Pandora's box of ever-expanding psychological phenomena that the company has to pay for. Consider, for example, the advice of Stanford University's Jeffrey Pfeffer (1998), who says that companies should try to make work both "fun" and "meaningful." This is the type of recommendation that sounds noble and may even be well-intentioned, but has very little bearing on life outside the languid confines of the faculty lounge. Nevertheless, executives who have already started down the slippery slope of trying to meet their employees' needs are at risk of feeling a certain compunction to follow Pfeffer's advice and try to make their workplaces fun and meaningful. This raises a key question: How do you do it? Think of all of the boring, tedious, unpleasant, meaningless jobs people do to make a living. If you ask the employees who do those jobs what would make their jobs more satisfying, fun, or meaningful, most them would probably say "Pay me more money." Is that because more money would actually make jobs like slaughtering chickens, processing paperwork in an uninspired bureaucracy or selling long distance service more meaningful or satisfying? No, it is because the neo-Marxist proponents of the Noble Employee Myth have led workers to believe that more money can assuage the chronic ache of a vacuous, mercenary existence.

A program of Radical Demotivation™ counterbalances the shallow, materialistic lies of the Noble Employee Myth and restores honesty and integrity to the workplace. It acknowledges the inherent meaninglessness of what your employees do for money and refuses to cheapen their lives any further by pretending they can be bought off with a few—or even many—dollars. Radically demotivating executives have to realize that the challenge to create an organization that is "satisfying," "motivating," or "meaningful" is really nothing more than a trap designed to get them to pay for things that cannot be bought. Your employees may not know that money cannot buy love or happiness, but there is no reason for them to learn that costly lesson at your expense.

BENEFIT BONANZA

Executives who are seduced into believing they are responsible for meeting their employees' psychological needs before they can expect those employees to live up to the conditions of their employment agreements end up getting fleeced via the Benefit Bonanza. As the name implies, the Benefit Bonanza is the ever-increasing smorgasbord of benefits, perks, and payola that are postulated by compensation experts and human resource professionals to make the workplace satisfying, meaningful, and motivating. There was a time when these benefits were, for the most part, limited to retirement, health care, and various profit-sharing plans, but those days are becoming a thing of the past. As compensation consultant Derek Pritchard and his colleagues put it, "The old assumptions—an adequate salary, a reasonable package of benefits, and the prospect of secure, long-term employment—just don't work anymore" (Pritchard, Watson, & Alcock, 2001, p. 239).

Instead, the new trend is to make executives and shareholders pay for increasingly large portions of the employees' lives via what are called "work-life benefits." The alleged goal is for "employees and employers to work together to enhance the balance between the frequently conflicting demands of job and family" (Kisela, 2000, p. 592). Do any of you believe this will result in your employees being more productive at a lower cost? Of course not! The "work-life benefit" is obviously a euphemistic way of saying that employees have discovered a new category of "needs" that they can use to justify getting more from their employers while at the same time doing less. Consider some of the work-life benefits that compensation expert James Kisela expects to become increasingly common:

- On-site day care
- Odd-hour child care
- Elder care
- Multimedia family resource center
- Financial planning
- The ability to work from home

- Dry cleaning
- Auto washing and servicing
- Concierge services
- Hair care
- Travel services
- "Grab-and-go" food services
- Company convenience store

Sadly, the expansion of this largesse shows no sign of stopping in most organizations. In fact, it will continue to balloon out of control as long as organizations believe this is a viable way of attracting and retaining their employees (Kisela, 2000).

As you scan this list you can see that it represents a topsy-turvy vision of the employer/employee relationship, one in which the employer bears increasing responsibility for the employees' welfare. Rather than earning or inheriting the money necessary to enjoy these services, employees have found a way to use the wealth of the executives and shareholders of the companies they work for to indulge in a lavish lifestyle of convenience and ease. It should be obvious that the bloodless proletariat revolution, which has long been the fantasy of the proponents of the Noble Employee Myth, is gradually being advanced via increasingly influential Human Resources departments and compensation experts. Corporations and the executives who run them are being transformed from icons of capital accumulation into the butlers, bankers, nannies, nurses and servants of their employees. Any executive with the foresight to see what is happening has to hear the distant whisper of Ray Bradbury and conclude that something wicked this way comes.

Radically demotivating executives have to recognize that their companies are not treatment facilities for the socially, psychologically, or economically infirm. Nor are they doting, wealthy supra-parents whose primary goal is to buy the affection of their employee-children by preventing them from experiencing the challenges and difficulties of life. Instead, they are impersonal economic engines that create goods and/or services and provide for the equitable distribution of wealth. Employees should only share in that wealth to the degree that they provide enough utility to warrant the transfer of a specific amount of capital as a fair exchange for the their labor. By refusing to over-compensate employees via the Benefit Bonanza, executives can restore a sense of dignity to employees who have been unduly rewarded for marginal, or even imperceptible, contributions. It is only by denying them the benefits they have not earned that your employees will begin to learn the true limits of their value to the economic system they support, and this is a lesson that must be learned by every employee as part of a comprehensive program of Radical Demotivation™.

PRINCIPLES OF A RADICALLY DEMOTIVATING APPROACH TO COMPENSATION

Given the number of different types of organizations available, the significant differences among industries, and the vast differences in size, it is impossible provide a detailed plan that will apply to every organization. Nevertheless, I do want to provide some general principles for developing a Radically Demotivating compensation plan that can be applied in virtually any organization. Some of you may want to begin by targeting a particularly troublesome division or department to help the organization adapt in a more gradual fashion. After all, when a patient is desperately ill, doctors sometimes have to treat the most life-threatening illness to build up the patient's strength before they begin to treat other illnesses. Others of you undoubtedly believe that you need to take dramatic, comprehensive action if your organization is going to survive. I should note, however, it's important that you use the dispassionate, inhumane judgment of an IRS bureaucrat when deciding the best course of action, and that you implement your plan with the unscrupulous determination and ruthlessness of a trial attorney who has picked up the scent of money.

Before I get to the principles of a Radically Demotivating compensation plan, I feel the need to reinforce two important ideas that should help dislodge your biases and make it easier to apply new thinking to your organization. First, your goal is to maximize share-holder value, not save the world. Many executives have been duped into believing that they are the "good shepherds" of a secular religion who have a responsibility to care for their flocks. You are not shepherds, and despite their obvious similarities in discipline and achievement, your employees are not sheep. You are an executive with a fiduciary responsibility to your shareholders, and your employees are vendors who are doing everything they can to sell their product at the highest possible price. You have a solemn duty to attend to the economic health of the company and its owners, not its vendors and suppliers.

Second, you should give no thought as to whether your employees will be "satisfied" with your compensation plan. The proponents of the Noble Employee Myth have been very successful at making this a criterion for compensation plans because it is supposed to "facilitate acceptance" among your employees. But it serves no genuine purpose other than to siphon money away from your shareholders to your employees by raising the price for an acceptable plan. You should give no thought to the satisfaction of your employees because those who do not accept the plan can be replaced with those who will, and because employees are almost never satisfied anyway. As Edward Lawler, the founder of the University of Southern California's Center For Effective Organizations, points out,

> Pay is an area of great—indeed, often the greatest—employee dissatisfaction. . . . Typically, 50 percent or more of all employees in an organization report dissatisfaction with their pay. . . . *Even when pay is high, employees can always find comparisons that make their pay look lower than it should be.* (Lawler, 2000, p. 82, emphasis added)

Despite all of the time, money, and attention spent to develop satisfying compensation plans, employee satisfaction is nothing more than a chimera concocted by the proponents of the Noble Employee Myth. Most employees are never satisfied until they see the corporation beaten and bloodied by their own greed and self-interest.

KEEP PAY LOW

The first, and perhaps most important, principle of a Radically Demotivating compensation plan is to *keep pay as low as possible*. Obviously, the actual pay level needs to be determined in the context of a realistic compensation survey, but suffice it to say that you should attempt to set your compensation in the lowest 25% of the range.

There are several good reasons why this should be done. First, you are fulfilling one of your responsibilities as an executive by keeping labor rates down; this will be a breath of fresh air to your Board of Directors and your shareholders. Sadly, executives who are guided by the Noble Employee Myth often *boast* that they pay their employees "better than average." Assuming that compensation is normally distributed, paying their employees better than average simply means that it cost them more for their labor than it does for more than 50% of their competitors. Would these same executives boast if they purchased their office equipment for 30% more than their competitors? Or if they sold bonds at 2% higher than market rates? Of course not! The fact that they boast about excessive labor expenditures is a sign that their Noble Employee Myth puppet-masters have so marred their judgment that one of their greatest sources of shame has become an irrational source of pride.

A second reason why employee compensation should be kept as low as possible is that it sends a strong demotivational message to your employees about their relative value in the presumptively rational economic system in which they live. Compensation has both substantive and symbolic dimensions. Substantively, it enables your employees to eke out a certain standard of living by enabling them to pay for their housing, transportation, leisure activities, and so forth. Symbolically, however, it provides a very visible ranking of their status in a pervasive, all-encompassing economic hierarchy. Employees who are paid less than their cohorts are often unable to display the same symbols of wealth and achievement. They live in different neighborhoods, drive different cars, take different vacations, and send their children to different schools. As they see others outpace them in the conspicuous consumption of the tokens of wealth, they are bound to conclude that their unsatisfied yearning to do the same is the emotional sign that they "just don't have what it takes" to lead that lifestyle. This is an important step in the process of Radical Demotivation™.

A third reason why employee wages should be kept low is that high wages are a magnet for money-grubbing hucksters who will say or do just about anything for a chance to cast their nets into the cascading streams of mismanaged capital, and they'll hang around until their nets are full and the streams are empty. They figure that if executives are foolish enough to over-pay for labor, then they are also foolish enough to fall for whatever line the hucksters are able to concoct to oversell their labor. These are the type of people who buy their academic credentials from diploma mills, exaggerate their previous accomplishments, and manage to advance to increasingly compensated positions by moving from one mismanaged company to another. We have all seen them and marveled at their ability to speak glibly about almost any subject, but still retain the ability to say nothing. They are the incarnation of the Peter Principle, rising to the level of their incompetence and then selling themselves to another company before the damage they have done can be discovered. These people avoid Radically Demotivating companies because they know their hucksterism will be seen for what it is and they fear the economic "smackdown" that would naturally ensue.

Fourth, high pay feeds your employees' already bloated self-regard and causes them to overvalue their contributions. Research shows that when employees are overcompensated they tend to feel guilty about this unjust largesse. Unfortunately, their guilt is short-lived. According to equity theory, they should attempt to relieve their guilt by working in a way that is commensurate with their overpayment; i.e., they should be more productive. If that really happened, perhaps a weak argument could be constructed for paying high wages, but that is not what happens in most cases. Instead, employees relieve their guilt by simply raising their estimation of themselves, and in some cases, even *conclude they are underpaid* (Lawler, 2000). Radical Demotivation™ counteracts this immoral pathology by lowering your employees' self-assessment to match their lower than average pay.

Fifth, low pay increases job security. We have all seen young children who, when offered a piece of candy from a jar, are unable to satisfy their desires because they greedily attempt to take an entire handful. With their hand filled with candy, they are unable to remove it from the jar. They are only freed from the jar when they let go of the candy and learn to demand less. This is a lesson your employees should learn, but they rarely do. As a result, they rarely realize that demanding too much money from the company places the company and their very jobs at risk. Nowhere was this more obvious than in the case of Schwab. In 2000 the company was flying high as a result of the economic bubble of the late 1990's, and as *Fortune* magazine reported, cash and stock options were distributed "liberally" to non-officers throughout the company. As a result, in January 2001 Schwab was ranked 5th in *Fortune* magazine's annual list of the top 100 Best Companies to work for (Levering & Moskowitz, 2001). Ironically, that same month Schwab was attempting to respond to declining revenues from the recent burst of the economic bubble, and in an attempt to avoid layoffs, proposed that 13,000 employees take unpaid three-day weekends. As Forbes.com later reported, the proposal was ridiculed by the employees and quickly abandoned (Bernhard, 2001). As a result of their inability to prevail over their employees' overcompensation-induced, irrational demands, Schwab eventually had to lay off close to 10,000 employees in order to save the company. It is unclear how many of those jobs could have been saved if the employees had simply realized that in the face of seriously declining revenues, they provided no more utility than lead cargo on a sinking ship.

The real tragedy of this story, however, is what happened outside of the company. After years of overcompensating his employees and several attempts to save their jobs, billionaire Charles Schwab was "thanked" in August, 2003 by having bombs placed outside of his newly constructed mansion overlooking the world famous Pebble Beach golf course and outside of his offices in the posh community of Carmel, California. The authorities could not say that the bombs were definitely the work of any of Schwab's current or past employees, but they did note that the bombs were poorly constructed and had no means of detonation, so draw your own conclusions.

Finally, low wages perform a culling function in that they help identify potential executives. By keeping wages low, you are able to differentiate between those employees who take their roles seriously and are willing to be productive at the wage they agreed to accept and those who are simply hoping to sponge off your generosity. Naturally, those who remain focused, disciplined, and responsible may have the potential to become executives, while the others become the targets of Radical Demotivation™ to ensure that you are able to extract as much utility from them as possible.

Before I move on to the next principle, I think it is important do dispel one of the most common suppositions of the Noble Employee Myth; namely, that higher wages produce high productivity. For example, Stanford's Jeffrey Pfeffer (1998) says that it is a myth that executives can lower their labor costs by cutting their labor rates. He then goes on to provide numerous examples of companies like General Motors, the SAS Institute, and Men's Wearhouse that pay higher wages than their competitors but are still able to operate at a lower cost because their employees are more productive. These examples are seductive and lead executives who have been influenced by the Noble Employee Myth to infer that higher wages will lead to higher productivity. Nothing could be further from the truth. The most likely reason why these companies are able to achieve lower labor costs in spite of higher labor rates is that they have done a better job of recruiting than their competitors. As a result, their employees provide more utility than the employees of their competitors and therefore warrant a higher level of compensation. This is consistent with a program of Radical Demotivation™. After all, it is clear that one will have to pay more for a Lexus than a Hyundai, but it is also clear that *no matter how much you pay for it, a Hyundai will never become a Lexus.* Similarly, executives who believe that overpaying their employees will transform them into the types of employees they wish they had hired in the first place are living an alchemist's fantasy that is destined to result in disappointment.

Include Incentive Pay As Part Of The Plan

Most of you probably know that compensation plans generally tend to be one of two basic types: merit pay plans or incentive pay plans. Merit pay plans are the most common. They typically include an annual performance review that eventuates in some percentage of an increase in pay based upon an evaluation of the employee's performance. In contrast, incentive pay plans involve paying employees a certain amount of money each time they complete a unit of work. Examples include hourly wages, sales commissions, and appropriately designed bonuses.

Each type of plan has its strengths and weaknesses, but the one most consistently criticized by the proponents of the Noble Employee Myth is incentive pay. Though their criticism is reason enough to include it as part of a Radically Demotivating compensation plan, there are several other reasons that make incentive plans particularly useful to a comprehensive program of Radical Demotivation™.

1. To the degree that employees find rewards or incentives desirable, *they have a controlling influence over the employees'* behavior (Deci, 1980; Lawler, 2000). This means that they actually do provide a boost to performance. According to speaker and author Alfie Kohn (1993) this performance boost is little more than temporary compliance. Though he meant this as a criticism, it is actually quite valuable to a program of Radical Demotivation™ because it indicates that incentive programs lead people to do what they do not want to do, and the experience of being *externally disciplined to do what you do not want to do* is clearly demotivating.

2. *Incentive plans promote ingratiation.* Your employees have an uncanny ability to miss the point of just about anything they do, and this includes the reason why they are employed. A well-designed incentive plan will zero in on the behaviors you want to reinforce, but many employees instead will spend their time and effort attempting to exploit any ambiguity in the evaluation process in the hope of influencing your judgment. Many of the employees who opt for ingratiation over achievement are

painfully aware that they would never earn the incentive based upon their accomplishments. It is quite funny to see them feign respect and loyalty toward you when you know they possess neither.

FLATTERY

IF YOU WANT TO GET TO THE TOP, PREPARE TO KISS A LOT OF THE BOTTOM.

3. An additional benefit of using incentives to control employees' behavior is that *it virtually eliminates intrinsic motivation.* After employees have traveled a distance down the emotional crag of Radical Demotivation™, they often attempt to find solace by abandoning their dreams and learning to be content with what they have. In these cases, the employee will often begin to derive a measure of enjoyment from whatever meaningless work she happens to do, for two basic reasons: (1) The decision to be content with less is an act of self-determination that increases her enjoyment of whatever she does, and (2) she figures that despite her unfortunate situation, it "could always be worse." Incentive programs, particularly those which offer large extra bonuses, have the Radically Demotivating effect of replacing any hint of self-

determination with the overwhelming controlling influence of something external. In so doing, the incentive eliminates any nascent intrinsic motivation the employee may have experienced, and with it, any attendant satisfaction (Deci, 1980).

4. *Incentives strain relationships among your employees.* Competition has the potential to bring out the best in people, but those people are usually talented artists, gifted athletes, or executives. When it comes to employees, competition generally brings out the worst in them. Rather than finding ways to improve their own performance, your employees will often attempt to improve their chances of success by engaging in various forms of subterfuge. It is not uncommon to see employees scapegoat or backbite their more productive co-workers in the hopes of making them look bad, while at the same time deflecting attention from their own unimpressive performances. In extreme cases, some of your employees will even attempt to sabotage the efforts of their co-workers by doing things like withholding information the co-worker needs to finish a project, providing them with incorrect data to throw them off track, or raising bogus objections to their ideas. This dynamic creates an increasing sense of frustration, paranoia, and mistrust among your employees, all of which are helpful to a program of Radical Demotivation™.

5. If handled correctly, *incentive plans are simply another occasion for failure for most employees.* The best incentive plans allow for only one or very few winners, and in so doing, they make everyone else a loser. In the vast majority of cases your employees will not be too disappointed by their losses because they have spent most of their lives learning to adapt to failure. Nevertheless, persistent losing reinforces the belief that they are unable to achieve a desired outcome by focused effort, which is inherently demotivating. As intrinsic motivation expert Edward Deci (1980) explains, as a result of repeated failure, one will experience a disconnection between their actions and their accomplishments. This, in turn, will diminish their sense of self-determination and increase demotivation.

As you can see, incentive plans can be a tremendous benefit to a comprehensive program of Radical Demotivation™. The combination of external discipline, duplicitous relationships, and almost certain failure creates an environment in which your employees learn that nothing they do will produce the satisfaction they seek.

Develop Compensation Goals And Plans
According To Employee Segments

Companies work harder to retain some employees more than others because they add more value to the organization. For example, a department manager in a retail store with ten years of experience is generally more valuable to the organization than a cashier with only six months of experience. Therefore it is important for the organization to develop different compensation strategies for different types of employees. Since it is too administratively complex to develop a separate compensation plan for every role in the organization, the best strategy is what is called Broadbanding. According to compensation expert Martin G. Wolf (2000), Broadbanding is an approach in which many positions are consolidated into a relatively few, very wide job categories that comprise the "bands" of the compensation strata. Each band represents a different type of employee in relation to the company's overall compensation strategy, and therefore different compensation plans are developed for each band.

Though you may find the need for a few more "bands" in your organization, our research suggest that any organization with 30 or more employees has four basic types of employees: (a) executives, (b) managers with the potential to become executives, (c) managers with little or no potential to become executives, and (d) wage earners. Each of these types of employee represents a different band and therefore warrants a different compensation plan. Moreover, the type of plan should be dependent upon the goals for the employee relative to the organization. I recommend the following general guidelines for each type of employee.

- **Wage earners.** This is the largest group in your organization. Therefore your goal is to pay them as little as possible. They are the flotsam and jetsam of the economic system and overpaying them is likely to turn the pristine shores of your organization into a debris field of employees who were forced to walk the plank by your competitors. Turnover in this group will be high if they are offered a position with a competitor before they have had a chance to be demotivated. This is okay, though, because turnover in this group is as necessary as the process of elimination is for the body.

- **Managers with little or no chance of becoming executives.** These employees have proven their value to the organization and their compensation plan should have two primary goals: First, to leverage their knowledge, skills, and abilities to increase the productivity of the wage earners who work for them, and second, to give them a reason to be interested in the long term success of the organization.

- **Managers with a chance of becoming executives.** The compensation plan for these employees is a mentoring program as much as it is anything else. These employees should be exposed to many of the sources of compensation experienced by executives, though at a dramatically lower level, so that they can learn to handle the burdens of wealth.

- **Executives.** Executive compensation has three fundamental goals: (1) To express appreciation for leadership; (2) to reduce as much as possible the temptation posed by executive recruiters; and (3) to provide access to the symbols of wealth and power.

With these goals in mind, it is possible to develop a basic compensation plan suited to each employee segment of the organization that is consistent with a robust program of Radical Demotivation™. As with traditional compensation plans, Radically Demotivating plans include a strategic mix of benefits that can be used for different segments of employees. The five basic types of compensation are as follows:

- Base Pay (BP). This is the employees' base salary or hourly wage.
- Variable Pay (VP). This can be any number of different types of incentive pay, such as bonuses, commission, profit sharing, prizes, and awards.
- Ownership (OWN). This includes stock grants, Employee Stock Option Plans (ESOP), Employee Stock Purchase Plans (ESPP), and other ways of granting employees ownership in the company.

- Perquisites (PERKS). Perquisites include access to company owned properties such as club memberships, VIP seats at sporting events, corporate jets, ski chalets, and island retreat centers. It also includes services paid for by the company, such as limousine and driver services, catered meals while at work, and day care services.

- Extra Benefits (EB). It is assumed that most companies will have a basic health insurance plan for its employees. Extra benefits are those related to the employees' health and well being that go beyond the basic plan. Examples include lower co-pays and deductibles, substituting PPOs for HMOs, private chefs, health club memberships, spa visits, stress reduction visits to various resorts around the world, and regular visits by a private masseuse or masseur.

The basic distribution of the different types of compensation in Radically Demotivating companies is shown in Table 5. You will notice that it is not only designed to counteract the subversive wealth distribution schemes of the Noble Employee Myth, it is also consistent with commonsense notions of fairness and justice. Naturally, the greater one's contribution, the more one should be rewarded (Lawler, 2000). Along that line, a Radically Demotivating compensation plan restores an equitable distribution of company resources and rewards by concentrating wealth in the hands of those who deserve it most.

Before I move on to the next guideline, I think it is important to highlight a few features of the compensation model outlined in Table 5 that make it so effective.

First, notice that the compensation plan for wage earners is a combination of low base pay and low variable pay. Some have feared that the low variable pay might not produce enough of an incentive to strip the employees of their sense of self-determination, but there are a variety of ways in which you can keep your overall costs low and still have the intended effect on your employees. The key is to design the variable part of the compensation plan so that only a small percentage of the employees will benefit from it. If done correctly, you can offer relatively large, very controlling incentives but still only spend a fraction of what you would have spent if you paid everyone more money. For example,

TABLE 5. BASIC COMPENSATION MIX FOR EMPLOYEE SEGMENTS
AS A PART OF A PROGRAM OF RADICAL DEMOTIVATION

	BP	VP	OWN	PERKS	EB
Executives	High	High	High	High	High
Manager with hope of being an Executive	Moderate	High	Moderate	Low	Moderate
Manager with no hope of being an Executive	Low	High	Low	N/A	N/A
Wage Earner	Low	Low	N/A	N/A	N/A

suppose you have a department of 100 employees who make an average of $25,000 per year while the average salary for that job is $28,000 per year. Now suppose you have a variable compensation plan in which the top 20% of the employees in that department will earn an extra $5,000 bonus at the end of the year. A bonus that represents a 20% increase in one's pay has a very controlling influence, but if the bonuses were averaged among the entire department they would represent only a $1,000 increase in pay per person. In this example, paying a large bonus would still generate a 9% savings over the average salary rate.

Another way you can offer very controlling incentives without spending much money is to offer very expensive, non-cash awards such as vacation packages. I heard from one company that serendipitously discovered an innovative way to maximize the impact of this type of plan. It has been so successful that it is now a regular feature of their compensation plan. They developed four criteria for their program: (a) The award has to be something which is non-transferable and non-sellable, which is why vacations work so well. (b) They choose vacations that the employee would typically not be able to afford, but would find very desirable. For example, one year the prize was a 9-day trip to one of the nicest resorts on Oahu, Hawaii. The package included first-class airfare, hotel fees, spa services and golf. (c) The package has to be expensive, typically worth $15,000 or more. (d) It has to be awarded in December.

This last criterion may seem a bit odd, but it is essential to their strategy and adds the Radically Demotivating kick. By awarding the prize in December they add at least $15,000 to the employee's taxable income. For many employees, this moves them into the next tax bracket and they are faced with the prospect of a finding an extra $2,000–$3,000 to pay their taxes before April 15. When the employer sees the employee's distress over the tax implications of the award, the employer offers the employee a $500 cash prize instead. So far, the cash has been taken over 50% of the time, thereby reducing their average variable pay expenditures to a negligible sum. Most importantly, though, when the employee realizes that the IRS has virtually stolen the vacation they worked so hard for, it creates a sense of powerlessness at the moment of their most stunning achievement.

As an aside, the executives at this company have known the malignant, wealth-diminishing impact of a "progressive" tax policy for a long time, and they take great delight in introducing their employees to the same.

Another important feature of a Radically Demotivating compensation plan is that middle managers have a high variable pay component. The payout of this component *must be made contingent upon the productivity of their employees.* In so doing, you will teach these managers to view their employees in purely utilitarian terms. This is an important transformation that must take place for them to be effective. Many of these middle managers will have been promoted from the ranks of the wage earners and will still feel a sense of solidarity with their former cohorts. Still drunk with the folly of the Noble Employee Myth, newly promoted managers often believe they are going to "make a difference" and be "employee advocates" among the leadership of the organization. Then they realize that, despite all of their supposed solidarity and mutual respect, their former cohorts are no more willing to be productive for them than they are for anyone else. In fact, it eventually becomes clear that their "friends" believe it is the responsibility of the newly promoted manager to make their lives easier by expecting even less work from them. It eventually dawns on the new managers that the exploitative, one-sided friendship they have with their former cohorts is costing them a fortune and they finally begin to see their friends for what they really are; namely, *former* friends who need to be controlled, not coddled.

Middle managers are also given an ownership stake in the organization in order to teach them the importance of increasing shareholder value. Some executives are a bit shocked at this, fearing that rising stock prices will lead the managers to think too highly of themselves and thereby nullify the lessons learned under the tutelage of a program of Radical Demotivation™. The fear is reasonable, but unnecessary for two reasons. First, if the share price soars the stock options will exert such a controlling influence over the manager that they will feel like "golden handcuffs." No matter how unhappy the manager is, she will realize that it is highly unlikely that she could earn anywhere near as much anywhere else, and therefore she will endure years of dissatisfaction while she waits for her options to vest. On the other hand, if the share price languishes, the manager will have to live with the gnawing reality that in lieu of cash, a portion of her compensation is comprised of "laughing stock" options, which is both humiliating and frustrating. Both of these phenomena, golden handcuffs and laughing stock options, reinforce the idea that the manager has very little control over her life, and this is Radically Demotivating.

A final note about what the compensation model outlined in Table 5 has to do with executive compensation. It is important that the variable pay for executives not be contingent upon the financial performance of the company, and instead that it be based upon a variety of factors such as tenure, popularity with the board, or something similar. We all know that the financial performance of a company is not always an accurate indicator of an executive's enduring value or contribution, and therefore executives should not be punished for leading their companies through the turbulent seas of financial difficulty. In fact, periods of financial difficulty may even warrant additional, unexpected perks or compensation as a way showing gratitude for an executive's leadership during difficult times.

Emphasize Intangibles And Non-Cash Awards

One of the more useful ideas developed by compensation experts is that intangibles and non-monetary awards have value as part of the total compensation mix. If used correctly, these strategies can be a low-cost way to recognize employees who exemplify the goals and values of the company and to improve performance (McAdams, 2000). Most of the recommendations you will find advanced by compensation consultants are more consistent with the Noble Employee Myth than with a program of Radical Demotivation™; therefore I think it is best that I give you a few examples of types of awards you can use in your organization.

- **Create a cult of personality.** People with a legacy of non-achievement love to bask in the reflected glory (Cialdini, Finch & DeNicholas, 1990) of anyone with a measure of celebrity. This is why so many people are willing to endure the irrational petulance of popular musicians and Hollywood celebrities, despite the absence of any real value they provide. You can leverage this same dynamic in your organization by becoming the object of your employees' admiration. If this is done well, something simple, like a 30-minute private conversation with you, can be used as the top award in an incentive program.[1] There are three keys to becoming a celebrity in your own organization, all of which are relatively easy to do: (a) Lead a lavish lifestyle that is vastly different than the lifestyle of your employees; (b) create a social distance between you and your employees by refusing to interact with them on a routine basis, and (c) publicize your achievements and public appearances throughout the organization. If you are unsure how to do this, any PR flack can help.

- **Reinforce the idea that your employees are lucky to be employed.** This can be done both generally and personally. Generally, you can place newspaper or magazine articles in the places where employees congregate, such as a break room, that include bad economic news or chronicle the lives of families who have fallen upon tough times. This will lead them to muse on their good fortunes, as unfortunate as they may be. More personally, your managers can remind employees that they are lucky to be employed and let them know that they have come close to being fired on several occasions.

---

[1] Remember to pay heed in any such encounter to the disconfirmational techniques outlined in the prior chapter.

- **Give the employees discounts on the products sold or produced by the company.** Employee discounts stimulate employee consumption. More importantly, when employees buy what they produce it provides a built in incentive to produce high quality products.

- **Offer the employees a line of credit.** If your company is large enough, you should start your own credit union and offer your employees a line of credit at lower than market interest rates. Moreover, you should offer them a slightly higher line of credit than their income and credit worthiness would normally suggest. This will prompt most of your employees to take advantage of the service and then spend to the limit of their line of credit to purchase the items their incomes do not allow them to afford. You should also include a clause in the credit agreement that says their reduced rate is dependent upon their continued employment at the company, and that if they quit or get fired the interest rate will be increased to 26% on any remaining balance. This is the type of intangible that has a very tangible affect upon employee retention, and also serves as an insurance policy against earnings shortfalls, which are invariably the fault of your employees. Terminations that instantly convert underperforming employees into holders of high-yield, short-term debt can produce a windfall in subsequent quarters. In short, these are layoffs that *pay* off!

- **Reward top performing employees by giving them special privileges.** Special privileges can be just about anything consistent with the organization's culture and business processes, from a reserved parking spot to choosing which project to work on. Radically Demotivating executives need to be a bit more innovative than traditional executives, however, to ensure that the privileges they offer have the appropriate demotivational impact. Let me give you two examples of intangible incentives that have been especially effective with a few early adopters of Radical Demotivation™. One company created a monthly "Manager for a Day" program that allowed top performing employees to take control of the department they worked in for a day. The initial goal was to teach the employees some of the challenges involved in managing the department, but the program has mutated into something much different. The natural dysfunctions in the relationships among the employees have taken over and now the employees seek the title so that they can make life difficult for the coworkers they like the least. The desire to take revenge is so intense that the employees work very hard for the chance to impose their brand of fairness over one another, even if it is just for a day.

A second company created a special break room that was reserved for the exclusive use of its top performers. Nobody is allowed to enter the room except the top performer who earned the right to use it. The room is very nicely decorated, but it has no windows, television, gaming console, or entertainment of any kind. Consequently, the employees who use it tend to get bored and end their breaks early and go back to work. On average, the top performers assigned to the special room spend about 20% less time on breaks than they are allowed.

It should be clear that intangibles and non-cash awards can be an important part of the total compensation package in organizations committed to a comprehensive program of Radical Demotivation™. Executives may need to be creative in the programs they develop, but the cost savings will be worth the effort.

Executives have a responsibility to increase shareholder value, but many of them have lost their way. There is a better than average chance that you're one of those executives. If ideologically driven compensation experts and wild-eyed human resource staff have caused you to see your company more like a social welfare agency for the economically infirm than the economic engine it is intended to be, then Radical Demotivation™ is the corrective you need. Employee compensation is a problem that is growing out of control as corporations continue to assume responsibility for ever-increasing aspects of their employees' lives. A comprehensive program of Radical Demotivation™ rejects the false morality of the Noble Employee Myth and reasserts the utilitarian nature of the employer/employee relationship. A Radically Demotivating compensation plan not only forces employees to live up to the conditions of their employment agreements, it also frees executives to live up to the conditions of theirs.

TEAMS:
Making the Most
of Your Employees

A few harmless flakes working together
can unleash an avalanche of destruction.
—DESPAIR, INC.

S everal years ago, prior to the founding of Despair, Inc., I
worked in a large high tech organization. One of the cor-
nerstones of the company's culture was the pervasive rhetoric of "teams." From the CEO on down, everybody was
part of a team: the executive team, the sales team, the engineering
team, the operations team, and so on. The intention of the ubiquitous
locution was clear—to foster a sense of collegiality among groups of
people with disparate needs and objectives.

Despite the presumably well-intentioned attempt at symbolic
unity, the organization had a very toxic political environment. Battles
raged over budgetary resources, the strategic direction of the company,
control over key operation centers, and the personal power of a small
group of pseudo-executive "teammates," each of whom sought to impose
his will over the others.

At one point I was forced to fight a political battle with a group of individuals who would not admit that the poor performance of their division was generating disproportionately high support costs in the company. Despite a mountain of objective data that proved my point, they attempted to avoid responsibility for their failures by blaming others. They eventually lost the skirmish and were ordered to make improvements.

One day not long thereafter, one of the political operatives from this group stopped by my office and gave me a gift. He said it was from the group's leadership team. Naturally, I was taken aback; not just because it was out of character for anyone in that cabal to extend an olive branch, but because it was wrapped in the same plain brown postal wrapping paper used by the Unabomber. Given my recent history with them and my awareness of copycat crimes as a particular type of psychological pathology, I felt the need to be cautious. I called one of my employees into my office and had him open the package while I stood safely outside the door. Fortunately, it wasn't a bomb; it turned out it was a framed picture of a crew team out on a lake, with a caption beneath the picture that read "Teamwork is the means by which common people work together to achieve uncommon results."

I was a bit touched at first. The plaque was similar to the motivational posters they had scattered throughout their offices, so I naturally assumed they wanted to let bygones be bygones and begin to work together for the common good. The gesture struck me as magnanimous, and I considered the possibility that I had misunderstood their intentions all along. But as time went on, I began to question the motive of the gift. Over the weeks and months following the gift they were just as uncooperative as they had been before, they still levied baseless charges at anyone who opposed their self-serving agenda, and they still seemed incapable of having a rational discussion over any controversial topic. Then one day, after a frustrating and difficult discussion with one of their operatives, I dug out the plaque from under a stack of papers in my office and read it again. This time it seemed to take on a meaning that was quite different than when I originally read it. Instead of being a gesture of goodwill, I began to wonder if it was actually a threat. I had thought the plaque was an appeal for our respective groups to work together, to recognize our interdependence and function like teammates instead of opponents, and to see if we could achieve "uncommon results" together. But that day I began to wonder if the real message was that their team was working together, united in a vision to destroy anyone who got in their way, and that if I were not careful, I would be the victim of the uncommon results they were hoping to achieve. I realized it was an unorthodox interpretation, but it certainly explained their pattern of behavior more closely than the orthodox reading. To this day I still remain ambivalent over the intended meaning of that plaque, but I'm not ambivalent about the malice of the "teammates" who gave it to me.

TEAMS AND RADICAL DEMOTIVATION™

The ambivalence that I feel over the meaning of that "Teamwork" plaque is similar to the ambivalence many people feel about working in teams. Harvard Business School's Jeffrey Polzer (2003) expressed this when he noted that sometimes teams are "truly remarkable," but other times they are "terribly dysfunctional." Academicians and motivational gurus alike have tried to sell us on the power, transcendence, and genius of teams. We've been told that teams make better decisions than individuals, that they create a sense of community in an otherwise impersonal work environment, that they facilitate organizational change, and give employees ownership in the direction of the company. Despite these supposed benefits, employees often find teams tedious, frustrating, and ineffective. This dynamic creates a tremendous opportunity for Radically Demotivating executives. My interest in teams is in using them as a *special context to advance a covert program of Radical Demotivation*™. Our research at Despair Labs indicates that teams often function as a dysfunctional microcosm in which the weaknesses of each participant are amplified and distilled in such a way that participants become emotionally disoriented and begin to do things that even they find hard to believe. They fight for positions they don't really care about, they behave in ways they don't respect, they forge social identities they find embarrassing, and acquiesce to ideas they find substandard in order to "move forward." Consequently, our research indicates that despite Polzer's observation that teams can be either "remarkable" or "dysfunctional," it's more realistic to say that teams are remarkably dysfunctional.

OUTSOURCING RADICAL DEMOTIVATION

The value of teams to advance a covert program of Radical Demotivation™ cannot be overstated. Few things are as Radically Demotivating as the powerlessness employees feel when forced to work in a team filled with defensiveness, dissimulation, irrationality, and self-aggrandizement. As a result, teams enable Radically Demotivating executives to leverage their efforts by enlisting unwitting employees to implement their demotivational agendas.

Getting employees to implement a demotivational agenda may sound difficult, but it is easier than you might imagine. As the normal "dysfunctions" of teams (Lencioni, 2002) begin to manifest themselves, employees become willing agents in their own collective demotivation. In essence, through the liberal use of teams, executives are able to "outsource" much of the process of employee demotivation to the very targets of the demotivation themselves. One of the chief benefits of this approach is that the participating employees become psychologically attached to the processes that lead to their inevitable demotivated state. As a result of this psychological attachment, any suggestion that they might be contributing to the emotional disorientation they feel is met with stiff resistance in the form of excuses for their own behavior and accusations of misconduct on the part of their teammates. This frame of mind makes them immune to any feedback that might prevent them from entering a state of Radical Demotivation™, thus, sealing their fate. The best part of this process is that in most cases the Radically Demotivating effects of team performance require very little executive intervention; they appear to be a natural byproduct of routine team functioning.

In this chapter I want to explain why teams are so effective in advancing a demotivational agenda. We have all been taught that using teams is an "enlightened" approach to tackling certain problems, but despite their theoretical promise, teams generally produce strained relationships and substandard results. It's important to understand why this is the case, and more importantly, how you can use this dynamic to your advantage. To that end, I want to dispel several of the myths that permeate contemporary thinking about teams. In the sections that follow, I'll argue that teams produce profound disappointment for three fundamental reasons: (a) they create a false sense of hope; (b) they bring out the worst in people; and (c) employees lack the skills necessary to perform well on a team. In the course of the discussion, it should become clear that so much of the disappointment produced by teams stems from the fact that their purported benefits are grounded in the Noble Employee Myth. Once executives lower their expectations and learn to see teams as a special context for the incubation of Radical Demotivation™, they will begin to find unanticipated uses for them.

THREE REASONS WHY TEAMS ARE RADICALLY DEMOTIVATING

REASON 1: TEAMS CREATE A FALSE SENSE OF HOPE

One of the reasons teams work so well in advancing a demotivational agenda is that *they create a false sense of hope that is destined to be unfulfilled.* Academic researchers and motivational gurus alike have oversold the benefits of teams, and as a result, employees expect too much from themselves and their teammates. When the promised benefits don't materialize, employees naturally become frustrated and disillusioned. The benefits employees have been taught to expect from their teams tend to fall into two general categories: achievement benefits and implementation benefits (Bradford, 1993; Leavitt, 1983). It's worthwhile to briefly discuss both of them to better understand the hopes employees bring to teams and how you can use them to your advantage.

Teams Create The False Hope of Better Achievement

Employees have been led to believe that teams produce "better" solutions than individuals, solutions that are more complex, creative, or satisfying. Consequently, employees tend to hope that the synergy of the team will transform their paltry contributions into something truly significant, something for which they can actually feel a sense of pride or accomplishment. They realize they don't have all the answers, but in the same way that horse dung can transform a sterile garden into a magnificent array of color, they earnestly hope their contributions will help their teams produce something they can be proud of. This hope, however, is not much different than the hope that overweight and undisciplined people feel when they buy a "revolutionary" new exercise machine from an infomercial. They *hope* their bodies will be trim and toned by the time summer rolls around, but by April or May it's pretty clear that they won't spend much time at the beach without turning at least a few stomachs. In the same way, employees who put their hopes in teams eventually realize that their team "solution," instead of being a source of pride, is just another reason to pursue a path of disciplined anonymity among their peers.

The reasons why employees don't experience the achievement they have been led to expect from teams are legion, but our research suggests that three reasons are most common.

Obstacle to achievement 1: Unacknowledged ignorance. Employees fail to realize the depth of their ignorance regarding the problem at hand. Rather than doing the research necessary to educate themselves and bring real expertise to bear on a problem, employees tend to rely on a toxic combination of a minimal apprehension of the issues, a strong desire to appear intelligent, and a craven need to achieve consensus. Moreover, they tend to see problem solving in teams as an extension of the old adage that two heads are better than one. They believe that each team member has a partial understanding of the problem, and if they work together and share their partial understandings they can develop a complete understanding. Presuming that a team has five members, this process can be illustrated with the following equation: $\frac{1}{5} + \frac{1}{5} + \frac{1}{5} + \frac{1}{5} + \frac{1}{5} = \textbf{100\%}$. Clearly, all employees do not make equal contributions in reality, but for illustrative purposes the principle is the same: Each employee has a portion of the solution and if they work together, they can reach a 100% solution.

The problem with this model is that it is naïvely optimistic. It focuses one's attention on the *partial knowledge* each employee has, but ignores the impact of the *partial ignorance* that each employee also brings to the group. When the ignorance of each team member is expressed as a similar equation, it clearly illustrates the difficulties teams have in developing a genuinely beneficial and workable solution. When the ignorance of the same team as was illustrated above is expressed as an equation it looks like this: $\frac{4}{5} + \frac{4}{5} + \frac{4}{5} + \frac{4}{5} + \frac{4}{5} = \textbf{400\%}$. In other words, the team in this illustration has 4 times more ignorance than it has information. This difficulty is compounded by the fact that employees are unaware of their ignorance. After all, error and folly do not feel any different than truth and insight. Consequently, the interactive confluence of error and information is narcissistically judged to be good and insightful.

This dynamic is, perhaps, an explanation for why some teams tend to enact what has been called the *risky shift* phenomenon; namely, that teams adopt extreme solutions with little chance of success in the hope of achieving a more substantial impact if the solution does happen to work. Interestingly, team members who enact the risky shift phenomenon admit that they never would have adopted such a poor solution if it were not for the influence of the team (Fisher & Ellis, 1990). Our observations lend support to the idea that the risky shift phenomenon along with its less extreme cousin, the *generally stupid team decision,* are byproducts of the unacknowledged and otherwise denied compounded ignorance of naïve team members who blithely believe that **n+1** heads are better than **n**. Or, as our Meetings Demotivator® so accurately characterizes it: None of us is as dumb as all of us. *(see illustration on folllowing page)*

Obstacle to achievement 2: Inadequate criteria for success. Most teams do not develop objective criteria for determining whether a solution is good or

MEETINGS

NONE OF US IS AS DUMB AS ALL OF US.

bad, and those that do generally produce vague or meaningless criteria that do not help them reject bad ideas. Most employee-led teams develop criteria like "Everyone on the team should be okay with the solution," "It should be doable by the end of the first quarter," and "It must be within budget." These types of criteria provide little guidance in developing a solution and no real value in judging whether a solution is good, let alone in judging whether one solution is better than another. To truly determine the relative value of proposed solutions, the team has to develop rigorous criteria that are rooted in the company's strategic and tactical objectives, its culture, and its core competencies. But this is precisely what teams do not do. As a result, the quality of a decision is generally based upon the team's "satisfaction" with the decision. Theoretically, satisfaction is a substitute for the quality of a decision because a team member should not be satisfied unless his individual objective criteria, rooted in the capabilities and constraints of his functional unit, are met.

In reality, however, team members are generally satisfied with the team's solution, no matter how bad it is. This is true for two fundamental reasons: (1) In the same way that bad artists see hidden beauty in their own art, team members tend to like whatever solutions they devise; and (2) it is too humiliating for team members to spend significant time and resources "working" on a project and then have to admit that they failed by collectively developing an unsatisfactory solution. This type of honesty could be a career-killer, so they convince themselves that bad ideas are good ideas and thus they are satisfied with the team's solution.

Obstacle to achievement 3: Conflict avoidance. Members do not know how to engage in constructive conflict. Constructive conflict is the means by which bad ideas and inadequate solutions are vetted by the team. It requires courage, the ability to listen and ask the right type of questions, and a purpose that is larger than one's ego. Since most employees lack one or more of these requirements, they tend to avoid conflict out of fear of losing and feeling humiliated. As a result, team decision-making tends to degenerate into a popularity contest. Team members with high levels of social power win the quick admiration and acquiescence of insecure team members who hope to increase their stature by ingratiating themselves with high-status team members. On the other hand, the suggestions of team members with low social power are routinely discounted or ignored to avoid the stigmatizing effect of being associated with a low-status team member. Consequently, the "team" decision tends to be no better than the decision of high status team member(s); the other team members add no value. The problems created by this dynamic are compounded by the fact that *social power is not correlated with intelligence or expertise relative to the problem at hand;* it can be based upon any number of irrelevant social attributes.

We saw a striking example of this dynamic in one of our experiments at Despair Labs. One summer we hired three college interns from a large public university. Breeze was a marketing major entering her senior year, Robert was an education major who wanted to be a school administrator, and Derrick was a computer science major who idolized Linus Torvalds and, like many nerds, viewed open source as kind of a liberation theology. Despite their stellar commendations from school administrators, they didn't work out the way we had hoped. We asked Breeze to examine our mailing list and flag addresses with bad data such as missing zip codes, misspelled cities, etc. Though she appeared busy, we later found out she was contacting male customers who lived in wealthy neighborhoods in Dallas and Houston and exchanging pictures with them over the Internet. Robert was given a job in our shipping department during the slowest time of the year, but still managed to repeatedly mislabel orders by mixing up the "From" and "To" fields in the shipping software. After he shipped about $3,000 worth of orders back to our warehouse, we realized he was in way over his head. Finally, Derrick was supposed to develop a screensaver for Despair, but based on our spyware logs, it was clear he spent most of his time either posting rants about "Micro$oft" on Slashdot or assuming the identity of a loincloth-wearing barbarian called "Looking4Booty" in Everquest. I was urged to fire them by several of their cohorts, but since they were just working for school credit I decided to use them in one of our team experiments.

I knew that Breeze intimidated Robert and Derrick because she was very assertive and charismatic. Unfortunately, her perceptual faculties were a bit less developed than some of her other attributes. Robert and Derrick, on the other hand, lacked several of the attributes generally associated with being "socially desirable," and tended to be somewhat shy. The team was given the task of developing a few new Demotivators®, complete with image, title, and quote. Breeze quickly took charge of the team, as I knew she would. After a few minutes of exchanging pleasantries and reviewing the task, the topic of conversation turned to who was in charge:

BREEZE: I'm really glad we were given this task. Reviewing addresses was really boring.

DERRICK: Yeah, it's cool. It's like Demotivators® are becoming open source. It's cool. It rocks.

BREEZE: Well, since I have a background in marketing, I think I should probably be in charge.

ROBERT: Sure, that makes sense to me.

DERRICK: <expletive>, that's cool.

In this brief interaction, neither Derrick nor Robert were willing to confront Breeze's non sequitur justification for why she should be in charge. Instead, they simply acquiesced to her vastly superior level of social power even though it was rooted in non-team dynamics.

The team continued to meet throughout the week without making any significant progress. Breeze was clearly in control because Robert and Derrick were too intimidated to challenge her. Instead, they repeatedly attempted to impress her by boasting about irrelevant achievements and feigning reflective analysis before their inevitable agreement with her suggestions. The real sign of their cowardice occurred on day four, however, when Breeze had a self-described "revelation" that she was sure would win my approval. Despite the unmitigated stupidity of her idea, neither Robert nor Derrick had the courage to enter into sustained conflict with her.

BREEZE: I was meditating behind this really hot guy last night at my yoga class and I had a great idea, like an amazing revelation.

DERRICK: Cool.

ROBERT: I had an idea too, but let's hear yours first.

BREEZE: Okay, you know how Demotivators® are a parody of motivational products?

ROBERT: Mhmm.

BREEZE: What if we do a parody of Demotivators®? We could do a parody of a parody. We could take Demotivators® in a whole new direction and tap into new markets.

ROBERT: Uhm, I don't think that will work, will it?

BREEZE: Sure it will. I've been working on some possible designs. The first one is Potential: There's a winner inside of you, but you have to let it out. Another one I thought about is Achievement: Nothing feels better than working through obstacles and achieving your dreams.

DERRICK: Wait a minute. These aren't Demotivators®, these are like those cheesy motivational posters they sell at the office supply store.

ROBERT: I think Kersten will fire us if we suggest this. If I don't get my internship credits, I won't graduate within five years. My Dad's really gonna kill me this time. He might cut me off, and this is the only job I was able to get.

DERRICK: Plus it's just stup. . . , uhm, I mean, it's been done already. It doesn't work.

BREEZE: No it hasn't. These are parodies of Demotivators®. They couldn't have been done before, because Demotivators® have only been out for a few years. Plus, I talked to a few of my friends about it, and they said my ideas were good. They said they liked them and they would buy them. They think regular Demotivators® are too negative and sometimes they're hard to understand. I mean, who ever heard of nepotism? Is that even a real word?

ROBERT: Uhhhmmm, well . . .

BREEZE: Anyway, if we made parodies of Demotivators®, Despair, Inc. could tap into a whole new market, like sales managers and HR directors.

DERRICK: I see your point. It's like Red Hat making money off of Microsoft; that rocks!

ROBERT: That is a good idea, Breeze. I didn't get it at first. It's like a whole paradigm shift, like teaching students to feel good about learning rather than teaching them how to learn. I like it, it makes me feel good.

BREEZE: I'm glad you guys finally see my point. I think this is really gonna change Despair for the better. I'm gonna share the credit with you guys, and I bet Kersten decides to hire us permanently.

DERRICK: We should demand stock options or profit sharing. We'd make a fortune, like Bill Gates—who I hate.

ROBERT: I can't wait to ship out these new designs.

BREEZE: Okay, let's get to work and think of some new designs.

This interaction between the interns provides a good example of the three most common reasons why teams make poor decisions: unacknowledged ignorance, the lack of criteria rooted in the company's strategic objectives and core competencies, and the inability to engage in constructive conflict. Needless to say, Breeze and her cohorts blew out of Despair as unceremoniously as they blew in.

Teams Create The False Hope Of Improved Implementation

In addition to claiming that teams make better decisions, team advocates claim that teams provide various implementation benefits to both the organization and the employees. Theoretically, the organization benefits because team members are able to support any institutional decision that is made as a result of the team's recommendation. Since the team members are the resident experts, they can function as apologists among their peers when their recommendations are implemented. The employees are said to benefit too. Those who participate on the team benefit because it gives them a chance to have an influence on the direction of the organization, to develop their expertise in a given area, and increase their stature in the organization. Finally, the remaining employees benefit because their peers represent them in the decision-making and direction of the organization.

This sounds good, but these positive results only seem to occur in the anecdotes of team advocates and the research reports published by consultants and academicians. The reality of the situation is that organizations are replete with the bureaucratic carcasses of failed initiatives that were prompted by team recommendations. This is due to an often unacknowledged but immutable law of corporate life: the tendency for employees to resist anything that will require them to learn 1 byte of new information or burn 1 calorie of additional energy to implement the solution. Instead, they would prefer to skip lunch and work overtime, generating gigabytes of information to justify their resistance to change. Every executive has witnessed this phenomenon. What is unrecognized, however, is that *this energy-wasting reaction is exacerbated when a policy or procedural change is initiated by a peer rather than a superior.*

In the fantasy world of the team advocate, peer-initiated change is said to be more readily accepted than executive-mandated change because it better represents the interests of the general population of employees. In reality, however, peer-initiated change is like a chemical reagent in the unstable structure of workgroup politics. Employees vehemently resist any productive change suggested by their peers because to do otherwise would entail submitting to the control or influence of a peer, even if the influence is exercised indirectly through the recommendation of a team. All but the most brutish employees instinctively know that to cooperatively acquiesce to the recommendations of a peer necessarily implies taking a position that is subservient to the peer, and that the only way to maintain their status in the dysfunctional nexus of workgroup power is to resist the change and attempt to maintain the status quo.

These situations are not just entertaining, they also create a vital context for the incubation of Radical Demotivation™. They do this in two complementary ways. First, employees who resist the change naturally put themselves in a place in which their goals are out of alignment with that of the organization. This misalignment produces psychological dissonance, which in turn leads to stress, grief, and anxiety. Moreover, they know that their open rebellion against company policy places them at risk of being punished, and their ever-present awareness of this fact contributes to a climate of defensive paranoia. All of this produces a toxic emotional cocktail that eventually leads to Radical Demotivation™.

The second way these situations lead to Radical Demotivation™ has to do with the way they affect the employee who serves on the team. As the resident expert and putative co-author of the recommendations leading to the currently resisted change initiative, he is generally regarded as a management shill, an icon of un-coerced productivity who can no longer be trusted. Consequently, he is typically made the focal point of resistance by rebel employees who used to be his friends and coworkers, but who now use a variety of means to communicate his outsider status. He is no longer made privy to inside jokes, conversations stop when he joins the group, and he finds himself eating lunch alone a lot more than he used to. Moreover, he becomes the scapegoat for every hiccup and difficulty encountered during the implementation. Rather than being a resident expert and "change agent," he finds himself searching for ways to justify the team's recommendations to an unreceptive audience. This is frustrating enough, but he also becomes increasingly cognizant of the fact that he is failing as an implementation facilitator. His previous status as an "insider" with his peers has provided no benefit in the implementation. Instead, he is now faced with a dual stigma: In the eyes of his peers he is a pawn of management, while in the eyes of the executives he's just another employee who was given a chance and failed. Despite his hope that serving on a team would increase his stature, the employee becomes a proverbial "man without a country," a pariah whose only remaining hope is that one day people will forget what he has done.

Stanford University's Kathleen Eisenhardt and her colleagues observed this Radically Demotivating dynamic in their study of team conflict. After a protracted period of resistance from his peers, one of the team members they observed eventually gave up while the others dug deep inside and got in touch with the baser parts of their natures. They described the scene in the following way: "As positions hardened, the conflict became more pointed and personal. The animosity grew so great that a major proponent of change quit the company in disgust *while the rest of the team either disengaged or slipped into intense and dysfunctional politicking*" (Eisenhardt, Kahwajy, and Bourgeois, 1997, p. 80, emphasis added). Though this is just one example, similar results are being achieved in scores of organizations throughout the world. It should be clear that, in stark contrast to the theoretical benefits claimed by team advocates, the true implementation benefits of teams are reserved for Radically Demotivating executives.

As you can see, there are several reasons why teams don't live up to the hype that is the foundation of the hope that they will produce "better results" than a well-informed individual. These reasons all have their root, in one way or another, in the personal weakness of your employees.

REASON 2: TEAMS BRING OUT THE WORST IN PEOPLE

A second reason why teams work so well in advancing a demotivational agenda is that *teams bring out the worst in people.* Team advocates like to talk about theoretical phenomena like "unified diversity," but the truth of the matter is that any difference that makes a difference tends to divide people rather than unite them. Despite the Pollyanna rhetoric of the hope and optimism merchants, there is plenty of evidence that the primary unity team members experience is in their tendency to judge and blame others for their problems, and the only substantive uniqueness they bring to the team is in the way they manifest their hidden contempt for one another. This is why conflict is usually *destructive rather than constructive.* Consequently, quite apart from what you have been told, teams are best understood as the an institutionalized context of "Destructive Diversity™."

The reason why teams are so destructive should be obvious: it is the employees who comprise them. More specifically, it is due to the basic beliefs employees bring to the teams about themselves, their teammates, and the rules of engagement. These basic beliefs are what Harvard's Chris Argyris and MIT's Donald Schön have labeled the employees' "theory-in-use." An individual's theory-in-use is a tacit set of beliefs that generally operate below a person's level of conscious awareness and guide their behavior. One's theory-in-use is contrasted with their "espoused theory," which refers to the articulated or espoused justification or explanation for their action. An espoused theory almost always meets the team's standards for political correctness and social decorum, whereas an individual's theory-in-use is often an expression of their baser natures and political strivings.

In their 30+ years of studying teams, Argyris and Schön (1996) have found that team members are almost always governed by a theory-in-use that includes the following four core desires:

1. To control the direction of the team;
2. To maximize winning and minimize losing;

3. To minimize the generation and expression of negative feelings; and

4. To be rational.

As these tacitly held desires are expressed in the team members' interactions, the team climate tends to become defensive and competing positions harden.

As this process continues, team members become less rational, less open to learning, less cooperative, and more combative. They begin to malign one another as being manipulative and political, all the while defending their own political machinations, which are intended to defeat their teammates. Eventually, the thin veneer of civility that governed the initial team interactions gets stripped away and the teammates begin to reveal the true poverty of their souls. Over time, team members begin to behave in ways consistent with a primal "fight or flight" instinct: The confident employees find ways to fight on with increasingly personal attacks and the cowards line up behind whoever they think will win. Eisenhardt et. al. (1997), for example, observed that teammates often fragmented into cliques and ceased cooperating with one another, and as a result, the conflict in the group became person-oriented rather than issue-oriented.

This is all done in a way that can be explained away or justified by the employees' espoused theories. But for executives who have eyes to see and ears to hear it is a glimpse into the cesspool of human weakness that is forced to the surface by the Destructive Diversity™ which is the hallmark of teams.

It should be clear that the desires which are the foundation of your employees' theory-in-use are a subconscious codification of their narcissistic impulses. As Argyris (1991) rightly identified, the goal of your employees' theory-in-use is to prevent them from feeling vulnerable, embarrassed, or incompetent by disguising the motives and inferences that guide their behavior. In other words, the goal is to avoid revealing the truth in order to look good. The narcissistic nature of the theory-in-use mentioned above was clearly evident in a team of "professionals" (i.e., a modern, Noble Employee Myth-inspired euphemism for an "employee" who wears a suit Monday–Thursday) studied by Argyris. At the completion of a project that delivered less to their client than had been promised, the manager of the team tried to get team members to reflect on their performance and determine how they could have done a better job. Rather than reckon with the reality of their failure, the professionals criticized the client and narcissistically distorted the situation and cast themselves as victims: They actually thought they should be commended for enduring their own poor performance.

Your employees' narcissistic impulse is one of your most effective and reliable tools in a covert program of Radical Demotivation™. When it is combined with the Destructive Diversity™ inherent in teams, it virtually guarantees the development of the intense bitterness and cynicism that are so characteristic of Radically Demotivated employees.

Before we move on it is important to note that the disjuncture between a theory-in-use and an espoused theory is different than the simple hypocrisy enacted by an employee when he or she knowingly feigns a persona in the pursuit of a hidden agenda. This is because employees lack the lucidity to truly understand what drives them, or the humility to learn and grow from their errors when confronted with their hypocrisy. Instead, they tend to develop sophisticated rhetorical maneuvers designed to explain away or defend against the warning signs of impending failure, their lack of intellectual rigor, and their glaring interpersonal weaknesses. Consequently, your employees' espoused theories are not just a way of deluding their teammates, they are also a socially acceptable way of deluding themselves. If they can get their teammates to accept their espoused rationalization for their behavior, it makes it easier for them to silence the pangs of conscience that beckon them to be a different type of person. (This is one of the reasons employees shamelessly blame executives for their failures. They are more skilled at blame and self-deception than they are at success and self-reformation. *This is why it's important to ignore employee "advocates" and "spokespersons."* They're typically just the least successful at work and the most articulate at expressing their delusion.)

REASON 3: EMPLOYEES LACK SKILLS

A third reason why teams work so well in advancing a demotivational agenda is that *most employees lack the skills or disposition to perform well in teams.* University of Southern California management professor Edward Lawler (1996) drove this point home when he said: "The saying that a camel is a horse designed by a committee, although a bit unkind to camels, is an all-too-accurate characterization of a team whose individual members do not have the skills to work in a new logic organization" (p. 158). Team advocates agree that it takes certain skills to perform well on a team. Katzenbach and Smith (1993) described three distinct categories of skills that team members need to be effective: Technical or functional expertise, problem-solving and decision-making skills, and interpersonal skills. Despite the rather garden-variety nature of these skills, there is good reason to believe that most employees do not have them. To prove my point, we will take a look at each skill identified by Katzenbach and Smith more closely and compare them with some observations about routine team performance.

Employees Lack Technical Or Functional Skills

Technical or functional expertise simply refers to knowledge about a specific domain of understanding required to address the issues encountered by the team. Examples include things such as knowing how to execute a marketing campaign, the pitfalls of data migration, or the finer points of intellectual property law. If team members do not have the requisite technical expertise, they are likely to respond in one of two ways. The first response is *lucid passivity:* They find themselves mute during team meetings because they realize they have nothing substantive to contribute. They are painfully aware of how irrelevant they are to the success of the team and they keep quiet in the hope that nobody else will discover what they regard as their secret. Anybody who has participated on a team in which 70% of the team members have nothing to contribute other than "Sounds good," "Works for me," "I don't have any questions," or any number of equally worthless expressions of follower-ship, knows how frustrating it can be.

Despite the frustration that can be created by lucid passivity, its impact is far better than the second alternative, *enthusiastic folly*, in which gregarious but technically incompetent team members enthusiastically share their "perspective" and "insights," blissfully unaware of their ignorance. Obviously, these team members can be positively dangerous if their "contributions" are not checked by someone with the technical competence to stop them.

These scenarios may seem remote to people who have spent more time reading about teams than participating in them, but there is good reason to believe they are the norm. Moreover, their normalcy suggests that most team members lack the technical expertise to perform well on a team. In a review of team process and performance, Crowe (1996) cited research indicating that less than 13% of 179 companies who planned to increase their use of teams had what could be considered "excellent" cross-functional teams. Additional research suggested that one of the primary reasons for the lack of success was technical incompetence. Interviews done with 569 employees who had disengaged from their team's decision-making process yielded a variety of reasons. The three most common causes in descending order were: (1) There was present on the team someone who they believed was an expert; (2) they were silenced by "compelling" but inadequate ideas; and (3) they lacked confidence in their ability to make a contribution. Clearly, the first and third reasons are evidence of lucid passivity, while the second reason is evidence of enthusiastic folly. Team members who are technically competent are unlikely to have any of these responses. They are aware of what they know and there is no reason for passivity. Consequently, they lend their expertise to the team. Similarly, they know enough not to be duped by compellingly inadequate ideas and they check the errors of the enthusiastic fools. Therefore, given the primacy of lucid passivity and enthusiastic folly, there is good reason to conclude that employees with the technical competence to perform well on teams are the exception rather than the rule.

Employees Lack Problem-Solving And Decision-Making Skills

In addition to technical expertise, employees need *problem-solving and decision-making skills* to perform well on a team. This refers to the ability to identify potential problems with alternative solutions, to evaluate the benefits and liabilities of potential solutions, and to eventually make a decision based upon that evaluation. Team members who lack these skills tend to spin their wheels with endless meetings and analyses, always searching for additional data in the hope that the decision they have to make will be made easier. The sad fact, though, is that if they do not have the skills to process the data, the added information they generate simply bogs them down, confuses the issues, and delays decision-making. Moreover, if they are unable to distinguish between essential issues and irrelevant details, they tend to get side-tracked into issues that do not matter. As a result, team members become confused, fragment into cliques, and settle on sub-optimal solutions (Katzenbach and Smith, 1993). The ubiquity of this problem is indicated by the all too common complaints that teams are a waste of time and that they fail to make any progress. As Bradford (1993) put it, these weaknesses "contribute to the common complaint of low productivity, high frustration, and poor morale. Members complain about hidden agendas with the real issues not being put on the table, endless discussions, sniping and noncooperation, mediocre decisions, and less than full commitment to implementation. 'We keep minutes but waste hours' is a frequent charge" (p. 41).

Employees Lack Interpersonal Skills

The third essential skill set for team members *is the ability to communicate with and relate to one another interpersonally*. Very simply, this includes the ability to listen carefully to others, provide input, seek understanding, reflect on theirs and others' input, ask probing questions, critique others' ideas in an objective, non-threatening way, and help move the discussion along. Most employees are confident they have all these skills, largely because they appear so pedestrian, but they clearly don't.

If they did have these skills, teams would not pack the demotivational punch that they do.

Most employees are unaware that they lack even the most rudimentary communication skills required to be a productive team member. For example, you have probably wondered how your employees can misunderstand you so frequently. If you have listened to consultants schooled in the Noble Employee Myth, you have probably tried to be clearer, more concrete, more specific, and use words with fewer syllables, and though you may have seen a slight improvement, you still marvel at your employees' frequent misunderstandings. This is because the problem is not with the messages you send. It's with your employees' ability to listen and understand them. Rogers and Roethlisberger (1989) argued that most people do not really know how listen in such a way that they truly understand another person. Instead, they listen long enough to form an evaluation and then begin to formulate their response. This is what your employees do, and as a result, they miss much of what you intend to communicate.

Poor listening skills are common and they impede understanding, but the biggest communication problem your employees have is their strong tendency to engage in defensive communication. This a natural manifestation of Mentropy™; it's easier for your employees to take the "low road" of defensive interaction than it is to take the "high road" of supportive interaction. Argyris and Schön (1996; Argyris, 1991) argue that most defensive interaction is a natural consequence of the self-protective, narcissistic theory-in-use discussed above. Once a defensive climate is created in a team, the interaction among the members becomes increasingly more hostile and correspondingly less productive. In a classic study of defensive communication, psychologist Jack Gibb (1990) noted that defensiveness prevents listeners from focusing on the content of a message. Instead, they concentrate on the relational definition between them and the sender that the message seems to imply. Moreover, as their defensiveness increases, so does their tendency to misinterpret the motives, values, and emotions of the sender. In other words, defensiveness creates an interactive distortion field that compounds and intensifies the miscommunication and misunderstanding

TABLE 6. SUPPORTIVE AND DEFENSIVE COMMUNICATION PATTERNS

Defensive Climate		Supportive Climate
Evaluation ⟵————————————⟶		**Description**
Messages that express a judgment or evaluation tend to evoke defensiveness, whereas messages that are seen as a genuine request for information or lack an evaluative dimension are seen as descriptive and tend to reduce defensiveness.		
Control ⟵————————————⟶		**Problem Orientation**
Messages intended to control another person via persuasion, coercion, or manipulation increase defensiveness. In contrast, messages that communicate a desire to collaborate to find a mutually satisfying solution to a problem tend to reduce defensiveness and evoke the same response from others.		
Strategy ⟵————————————⟶		**Spontaneity**
Ambiguous or disingenuous messages that suggest a hidden agenda inspire defensiveness, while those that appear spontaneous and sincere reduce defensiveness.		
Neutrality ⟵————————————⟶		**Empathy**
Employees who demonstrate a lack of care for their teammates' welfare evoke a defensive response, while those that communicate respect and empathy reduce defensiveness		
Superiority ⟵————————————⟶		**Equality**
Teammates who communicate an air of superiority on any relevant dimension arouse defensiveness, particularly in insecure teammates. In contrast, communicating a sense of equality helps produce a support climate.		
Certainty ⟵————————————⟶		**Provisionalism**
Team members who are so certain of their positions that they are not interested in additional information contribute to a defensive climate, while those who form provisional judgments, who are more interested in solving problems than in taking sides, help reduce defensiveness on the team.		

among the team members. Eisenhardt, et al. (1997) witnessed this in their study of teams in the Silicon Valley. They noticed that when a team climate was defensive, "A comment meant as a substantive remark can be interpreted as a personal attack. Anxiety and frustration over difficult choices can evolve into anger directed at colleagues" (p. 78). Clearly, extended exposure to these types of toxic team environments will be Radically Demotivating for even the most dimwitted optimists.

In an eight-year study of team interaction, Gibb found that a defensive team climate was clearly associated with certain message characteristics. He identified six pairs of message characteristics that represent the opposite poles on a continuum between supportive and defensive communication. He found that the degree to which a team's climate was supportive or defensive was dependent on how the team members spoke to one another. The message characteristics he identified are described on the previous page in Table 6.

It is not necessary to discuss each pair in detail, but it should be obvious that your employees are more prone to communicate in ways that are consistent with the message characteristics on the left side of the table than on the right. Supportive messages are rare, and when they do occur they are quickly exploited as weaknesses by teammates who are driven by their narcissistic impulses. When was the last time you saw an employee humbly and dispassionately consider the views of a lower status teammate with an opposing viewpoint? Instead, they will almost never pass up a chance to belittle one another if they believe they can move up another notch on an irrelevant totem pole of employee stature. When was the last time you saw an employee demonstrate an adequate grasp of the limits of his own understanding and temper his inferences and suggestions based upon those limits? Nope, that's not the "stuff" of employee-led teams. Instead, they will use every logical fallacy ever codified to support their position and avoid being proven wrong. The truth of the matter is that it is unnatural and counter-intuitive for your employees to engage in genuinely supportive communication. They feel much more comfortable and are much more skilled at being defensive and egocentric, and this is the reason they do not have the interpersonal skills to succeed on a team.

At this point it should be clear why teams work so well at advancing a covert program of Radical Demotivation™. Despite the hypothesized promise and potential of teams sold by team advocates, their real potential lies in being an employee-led context for Radical Demotivation™.

As lamentable as it may seem, this is the true, unvarnished state of the art of employee-led teams. Though you have been taught to see your employees' toxicity as a "problem" that you have to solve, the good news is that you can stop fighting nature and leave your employees as they are. The predictability and toxicity of your employees' behavior is your greatest ally in a covert program of Radical Demotivation™. It may sound odd, but your employees find their behavior as frustrating and exasperating as you do, and this is why they are able to serve as agents in the implementation of their own Radical Demotivation™. The difference, of course, is that you see the situation as it really is, but they, in an effort to protect against a humiliating confrontation with reality, justify their behavior and choose to blame you and one another for their problems. This may not seem "smart" or "fair," but having been a part of the most prosperous, forgiving, opportunity-laden labor context in history has made them weak and lazy. Your employees would rather gripe, whine, and blame others for their troubles than evaluate themselves and change. The beauty of the situation is that as long as they continue to blame you or anyone else they will never climb out of their current situation. Instead, they will continue to demotivate themselves and one another by their toxic patterns of thinking, speaking, and acting. In their current state, they will never learn that it is the poverty of their souls that has led to the poverty of their bank accounts. It's your responsibility to realize that it is okay for them to be who they are, and that it is not your job to change them. *You just have to find a way to use them.*

OPTIMIZING TEAM DEMOTIVATION

In the previous section I discussed why teams work so well in advancing a demotivational agenda. As I mentioned above, many executives are ambivalent about teams because they rarely produce the results promised by team advocates and academicians. As result, the executives foolishly begin to wonder if they are doing something wrong. This self-doubt, of course, stems from the belief that executives have a responsibility to create an environment that will protect their employees from themselves and magically transform their weaknesses into strengths.

Clearly, this is impossible. As I have argued, executives will be much more successful if they stop wasting money trying to overcome employee weakness, face the facts and learn to exploit those weaknesses. (I mean this in the positive sense of the word, in which weaknesses are capitalized upon and nurtured for the company's profit.) Executives need to realize that employees will never be motivated, inspired, trained, incentivized, or otherwise manipulated to be more than they are, in stark contrast to the claims of the pseudoscientific social engineers in the motivational industry. If 12 to 16 years of formal education have not taught your employees to think, speak, and reason like adults, two days of jokes, high-fives, hugs, parables, stuffed animals, and seminars in which they learn to divide people into any number for "four types" of anything (Marks, 2005) will not change them.

Having said this, I also realize that teams sometimes produce truly noteworthy accomplishments. This shouldn't seduce you into believing that noteworthy accomplishments can be made the norm for teams in your company—even if you were promised it could be by high-priced, well-dressed, highly-educated consultants. Blind squirrels occasionally stumble upon a nut and are able to enjoy a feast, but that does not mean that blindness is the key to the survival of the squirrel population. When I hear about executives who have been charged with maximizing shareholder value squandering investor dividends on consultants who have promised to provide the "formula," "secret," or "key" to "optimize team performance," it truly grieves me. Not just because I know that it's a waste of money that could be better spent on non-essential luxury items by those who deserve them most, but because there is a chance they will be duped by an anomalous team success and end up ever more shackled to the Noble Employee Myth and all its nefarious implications. Moreover, sporadic team success has the potential to have a long-term negative influence on the organization. It does this by tempting employees to begin to develop a Progressive Achievement Narrative. When employees work through the natural difficulties inherent in teams and succeed, they begin to realize that obstacles are not an unequivocal sign of failure and that there is a better than average chance that disciplined persistence will pay off. If allowed to fester, this type of thinking can prove to be a serious setback to a covert program of Radical Demotivation™.

Given this risk, however remote and unlikely it may seem, it is important to use teams in a way that provides the maximum demotivational impact. The following guidelines can be used to guarantee that your teams will be Radically Demotivating.

1. **Create unrealistic expectations for the team's performance.** There are several ways you can do this, but I like to feed my employees a few maxims by motivational gurus and team advocates and lead them to believe that I am eagerly anticipating their recommendations. I generally let them know that I have a pretty good idea how I think the company should proceed, but that teams are supposed to be more creative than individuals and that I genuinely hope they develop a solution that is better than my own. I then explain that I'm not going to tell them my idea because I don't want to bias them in any way; I just want to reinforce that I have very high expectations. I will occasionally give them a plaque or mousepad with a motivational maxim, similar to the one given to me, to activate their narcissistic impulse. This sets the tone for the team: Some immediately get defensive because they instinctively know that they will not live up to my expectations, while others bask in the glow of their own self-love, wistfully musing about how they are going to succeed this time. The two worldviews are destined to collide—confirming one and destroying the other in the process.

2. **Use the right reward program.** There are several ways to incentivize teams, but the *Reward Equally* and *Relative Ratio* incentive programs are the two most Radically Demotivating I have found. Both of them are rooted in a quasi-socialistic view of reward distribution that will appeal to your least competent employees, while the most competent will be demotivated but still have a difficult time explaining why the schemes are unfair. The Reward Equally incentive structure is the easiest to understand and implement and should be used when it is difficult to identify the relative contribution of each team member. Very simply, it rewards everyone on the team the same. As is always the case in such systems, the highly motivated will work hard as long as they think they have a

chance to succeed and the slackers will simply ride their coattails and make moral pronouncements about the importance of "working together" and team loyalty. Inevitably, one of two things eventually happens: (a) The highly motivated meet with a modicum of success and end up resenting the slackers because they are receiving a reward that was earned by the highly motivated; or (b) the highly motivated eventually grow weary of compensating for the poor performance of the slackers, realize they are not going to reach their objectives, and give up and accept failure. When this happens both groups develop a deep and bitter resentment toward one another: The highly motivated resent the fact that the slackers added no value to the teams, while the slackers resent the highly motivated for robbing them of their only chance of success. Either result is very effective in advancing a program of Radical Demotivation™.

The Relative Ratio incentive structure is a bit more complicated and should be used when individual employee contributions can be easily tracked, as with the individual contributions of a sales team. Under this program, each team member is rewarded for her individual contribution until the reward of the most successful teammate is double that of the least successful teammate (Katz, 2001). At that point, the future rewards of the most successful teammate are given to the least successful to help balance out the team. In such cases, instead of talking about the fairness of the program, you should refer to the "responsibility" of the most successful to help the least successful. As an executive, you know that this is nothing more than an artificially imposed cap on compensation that punishes achievement and rewards indolence, but this is precisely why your employees will find it so appealing. Moreover, its Radically Demotivating affect on teams is unparalleled. As Katz observed in her experiment on team incentive structures, the teammates were intensely competitive and overly concerned with their performance relative to one another. As a result, they withheld information that might help their teammates and stole resources from them.

As a final note regarding team incentives, avoid reward systems that can be considered truly equitable. In such cases treatment will be both fair and unequal, and you will run the risk of circumventing an otherwise successful program of Radical Demotivation™.

3. **Assign teams relatively unimportant tasks.** When team members do not believe a task is important or worthwhile, they naturally begin to resent the team and consider it a waste of time (Bradford, 1993; Katzenbach & Smith, 1993). As this dynamic progresses and intensifies, the teammates begin to direct their frustration toward one another. Personal animosity develops and the team members begin focusing their attention on how to ensure that their teammates fail rather than on how they themselves can succeed. Moreover, all of this is fueled by a feeling of futility that is compounded and intensified by every irrelevant interpersonal "victory." Once you see this dynamic play itself out in your organization with so little direction on your part, you will be tempted to ask yourself, "Why didn't I do this sooner?"

4. **Routinely discount team proposals.** There are few things as demotivating as spending weeks or months with people you resent in order to generate a proposal, only to have it ignored or rejected. Therefore, do this often. Discounting team proposals will reinforce to your employees their expendability, both individually and as a group. As this begins to occur with greater frequency in the organization, the futility of team effort will become more and more apparent. Though you will see some immediate short-term benefits, you have to be careful if you expect to use this tactic as a long-term source of demotivation. If this process is not handled deftly, you are at risk of having your employees learn how futile their effort will be and they will remain emotionally disengaged and make only a half-hearted effort on the team. If this happens, the team will not have the demotivational impact that you intend. It's important to do two things to prevent this: (a) Declare the importance of the task as was described in the first recommendation above, and (b) couple the rejection of a team proposal with an additional punishment of some sort so that even if your employees are not motivated to succeed, they will be motivated to avoid punishment.

5. **Use team participation as a form of punishment.** If you follow the recommendations above, the very fact of being selected to partici-

pate on a team will be viewed as a punishment by your employees. This was one of the fortuitous unintended consequences that we heard over and over again from executive beta testers of Radical Demotivation™ in organizations in the US, Canada, and Europe. Since teams were never given crucial assignments, managers never wanted to waste the time of their best employees on team projects. Over time, the unspoken understanding throughout the organizations was that only the most expendable employees were assigned to participate on the teams. Consequently, being selected to participate on a team was like being marked with a modern day scarlet letter; it was a stigma that signaled that the employee had a unique worthlessness that distinguished him from his cohorts. Though many of those selected for the teams were too dim to feel the sting of the stigma, the more lucid employees increased their individual productivity to avoid being placed on a team.

6. **Make sure your teams include one or more enthusiastic fools.** As I described above, enthusiastic fools are both unaware of their ignorance and driven by their narcissistic impulse. They love to hear themselves talk, but they generally have no idea what they are talking about. Enthusiastic fools will quickly take charge of the group and get it considering all sorts of unworkable, intellectually incoherent propositions. If they are challenged by one of the more lucid teammates, they will justify their folly by saying they are "thinking outside the box." Since they do not really know that the expression means, they will use it as a justification for all manner of stupid ideas. When the team includes two or more enthusiastic fools, the battle between them for the supremacy of their own respective bad ideas will drive them to develop increasingly novel and unworkable "solutions." The fools will become intensely partisan and defensive, and their interaction will degenerate into passive-aggressive sniping, attacking, and withdrawal. As this process continues, the more lucid teammates will feel increasingly alienated and hostile toward the fools, as they develop greater clarity regarding the form their inevitable embarrassment will take. As unrealistic as this may seem, it is quite attainable if you are careful to choose the right people for the team.

7. **Make teams as diverse as possible.** To parlay the potential of Destructive Diversity™ to their advantage, executives have to think in terms of a deeper diversity than that which typically shows up in demographic profiles. The type of diversity that will be most effective in a covert program of Radical Demotivation™ has to do with worldviews, standards of decorum, intellectual acuity, and morality of their employees. Diversity in these dimensions will inevitably lead team members to view one another as enigmatically depraved, untrustworthy, unintelligent, and barbaric. Though they will be correct in their assessment of one another, they will narcissistically exempt themselves from such unflattering assessments and thereby regard their teammates as "Others" who are impervious to reason and justice. As a result, they will see the team project as a long, hard slog in which they must protect themselves from the ominous destiny of the cretins and fools who are their teammates. Since the only thing missing from their assessment is the reflexivity that could lead to self-reformation, the teammates will naturally begin to treat one another as the as the enemies they have become.

If you have been frustrated by the inability of teams to live up to the hype, and if you've been searching for a way to make them more effective, Radical Demotivation™ is the solution you've been searching for. Teams have a very important role to play in modern organizations, though not the role that the purveyors of the Noble Employee Myth have tried to sell. Rather than being the sources of ingenuity and organizational transformation that you have been promised, the Destructive Diversity™ created by the "teammates" makes them a potent source of Radical Demotivation™. As such, the liberal use of teams is an effective tool for executives, particularly those in large organizations, who are looking for a way to multiply their demotivational impact throughout the organization. Therefore, I recommend that you put your most stiff-necked employees on teams with one another and then sit back and watch the sparks fly as they inflict themselves on one another. At that point you will see the true genius of teams.

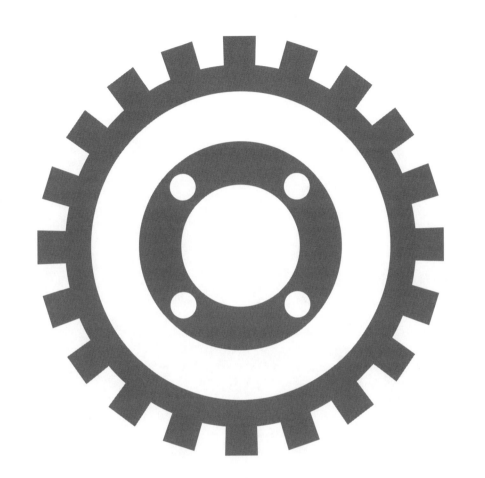

CONCLUDING THOUGHTS:
Getting Started

Many executives who grasp the transformational potential that Radical Demotivation™ holds for their organizations are eager to get started. They report experiencing a sense of hope and excitement unlike anything they've experienced since the day they first learned that they would bear the mantle of an executive. As on *that* day, the enthusiasm they feel is often tempered by a fear that they might do something wrong, and in so doing they would render their fledgling attempts at Radical Demotivation™ impotent. Fortunately, Radical Demotivation™ can be achieved any number of ways, and once you've determined to make it a defining characteristic of your organization it's almost impossible to fail. Nevertheless, before we conclude our journey through the valley of hope, I feel it's necessary to offer a few final recommendations that will help you become a more effective Radically Demotivating executive. I also want to encourage you to develop new demotivational techniques. To that end I've included a few examples of ideas submitted by early adopters of the program. My hope is that they will spark your imagination and enflame your passions, and in so doing, help you to make your dream a reality.

PUT THINGS IN PERSPECTIVE

Since Radical Demotivation™ seeks to reestablish the natural divisions between executives and employees, it's important that you develop a worldview that reflects these divisions. There is a reason that you enjoy the unique privileges, superior authority, and higher compensation that you do, and—contrary to the reflexive grumblings of your employees or the incorrigible beliefs of doctrinaire academics —it isn't because of luck or societal advantage[1]. As a Radically Demotivating executive, you must see yourself as being fundamentally *different from your employees,* and more importantly, you're different in a way that makes you *better than your employees.* This worldview is so important that it's virtually impossible to implement a program of Radical Demotivation™ without it. If this worldview is not something that comes naturally to you, you should develop a list of the ways in which you are better than your employees and reflect on it often. If done correctly, your list will not only transform the way you see the world, but it will also provide a cogent summary of the reasons why you enjoy the many economic and social privileges that your employees can scarcely comprehend.

FOCUS YOUR ENERGY

In addition to developing a Radically Demotivating worldview, it's very important that you learn to *channel your emotions* into the program. Most executives go through a stage in which their emotions fluctuate between vindication and indignation. They feel vindicated because they realize that their instincts have been right all along, and this recognition boosts their confidence in their native ability to judge others. Vindication eventually gives way to indignation, however, when an executive considers how much money he has wasted on ineffective programs inspired by the Noble Employee Myth. If you experience these two powerful emotions, it's important that you not get bogged down trying to set the record

[1] I realize that some of you *are* riding on the coattails of your ancestors. That's okay, just focus on the main point being made.

straight or exact revenge. Simply use them to drive you even further in the relentless pursuit of Radical Demotivation™.

DEVELOP A CLEAR VISION

Radical Demotivation™ is not just a journey, it's a destination. Therefore, it's important that you *develop a clear vision* of what you want your company to look like at the conclusion of the demotivational process. When done correctly, the vision will provide a strong incentive to press on even in the face of criticism. I should warn you, however, developing a clear vision of a Radically Demotivated company is generally more difficult than it sounds. As the vision becomes clearer, your mind will inevitably raise objections. Some confuse these objections with the voice of conscience and end up getting thrown off track. In reality, the voices are nothing more than the residual influence of the Noble Employee Myth. Be ruthless in your determination to ignore them! If you do, you will also find it much easier to ignore the objections of your employees as they mount their resistance to Radical Demotivation™.

PRESENT A UNITED FRONT

Your efforts will be more effective if you get the entire executive management team on board. The effects of a program of Radical Demotivation™ may be slowed (though not stopped) if part of the management team is still laboring under the delusion of the Noble Employee Myth. To that end, you should purchase copies of *The Art of Demotivation* for every executive and manager-with-executive-potential in your organization[2]. Having said that, I am aware that hierarchies exist and are important, even within the managerial ranks. Therefore, we have created two trade versions of this book, an "Executive Edition" and a "Manager Edition," so as to simultaneously acknowledge and reinforce that traversable but nevertheless considerable divide between the two groups. In substance,

---

[2] Volume discounts available at http://www.despair.com

there is little difference between the two editions, but in style, the differences are profound. The Executive Edition is for those who are accustomed to the S-Class on the road and first class[3] in the air, while the Manager Edition is for those accustomed to C-Class on the road and who can still only *hope* for an upgrade in the air. Let your purchases of each edition serve to reinforce the important differences in rank, stature, and value in your organization.

RECLAIM LOST TERRITORY

After you and your team are mentally and emotionally prepared, it's important that you begin to *reallocate resources* as quickly as possible. One of the great benefits of Radical Demotivation™ is that it reclaims resources that are wasted on employee perks and motivational programs and sends them straight to the bottom line. It's essential, therefore, as quickly as possible that you develop a list of items you intend to reduce, or in some cases, eliminate altogether. The list should be considered a "living document," subject to revision and expansion as the need arises. When you begin the cutbacks, I recommend that you start small. Begin with items that your employees will find deeply annoying, but they should not be so grievous as to prompt them to look for another job. For example, if you provide free coffee in the morning, begin charging them 50¢ per cup. Employees will hate this, but it's a fraction of what they would pay for coffee at coffee bar. Similarly, if you provide free parking, start charging them $5.00 or $10.00/month to park. Once again, they'll find this aggravating, but the cost is not high enough to warrant a change. Over time, though, these small changes send the clear message to your employees that they are an economic drain on the company and that there are "no free lunches"—or coffee, or parking spaces for that matter. Once they get used to accepting small changes like these, you can gradually stop spending money on big-tick-

[3] For those rarest of readers for whom a private jet travel is the preferred means of transportation, we offer our Chairman of the Board Edition. Commissioned expressly for collectors of literary objets d'art, this limited, letterpress edition bears the author's signature and serves as an elegant reminder that privilege has its privileges. Please have your personal assistant see our website, www.despair.com to order your copies.

et items like holiday parties, state-of-the-art office equipment, and premium health insurance[4].

SHARE BEST PRACTICES

As we all know, it can be lonely at the top. At no time will this be more true than as the effects of Radical Demotivation™ begin to be felt throughout your organization. Therefore, it's important that you associate with others of like mind. One of the best ways to do this is to buy a copy of *The Art of Demotivation* for your peers and colleagues in other companies, particularly those of your suppliers and business customers[5]. This will help to create an interdependent community of like-minded visionaries who can share their experiences and serve as resources for one another. By sharing best practices, we all stand to benefit. Radical Demotivation™ is a paradigm in its infancy—a new kind of social science. As such, it is my hope that other progressive thinkers will catch the vision of its potential, and that it will continue to be improved and refined through testing and experimentation in different companies, industries, and countries around the world.

FIND A MENTOR; BE A MENTOR

As you share your enthusiasm for Radical Demotivation™ with others, you will invariably discover that a few of your colleagues already have plenty of experience with its principles. As I mentioned earlier, some executives have been experiencing the benefits of Radical Demotivation™ for years, but they have never quite understood why; they simply ignored the faddish lunacy of the Noble Employee Myth and followed their instincts. When you find these rare jewels of industry, listen to

---

[4] I should note that the long-term psychological impact of Radical Demotivation™ is unknown. We know that stress can have a deleterious impact on one's mental state, and there is evidence that some employees find Radical Demotivation™ stressful. Therefore, it's prudent to allocate a portion the savings achieved by a program of Radical Demotivation™ to a robust mental health program for your employees, lest your good intentions backfire.

[5] As a strategic matter, you may want to give a copy of the latest Noble Employee Myth inspired management book to your competitors.

them. Allow them to become your mentors, either formally or informally. Their experience and encouragement will help you maintain your resolve in the face of criticism, legal challenges, and other forms of opposition[6].

As you become more skilled at Radical Demotivation™, it's also important that you become a resource for others. Your wisdom and experience are too valuable to be kept to yourself. Dare I say that you have an *obligation* to share what you've learned with those who are following in your footsteps. Though this may sound like a burden, it isn't. I can guarantee you that you'll get more *from* the process than you'll give. There are few things more satisfying then helping a beleaguered, weary fellow executive reignite the fire that the Noble Employee Myth zealots have almost snuffed out.

LEARNING FROM OTHERS

In the spirit of practicing what I preach, I think it's a good idea to conclude with a few examples of best practices from others. Even before the publication of this book, I received a deluge of exciting suggestions and testimonials from early adopters of Radical Demotivation™. My hope is to further encourage those for whom the spirit is willing and the flesh is strong.

FINALLY, AN HONEST ORGANIZATIONAL CHART

Organizations of any size can take immediate advantage of the simple but brilliant demotivational power of an improved organizational chart suggested to me by a partner in a San Francisco architecture firm.

As a founder and senior partner of the firm, he has long enjoyed what he described as "Class A real estate" on the company organizational chart. And yet, in spite of his position at the top of the depicted hierarchy, he confessed to having always felt "ill at ease" at the sight of it,

---

[6] Mentoring services also available directly from Dr. E. L. Kersten. The service includes up to 6 hours of private phone consultation per month. Unused hours expire at 1:00 PM on the last business day of the month. Fees as of January, 2005 are $30,000/month with a 6 month agreement; $22,500/month with a 12 month agreement. Volume discounts available for organizations that purchase mentoring services for 3 or more executives. Contact *mentor@demotivation.com* for current pricing.

writing, "It has long seemed in some indeterminate way to be a dishon-est rendering of the organization's true nature."

In reading about the pervasiveness of the Noble Employee Myth in an early draft of *The Art of Demotivation*, he experienced an epiphany, one that amazed both of us in its shocking obviousness. Though the vertically organized chart was a clear picture of employee rank, it struck him that the uniformity of the size of the boxes was a gross misrepre-sentation of the value of the persons or roles depicted on the chart. It made no sense to him that an entry-level draftsman would have the same size box on the chart as the founding partner of the firm. As such, he realized that something as mundane as the organizational chart has been, since its invention, yet another vessel for the delivery of the Noble Employee Myth to the workforce!

In a design innovation worthy of Edward Tufte himself, the architect commissioned his human resources department to create and circulate a revised org chart; one that incorporated employee compensation into the calculation of box size: each box was sized proportionate to the income of the person occupying that position[7].

FIGURE 9. SALARY SENSITIVE ORG CHART

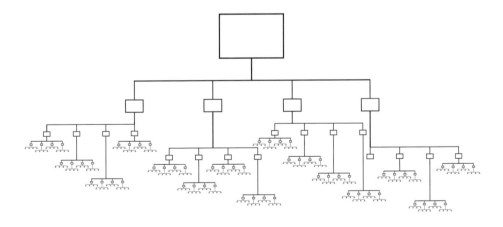

---

[7] Organizational charts that use a single box to represent many people who fill a role should use an aver-age salary number to determine the size of the box. It should be clear that using the total expenditure for those who fill that role could create a distortion even more egregious than that inspire by the Noble Employee Myth.

With understandable pride, he observed:

"It is, in my estimation, the world's first truly honest organization chart—possessed of a candor, immediacy and power that no chart before it has known. For most here, its circulation has delivered a demotivational confrontation with organizational insignificance. Several employees were amazed to discover how little ink or space were required to signify their presence in the firm. And yet it has done so only by visually depicting a disparity already manifestly obvious. We are not of equal value to the organization, and any pretense to the contrary only demeans us all."

MYSTICAL DEMOTIVATION

Those with a large enough budget and a theatrical flair might consider this Radically Demotivating experiment, which was recounted to me by a VP of Marketing from a publicly-traded specialty cataloger.

Prior to being exposed to *The Art of Demotivation,* the VP had already committed to take his thirty person marketing department on a firewalking retreat. He had even paid a $5,000 non-refundable deposit. Naturally, after reading the manuscript, he was aghast at the prospects of spending $10,000 on an event that would only serve to convince his underlings of their godlike potential. For a moment, he considered canceling retreat altogether. But after a careful contemplation of the chapters on Organizational Storytelling and Self-Narrative, he realized that a firewalking retreat might actually be made to serve a useful purpose, and with only slight modifications to the standard program.

Unbeknownst to his employees, he arranged to have a number of minimally conductive "stepping stones" placed within the coals of the firewalking pit, along with dozens of metallic utensils. He then started the session by removing his shoes and walking slowly across the special stones, giving the impression that he could walk on fire. After completing the firewalk, he spent about half an hour speaking to his employees about the importance of focus, mental discipline and determination when confronting obstacles. Being unaware of the existence of the special stones, his employees were both impressed and inspired. At the conclusion of his presentation, he challenged volunteers to prove their worth by walking across the fire pit, just as he had.

Most of them whipped off their shoes and socks (or stockings) and lined up before the pit, eager to prove their own courage and capability. The first employee who tried to walk across the embers made it about two feet before letting out a terrified shriek and leaping out of the pit. As he writhed in agony before his shocked coworkers, the VP rushed to his aid, improvising a compress with socks and ice water. Then, to the utter amazement of all around, the VP lifted the injured employee up and *carried him across the fire without injury* to an ambulance that had already been prepared in case of any "mishaps."

After returning to the gathering of employees, he again challenged them to cross the fire as he had now done twice. A female marketing intern timidly approached the firewalking pit. But before she could take her first step, she burst into tears and ran back to the group, sobbing, "I can't do it! I can't do it!"

After that, no one else chose to attempt the feat. The lesson learned from the firewalking retreat was clear; the chasm that separates executives from employees is both vast and mysterious, and employees fancy themselves to be like executives as their own peril.

GOING FOR BROKE

One executive sent me an email that described an idea so innovative that I can honestly say, as has been said to me so many times in the past, "I wish I'd thought of that." He is the CEO of an underground coalmine in a state that must remain unnamed for legal reasons. Not long after reading an early draft of *The Art of Demotivation,* he had his driver stop at a convenience store on the way home to get a cold drink. Serendipitously, he let his driver stay in the car that day and he went inside to choose his beverage. Walking in, he was surprised to see at least ten people waiting in line, half of whom were covered in varying amounts of soot. They were clearly his own employees. Despite the fact that his name was on their paychecks, it was clear they did not know who he was. He nonchalantly grabbed a soda and got in line.

Predictably, some were buying beer for the weekend, others, cigarettes. One had a sports car magazine featuring exotic vehicles he would never be able to afford. To his surprise, he watched *as each employee also purchased one or more lottery tickets.* Though at one time he would have marveled at the irrational and gratuitous waste of money by those who could afford it least, he immediately grasped the dynamics at play. His employees, most of whom performed backbreaking labor in near darkness for very meager pay, were all victims of a Fantasy Self-Narrative. Somewhere, deep within, *each truly believed that one day things would change for the better.* He realized that purchasing a lottery ticket was little more than pathetic attempt to put themselves in Fortune's way, where they might realize in one instant the financial windfall that had eluded them their entire lives.

Behind the counter, the storeowner eagerly snapped up their money, smiled, and dispensed to each a losing ticket. It struck him as amazing that each employee would pay to be reminded that they were losers. When he thought about how much of the money he had paid to his employees that had passed straight from their hands into the pockets of the opportunistic storeowner it sparked an idea. He resolved to not allow the situation to go unaddressed.

Four weeks later his company became a state-certified reseller of lottery tickets. He implemented a new program that allows his employees to receive up to 15% of their paycheck in the form of lottery tickets. For every $4.99 they forego in cash, they can receive $5 in lottery tickets. His employees are happy because he's selling them lottery tickets at a discount. Each senses the corporation's largesse has brought them one step closer to realizing their dream of financial independence. The executive is happy because he's already lowered his payroll costs by four percent *and* created a new profit center in his company. Moreover, if one of his employees *does* happen to win the lottery, he gets a certain percentage of the prize as the seller of the ticket.

In less than 3 months, he has become the largest regional reseller of lottery tickets. This is an example of a truly inspired piece of Win/Win[8] thinking.

I hope my inclusion of these implementations of Radical Demotivation™ have given you hope and inspiration as you consider unveiling your own tailored programs within your organizations. The possibilities are truly endless for the enterprising executive with a Radically Demotivating agenda. With this public release of this book, I eagerly anticipate the feedback of future readers who are willing to share their own experiences with Radical Demotivation[9].

Even as I hope to encourage you, I must end this work as it began— with a warning. The revolution has begun. Those who ignore it do so at their own peril. We are all in a struggle that defines our era, though its true nature is misunderstood by the profane. Fifty years hence, when the victors of this modern conflict emerge, it will be those leaders who remember their obligations. For those who chose to put the interests of their employees above all others, it will be a time of reckoning with their folly amidst rubble and ruin they have wrought. But for those who acknowledged the primacy of shareholder value, it will be an era of triumph and celebration.

In the interest of that party which has the lasting relevance to your own destiny as an executive—I urge you to join the revolution, before it's too late[10].

---

[8] Odds of employees winning 1 in 47,000,000.

[9] Feedback can submitted via demotivation.com. All submissions become the property of Despair, Inc.

[10] It may also be a good idea to hire a competent employment law attorney.

References

Adams, J. S. (1965). Inequity in social exchange. In L. Berkowitz, (Ed.), *Advances in experimental social psychology, Vol. 2,* (pp. 267–299). New York: Academic Press.

Argyris, C. (1991). Teaching smart people how to learn. *Harvard Business Review, 69,* May-June, Reprint 91301, 5–15.

Argyris, C. (1998). Empowerment: The emperor's new clothes. *Harvard Business Review, 76,* May-June, Reprint 983012, 98–105.

Argyris, C. & Schön, D. A. (1996). *Organizational learning II: Theory, method, and practice.* Reading, MA: Addison-Wesley Publishing Company.

Beatty, R. W. & Schneier, C. E. (2001). Assessing the value of the individual. In C. H. Fay, M. A. Thompson, & D. Knight, (Eds.), *The executive handbook on compensation: Linking strategic rewards to business performance* (pp. 150–163). New York, NY: The Free Press.

Bennett, L. (1992). Legal fictions: Telling stories and doing justice. In M. L. McLaughlin, M. J. Cody, & S. R. Read (Eds.), *Explaining oneself to others* (pp. 149–166). Hillsdale, NJ: Earlbaum.

Bennett, W. J. (1993). *The book of virtues: A treasury of great moral stories.* New York, NY: Simon & Schuster.

Bernhard, M. (2001). Disaster of the day: Charles Schwab. *Forbes.com,* retrieved December 10, 2004 from http://www.forbes.com/2001/03/16/0316disaster.html.

Bolman, L. G., & Deal, T. E. (1991). *Reframing organizations: Artistry, choice, and leadership.* San Francisco, CA: Jossey-Bass.

Bossidy, L., & Charan, R. (2002). *Execution: The discipline of getting things done.* New York, NY: Crown Business.

Bradford, D. L. (1993). Building high-performance teams. In A. R. Cohen, (Ed.), *The portable MBA in management* (pp. 38–70). New York, NY: John Wiley & Sons.

Carey, J. F. (1994). *About pay: Discussing compensation.* Menlo Park, CA: Crisp Publications.

Cialdini, R. B., Finch, J. F. & DeNicholas, M. E. (1990). Strategic self-presentation: The indirect route. In M. J. Cody & M. L. McLaughlin (Eds). *The psychology of tactical communication* (pp. 194–206). Clevedon, Avon: Multilingual Matters.

Cissna, K. N. L. & Sieburg, E. (1990). Patterns of interactional confirmation and disconfirmation. In Stewart, J. (Ed.), *Bridges not walls: A book about interpersonal communication* (5th ed., pp. 237–246). New York, NY: McGraw-Hill.

Coffee, R. E., Cook, C. W., & Hunsaker, P. L. (1994). *Management and organizational behavior.* Homewood, IL: Austen Press.

Collins, J. C. & Porras, J. I. (1994). *Built to last: Successful habits of visionary companies.* New York, NY: Harper Business.

Covey, S. R. (1989). *The 7 habits of highly effective people: Powerful lessons in personal change.* New York, NY: Simon & Schuster.

Crawford, R. & Bowker, M. (1989). *Playing from the heart.* Rocklin, CA: Prima Publishing.

Crowe, M. (1996). Why the members of your team won't speak up, and what you can do about it. *Harvard Management Update,* Reprint U9611C, 1–4.

Csikszentmihalyi, M. (1990). *Flow: The psychology of optimal experience.* New York, NY: Harper & Row, Publishers.

Deal, T. E. & Kennedy, A. A. (1982). *Corporate cultures: The rites and rituals of corporate life.* Reading, MA: Addison-Wesley.

Deci, E. L. (1980). *The psychology of self-determination.* Lexington, MA: D. C. Heath and Company.

Dweck, C. S., Goetz, T. E. & Strauss, N. L. (1980). Sex differences in learned helplessness: IV. An experimental and naturalistic study of failure generalization and its mediators. *Journal of Personality and Social Psychology, 38,* 441–452.

Dweck, C. S. & Leggett, E. L. (1988). A social-cognitive approach to motivation and personality. *Psychological Review, 95,* 256–273.

Eisenberg, E. (1984). Ambiguity as strategy. *Communication Monographs, 51,* 227–242.

Eisenberg, E. M. & Goodall, H. L. (1993). *Organizational communication: Balancing creativity and constraint.* New York: St. Martin's Press.

Eisenhardt, K. M., Kahwajy, J. L., & Bourgeois, L. J. (1997). How management teams can have a good fight. *Harvard Business Review, 75,* July-August, Reprint 97402, 77–85.

Elliott, E. S. & Dweck, C. S. (1988). Goals: An approach to motivation and achievement. *Journal of Personality and Social Psychology, 54,* 5–12.

Employee Theft Still Costing Business (1999). Retrieved December 10, 2004 from http://www.inc.com/articles/1999/05/13731.html

Ernst & Young Estimates Retailers Lose $46 Billion Annually to Inventory Shrinkage (2003). Retrieved December 10, 2004 from http://www.ey.com/global/Content.nsf/US/Media_-_Release_-_05-13-03DC

Fisher, B. A. (1978). *Perspectives on human communication.* New York, NY: Macmillian Publishing Co., Inc.

Fisher, B. A. & Ellis, D. G. (1990). *Small group decision making: Communication and the group process* (3rd ed.). New York: McGraw Hill.

Fisher, W. R. (1987). *Human communication as narration: Toward a philosophy of reason, value, and action.* Columbia, SC: University of South Carolina Press.

Frankl, V. (1963). *Man's search for meaning.* New York, NY: Pocket Books.

Garfinkel, H. (1967). *Studies in ethnomethodology.* Cambridge: Polity Press.

Geary, L. H. (2002). Riches to rags: Millionaires who go bust. *CNN/Money,* retrieved December 10, 2004 from http://money.cnn.com/2002/05/08/pf/saving/q_gonebust/

Gergen, K. J. (1994). *Realities and relationships: Soundings in social construction.* Cambridge, MA: Harvard University Press.

Gerhart, B. (2001). Designing reward systems: Balancing results and behaviors. In C. H. Fay, M. A. Thompson, & D. Knight, (Eds.), *The executive handbook on compensation: Linking strategic rewards to business performance* (pp. 214–237). New York, NY: The Free Press.

Gibb, J. R. (1990). Defensive communication. In Stewart, J. (Ed.), *Bridges not walls: A book about interpersonal communication,* (5th ed., pp. 334–339). New York, NY: McGraw-Hill.

Goldhaber, G. M. (1993). *Organizational communication,* (6th ed.) Dubuque, IA: Wm. C. Brown Communications.

Gordon, T. (1977). *Leader effectiveness training.* L.E.T. New York: Wyden Books.

Gouillart, F. J. & Kelly, J. N. (1995). *Transforming the organization.* New York, NY. McGraw-Hill.

Hallowell, E. M. (1999). The human moment at work. *Harvard Business Review, 77,* January-February, Reprint 99104, pp. 2–8.

Herzberg, F. (1989). How do you motivate employees? In *People: Managing your most important asset, Harvard Business Review,* Reprint 68108 (pp. 26–35).

Hill, L. A. (1996). *Building effective one-on-one work relationships.* Unpublished manuscript, product 9-497-028, Harvard Business School.

Hill, N. (1960). *Think & grow rich.* New York, NY: Fawcett Books.

Jablin, F. M. (1985). Task/work relationships: A life-span perspective. In M. L. Knapp & G. R. Miller (Eds.), *Handbook of interpersonal communication* (pp. 615–654). Newbury Park, CA: Sage Publications.

Johnson , S. (1998). *Who moved my cheese?* New York, NY: G. P. Putnam's Sons.

Jones, E. E. & Harris, V. A. (1967). The attribution of attitudes. *Journal of Experimental Social Psychology, 3,* 1–24.

Kanter, R. M. (1989). The new managerial work. *Harvard Business Review, 89,* 85–92.

Katz, N. (2001). Getting the most out of your team. *Harvard Business Review, 79,* Reprint F0108B, 3.

Katzenbach, J. R. & Smith, D. K. (1993). The discipline of teams. *Harvard Business Review, 71,* 111–120.

Kisela, J. F. (2000). The role of work-life benefits in he total pay strategy. In L. A. Berger & D. R. Berger (Eds.). *The compensation handbook: A state-of-the-art guide to compensation strategy and design,* (4th ed., pp. 587–600). New York, NY: McGraw-Hill.

Klein, K. E. (2001). When good workers go bad. *Business Week Online,* retrieved December 10, 2004 from http://www.businessweek.com/smallbiz/content/may2001/sb20010529_956.htm

Kohn, A. (1993). Why incentive plans cannot work. *Harvard Business Review, 71,* 54–63.

Kuhn, T. S. (1970). *The structure of scientific revolutions* (2nd ed.). Chicago: University of Chicago Press.

Laing, R. D. (1969). *Self and others.* New York, NY: Pantheon Books.

Lasch, C. (1978). *The culture of narcissism.* New York, NY: W. W. Norton & Company, Inc.

Lawler, E. E. (1996). *From the ground up: Six principles for building the new logic corporation.* San Francisco, CA: Jossey-Bass.

Lawler, E. E. (2000). *Rewarding excellence: Pay strategies for the new economy.* San Francisco: Jossey-Bass Publishers.

Leavitt, J. J. (1983). Suppose we took groups seriously . . . In J. R. Hackman, E. E. Lawler, & L. W. Porter (Eds.). *Perspectives on behavior in organizations* (2nd ed, pp. 370–377). New York: McGraw Hill.

Lencioni, P. M. (2002). *The five dysfunctions of a team: A leadership fable.* San Francisco, CA: Jossey-Bass, Inc.

Levering, R. & Moskowitz, M. (2001). The 100 best companies to work for. *Fortune, 143,* pp. 148–168.

Ludin, S. C., Paul, H., & Christensen, J. (2000). *Fish!* New York, NY: Hyperion.

Maltz, M. (1960). *Psycho-cybernetics.* Englewood Cliffs, NJ: Prentice-Hall.

Mandino, Og (1972). *The greatest secret in the world.* New York, NY: Bantam Books.

Manzoni, J. F. & Barsoux, J. L. (1998). The set-up-to-fail syndrome. *Harvard Business Review, 76,* March–April, Product 861x, 101–113.

Martin, J., Feldman, M., Hatch, M. J., & Sitkin, S. (1983). The uniqueness paradox in organizational accounts. *Administrative Science Quarterly, 28,* 438–453.

Martin, J. & Powers, M. (1983). Truth or corporate propaganda: The value of a good war story. In L. Pondy, P. Frost, G. Morgan, & T. Dandridge (Eds.), *Organizational symbolism* (pp. 93–107). Greenwich, CT: JAI Press.

Marks, B. (2005). *Bearly motivated*. New York: Panda-Mania Press.

Maxwell, J. C. (1993). *The winning attitude*. Nashville, TN: Thomas Nelson.

McAdams, J. L. (2000). Nonmonetary rewards: Cash equivalents and tangible awards. In L. A. Berger & D. R. Berger (Eds.), *The compensation handbook: A state-of-the-art guide to compensation strategy and design* (4th ed., pp. 241–259). New York, NY: McGraw-Hill.

Morgan, G. (1986). *Images of organization*. Newbury Park, CA: Sage Publications.

Peale, N. V. (1996). *The power of positive thinking*. New York, NY: Fawcett Columbine.

Perrow, C. (1986). *Complex organizations: A critical essay* (3rd Ed.). New York, NY: Random House.

Peters, T. J. & Waterman, R. J. (1982). *In search of excellence: Lessons from America's best run companies*. New York: Harper & Row.

Pfeffer, J. (1994). *Competitive advantage through people: Unleashing the power of the workforce*. Boston, MA: Harvard Business School Press.

Pfeffer, J. (1998). Six dangerous myths about pay. *Harvard Business Review, 76*, May–June, Reprint 98309, 108–119.

Polzer, J. T. (2003a). *Identity issues in teams*. Unpublished manuscript, product 9-403-095, Harvard Business School.

Polzer, J. T. (2003b). *Leading teams*. Unpublished manuscript, product 9-403-094, Harvard Business School.

Pritchard, D., Watson, S. H., & Alcock, C. (2001). Emotional reward: Shaping reward for commitment and motivation. In C. H. Fay, M. A. Thompson, & D. Knight, (Eds.), *The executive handbook on compensation: Linking strategic rewards to business performance* (pp. 238–245). New York, NY: The Free Press.

Redding, W. C. (1972). *Communication within the organization: An interpretive review of theory and research*. New York, NY: Industrial Communication Council.

Robbins, A. (1986). *Unlimited power*. New York, NY: Fawcett Columbine.

Robbins, A. (1991). *Awaken the giant within*. New York, NY: Free Press.

Rogers, C. R. & Roethlisberger, F. J. (1989). Barriers and gateways to communication. In *People: Managing your most important asset, Harvard Business Review*, Reprint 5240, 19–25.

Schein, E. H. (1991). *Organizational culture and leadership*. San Francisco, CA: Jossey-Bass.

Seligman, M. E. P. (1998). *Learned optimism: How to change your mind and your life*. New York, NY: Pocket Books.

Sieburg, E. (1976). Confirming and disconfirming organizational communication. In J. L. Owen, P. A. Page, & G. I. Zimmerman (Eds.), *Communication in organizations* (pp. 129–148). St. Paul, MN: West Publishing.

Smircich, L. (1983). Concepts of culture and organizational analysis. *Administrative Science Quarterly, 28,* 339–358.

Swann, W. B., Jr., Pelham, B. W., & Krull, D. S. (1989). Agreeable fancy or disagreeable truth? How people reconcile their self-enhancement and self-verification needs. *Journal of Personality and Social Psychology, 57,* 782–791.

Taylor, F. W. (1911). *The principles of scientific management.* New York: Harper & Brothers.

Thompson, M. (2001). Competitive advantage through achieving pay and performance alignment. In C. H. Fay, M. A. Thompson, & D. Knight, (Eds.), *The executive handbook on compensation: Linking strategic rewards to business performance* (pp. 111–124). New York, NY: The Free Press.

Treacy, M. & Wiersema, F. (1995). *The discipline of market leaders.* Reading, MA: Addison-Wesley.

Waitley, D. (1983). *Seeds of greatness.* Old Tappan, NJ: Fleming H. Revell Company.

Waitley, D. (1995). *Empires of the mind: Lessons to lead and succeed in a knowledge-based world.* New York, NY: William Morrow and Company.

Walster, E., Walster, G. W., & Berscheid, E. (1978). *Equity: Theory and research.* Boston, MA: Allyn and Bacon, Inc.

Weick, K. (1979). *The social psychology of organizing (2nd ed.).* New York, NY: Random House.

Weiner, B. (1992). Excuses in everyday interaction. In M. L. McLaughlin, M. J. Cody, & S. R. Read (Eds.), *Explaining oneself to others* (pp. 131–146). Hillsdale, NJ: Earlbaum.

Wolf, M. G. (2000). Compensation: An overview. In L. A. Berger & D. R. Berger (Eds.), *The compensation handbook: A state-of-the-art guide to compensation strategy and design* (4th ed., pp. 41–54). New York, NY: McGraw-Hill.

Acknowledgments

I would like to begin by thanking Richard Melella for taking time out of his busy schedule to read the entire manuscript and provide helpful feedback. As a long time friend and fellow executive, he confirmed many of the principles contained herein and repeatedly encouraged me to "go further." He was especially helpful in developing the ideas on interpersonal confirmation in chapter eight.

I am also indebted to Mattie Akers, a true manager with executive potential, for managing the many details involved in the production process. If it were not for her disciplined attention to detail, several deadlines would have been missed.

Thanks to the feedback and insights of my editor, Bill Barol, the manuscript is much clearer than it would have been without his intervention.

A tremendous effort went into designing this book. I am grateful to BTDnyc for their leadership, expertise, and patience in designing the layout of the book. I am also grateful to Mark Melnick for his insightful and iconic cover design. Finally, I must thank Kevin Sprouls who did an amazing job transforming several of our Demotivators® into the beautiful illustrations used throughout the book.

I also need to give credit to my research assistants, Robert (or Roger?) from Massachusetts and the redhead with the eyebrow piercing. They tracked down numerous references, checked the accuracy of the quotations, and were a constant source of inspiration. Naturally, any errors and omissions in the final manuscript are their fault.

I should also note the inspiring observations of Stephen Glass. Exactly one year after his article, Writing on the Wall, was published in *The New Republic,* Despair was officially incorporated.

Finally, I need to thank my wife for her patience during the writing of this book. Her disciplined lack of interest in my work made it much easier to complete.

Index

A

Accufession, 69
Adams, J., 70, 227
Alcock, C., 154, 161, 232
Argyris, C., 8, 196, 197, 198, 202, 227
Armstrong, N., 105, 129
Attitudes
  as acquiescence, 111–14
  as alchemy, 107–11

B

Barsoux, J., 12, 13, 14, 26, 231
Beatty, R. W., 1, 227
Benefit Bonanza. *See* Compensation
Bennett, L., 80, 227
Bennett, W., 77, 227
Bernhard, M., 167, 227
Berscheid, E., 70, 233
Bolman, L., 53, 66, 71, 227
Bossidy, L., 43, 227
Bourgeois, L., 195, 228
Bowker, M., 96, 228
Bradford, D., 185, 201, 209, 227
Broadbanding.
  See Compensation

C

Carey, J., 151, 157, 227
Carnegie, A., 105
Charan, R., 43, 227
Christensen, J., 112, 231
Cialdini, R., 99, 139, 178, 227
Cissna, K., 128, 132, 133, 134, 138, 143, 148, 228
Coffee, R., 121, 228
Cognitive premises, 67, 71, 75, 78
Collins, J., 54, 228
Collusion, 56–57
  covert, 56–57
  demotivated, 57
  enlightened, 56
Compensation
  Benefit Bonanza, 161–63
  cannot assuage ache of a mercenary existence, 160
  golden handcuffs, 177
  Mission Creep, 157–60
  Responsibility Displacement, 155–56
  stock options, 177
  transformed by social scientists, 154
  unfair, 153–55

Compensation plans
  broadbanding, 172–77
  components of, 173
  emphasize intangibles, 177–80
  incentive pay, 169–72
  keep pay low, 165–68
  merit pay, 169
  principles of, 165–80
  principles of executive pay, 173
Concern reflex, 102
Confirmation
  defined, 128
  using to advance Radical
    Demotivation™, 147–48
Cook, C., 121, 228
Core values, 54–58, 60–64
  and cynicsm, 55
  avoid socially transcendant, 59
  burden of authenticity, 58
  defined, 54
  guidelines for developing, 59–61
  introduction to the organization,
    61–63
  reinforcing in daily life, 63–64
Covey, S., 64, 228
Crawford, R., 96, 228
Crowe, M., 200, 228
Csikszentmihalyi, M., 39, 228
Culture of blame, 118
Custer's Bluster™, 129

D

Deal, T., 53, 65, 66, 71, 227, 228
Deci, E., 118, 169, 171, 228
Demotivation Vortex, 49, 50
DeNicholas, M., 99, 139, 227

Destructive Diversity™, 197, 198, 211
Disconfirmation
  defined, 128
  elements of, 132
  strategem to confront the Noble
    Employee Myth, 128–31
  strategies
    for expressing disqualification,
      146–47
    for expressing imperviousness,
      143–46
    for expressing indifference,
      133–43
Dweck, C., 116, 228

E

Eisenberg, E., 7, 60, 228
Eisenhardt, K., 195, 197, 203, 228
Elliott, E., 116, 228
Ellis, D., 187, 230
Employees
  and infantile rage, 106
  and psychological obesity, 127
  artificially motivated, 44
    impact of, 45
  as paradigmatic failures, 79
  authentically motivated, 44
    critical of motivational
      programs, 45
    impervious to Radical
      Demotivation™, 46
  bad attitudes, 105–7
  become poorer value over time,
    152
  believe others have an unfair
    advantage, 105

believe they are inherently useful, 159

blame their failures on external factors, 105

confuse their personhood with their labor, 159

distort reality to justify exploitation, 126

existential crisis, 105, 108, 110

fail to acknowledge their ignorance, 186

ground of their identities, 125

hold unrealistic dreams of the future, 86

incorrectly conclude that they are underpaid, 166

inflated sense of entitlement, 26, 100, 124, 125, 128, 149

lack interpersonal skills, 201–5

lack problem-solving skills, 201

lack skills to perform well in teams, 199–205

lack technical skills, 199–200

manipulate executive compassion, 119

motivated to act, 4–5

narcissistic, 3, 10, 22, 23, 45, 59, 69, 74, 75, 104, 106, 117, 166, 198

narcissistic impulse of storytelling, 68

needs of, 126–29

organizational liability, 21

past failures omens of the future, 79

responsible for their failures, 155

riddle of productivity, 3–11

similar to gambling addicts, 110

source of company problems, 16–21

alienate customers, 17

exploit their employer's generosity, 19

make bad decisions, 16

make mistakes, 17

steal from their employers, 20

source of competitive disadvantage, 2

spurious identification with executives, 115

stuck in a quagmire of mediocrity, 105

tormented by inflated self-worth, 22

transformed into personal valets, 144

unable to benefit from rebuke, 125

units of labor, 22

unmotivated by over-compensation, 156

unwilling to do what it takes to succeed, 39

use narrative to make sense of their lives, 80

victims of the Noble Employee Myth, 125

violate the conditions of their employee agreement, 159

Enthusiastic folly, 200

Equity Theory, 70–71, 166

Espoused theory, 196, 198

Executive compensation
    and financial performance,
        177
    unfair, 152
Executives
    desire to be fair, 154
    fleeced by Mission Creep.
        See Compensation
    fleeced by the Benefit Bonanza.
        See Compensation
    foolishly overpay for labor,
        152–53
    hypothesized obligations to
        employees, 2
    must practice disciplined apathy,
        119
    rise above their circumstances,
        106
    should create a cult of personali-
        ty, 178
    victimized by Responsibility
        Displacement.
        See Compensation
    victims of plummeting compensa-
        tion, 151
    victims of Responsibility
        Displacement.
        See Compensation

F

Feldman, M., 66, 68, 231
Finch, J., 99, 139, 227
Fish! Philosophy, 112
    benefits of, 113–14
    components of, 113
    suitable complement to

    Radical Demotivation™,
        114
Fisher, A., 4
Fisher, B., 187, 230
Fisher, W., 80, 230
Ford, H., 105
Frankl, V., 112, 117, 230

G

Garfinkel, H., 130, 131, 230
Gates, B., 105, 192
Geary, L., 92, 230
Gergen, K., 80, 81, 87, 230
Gerhart, B., 19, 20, 230
Gibb, J., 202, 204, 230
Goetz, T., 116, 228
Goldhaber, G., 121, 230
Goodall, H., 7, 228
Gordon, T., 127, 230
Gouillart, F., 54, 230

H

Hallowell, E., 230
Harris, V., 105, 230
Hatch, M., 66, 68, 231
Herzberg, F., 7, 8, 230
Hill, L., 122, 230
Hill, N., 110, 230
Horatio Alger, 78
Human potential movement, 10
Human Relations Movement, 6–7
Human Resources Model,
    7–8
Hunsaker, P., 121, 228

I

Icarus, 77, 79
Icarus moment, 85
Irrational Enthusiasm. *See*
    Motivation Cycle
It Could Be Worse™ Program, 119

J

Jablin, F., 122, 230
Jones, E., 105, 230

K

Kahwajy, J., 195, 228
Kanter, R., 122, 230
Katz, N., 208, 231
Katzenbach, J., 199, 201, 209, 231
Kelly, J., 54, 230
Kennedy, A., 53, 65, 66, 228
Kisela, J., 161, 162, 231
Klein, K., 231
Kohn, A., 169, 231
Krull, D., 97, 233
Kuhn, T., i, 231

L

Labor unions, 153
Laing, R., 56, 57, 58, 127, 128, 129,
    133, 231
Lasch, C., 11, 231
Lawler, E., 164, 166, 169, 174, 199,
    231

Leavitt, J., 185, 231
Leggett, E., 116, 228
Lencioni, P., 184, 231
Levering, R., 167, 231
Lucid passivity, 199, 200
Ludin, S., 112, 231

M

Maltz, M., 110, 231
Mandino, O., 39, 231
Manzoni, J., 12, 13, 14, 26, 231
Marks, B., 206, 231
Martin, J., 66, 68, 69, 172, 231
Maxwell, J., 109, 232
McAdams, J., 154, 178, 232
ME-I Complex. *See* Motivational
    Educational Industrial
    Complex
Mentropy™, 39, 105, 202
Mission Creep. *See* Compensation
Morgan, G., 53, 66, 231, 232
Moskowitz, M., 167, 231
Motivation Cycle, 47, 48, 49
    irrational enthusiasm, 47
    rational disillusionment, 47
Motivational Educational Industrial
    Complex, 11
Motivational industry, 9, 10, 11, 21,
    42, 51, 103, 107, 108, 109, 111,
    112, 114, 206
    incompatible with Radical
        Demotivation™, 115
    modern day alchemists,
        107–11
    objective of, 10
Motivational Junkie, 49

N

Narcissism, 10, 11, 22, 45, 59, 68,
74, 75, 104, 108, 114, 117, 118,
122, 125, 128, 159
Narrative, 80
and cognition, 80–81
components of, 81–86
form, 87–95
Radically Demotivating self-
narrative. *See* Self-narrative
Noble Employee Myth, 11, 14, 16,
18, 21, 23, 24, 25, 35, 37, 38,
39, 41, 43, 67, 68, 70, 78, 102,
103, 104, 105, 112, 114, 122,
124, 125, 128, 129, 139, 146,
153, 155, 158, 159, 160, 162,
164, 165, 168, 169, 174, 176,
178, 180, 185, 197, 202, 206,
211
and superior/subordinate interaction, 123
defined, 11
eliminates powerful motivators
from workplace, 156
orthodoxy, 12
produces false criteria for evaluating employees, 44
robs employees of dignity, 156
sows confusion regarding compensation, 153
victimizes employees, 22, 33
Noble Savage Myth, 11

O

Organizational Stories. *See* Stories

P

Paul, H., 112, 231, 232
Peale, N., 108, 232
Pelham, B., 97, 233
Perrow, C., 67, 232
Peters, T., 134, 232
Pfeffer, J., 1, 160, 168, 232
Phlogiston, 3–4
Polzer, J., 183, 184, 232
Porras, J., 54, 55, 228
Positive Mental Attitude (PMA),
103
Power/Values Differential™, 55
Powers, M., 66, 231
Pritchard, D., 154, 161, 232
Productivity
defined, 3
ineffective approaches, 4–11
PVD. *See* Power/Values
Differential™

R

Radical Demotivation™, 22, 23, 25,
34, 35, 37, 38, 42, 44, 46, 49,
50, 54, 61, 63, 64, 66, 67, 68,
69, 70, 71, 75, 78, 79, 80, 81,
84, 85, 94, 95, 96, 100, 102, 103,
107, 111, 112, 113, 114, 115,
116, 117, 120, 122, 124, 125,
126, 128, 129, 133, 134, 137,
138, 148, 149, 153, 156, 160,
163, 166, 168, 169, 170, 171,
173, 175, 177, 178, 179, 180,
183, 184, 185, 194, 198, 204,
205, 207, 208, 209, 210, 211

a process of psychological starvation, 127

counteracts employee pathology, 166

discovery executives have hoped for, 24

easy to learn, 41–43

emotional ingredients, 33

enables executives to be themselves, 41

exploits weaknesses of your employees, 38–41

goal of, 22, 25

helps employees expect less, 28

highlights authentically motivated, 46

improves accurate self-perception, 32

increases job security, 167

increases productivity, 31, 32

maximizes impact of PVD, 55

mistaken weakness of, 32

outsourcing to employees, 184

prevents artificial motivation, 45

reduces turnover, 29

replaces inspiration with collusion, 58

requires collusive relationship with employees, 57

restores dignity to the workplace, 163

rooted in reality, 21

same results for less money, 46–50

separates authentic from artificial, 43–46

soft benefits, 126

targets employees' identities, 26

using self-narrative to drive deeper, 79

Radically Demotivated employees, 26, 27, 29, 31, 73, 198

acutely aware of stature gap with executives, 30

are acutely defensive, 30–31

chonically sullen, 34–35

chronically pessimistic, 33–34

compliant toward executives, 30

experience acute self-doubt, 31

experience low-self esteem, 32–33

feel like victims of a hostile fate, 28–29

feel powerless, 27–28

Icarus moment becomes continual present, 79

interpret contributions as inadequate, 34

lack emotional resistance, 31–32

must be pushed out of comfort zone, 33

overview, 27

regard success as luck, 34

risk averse, 33

work hard to validate their utililty, 31

Radically Demotivating self-narrative, 87–95

Rational Disillusionment. *See* Motivation Cycle

Reconfiguring the employee, 9–11

Redding, C., 123, 232

Responsibility Displacement. *See* Compensation

Risky shift phenomenon, 187

Robbins, A., 110, 232

Roethlisberger, F., 202, 232
Rogers, C., 202, 232

S

Schein, E., 66, 232
Schneier, C. E., 1, 227
Schön, D., 196, 202, 227
Scientific Management, 5–6
Self-narrative
  Progressive Achievment
    Narrative, 95
  Radically Demotivating
    Achilles Heel Narrative, 90–92
    and Zone of Opportunity, 92–95
    Fantasy Narrative, 94–95
    Lost Opportunity Narrative,
      89–90
    Optimist Narrative, 92–94
    regressive, 87
    Squandered Potential Narrative,
      88–89
Seligman, M., 34, 110, 118, 232
Set-Up-To-Fail Syndrome, 12–16
Sieburg, E., 128, 132, 133, 134, 138,
    143, 148, 228, 232
Sitkin, S., 66, 231
Smircich, L., 54, 233
Smith, D., 199, 201, 209, 231
Stikin, S., 68
Stockholm Syndrome, 35
Stories
  believability, 71–72
  need to cast employees in role of
    exploiter, 71
  need to cast executives in the
    role of victim, 71

  post-modern criteria of veracity,
    71–72
  principles of storytelling, 71–75
  questions answered by, 68
  used to control employees.
    See Cognitive premises
Strauss, N., 116, 228
Swann, W., 97, 233

T

Taylor, F., 5, 6, 233
Teams
  and ignorance. *See* Employees
  as a form of punishment, 209
  bring out the worst in people,
    196–98
  create a false sense of hope,
    185–95
  defensive climate, 204
  destructive diversity. *See*
    Destructive Diversity™
  employees lack skills to succeed,
    199–205
  espoused theory. *See* Espoused
    Theory
  Radically Demotivating incentive
    structures, 207–9
  risky shift. *See* Risky Shift
    Phenomenon
  should leverage Destructive
    Diversity™, 211
theory-in-use. *See* Theory-in-use
Theory-in-use, 196, 197, 198, 202
Thompson, M., 157, 227, 230,
    232, 233
Treacy, M., 60, 233

W

Waitley, D., 233
Walster, E., 70, 233
Walster, G., 70, 233
Waterman, R., 134, 232

Watson, S., 65, 154, 161, 232
Watson, T. Jr., 65
Weick, K., 54, 233
Weiner, B., 105, 233
Wiersema, F., 60, 233
Wolf, M., 172, 233

About the Author

E. L. KERSTEN is the cofounder of Despair, Inc., a publishing and media enterprise dedicated to the dissemination of contrarian wisdom. He holds a Ph.D. in Organizational Communication from the University of Southern California and is the author of several of the company's popular Demotivators® products.

E. L. Kersten

Kersten spent the early part of his professional career as a university professor, holding teaching positions at the University of Southern California, California State University, Fresno, and City University of New York, among others. In 1995, he was lured out of academia by a fledgling Dallas Internet startup. His experiences in the private sector managing the customer care operations for an explosive-growth ISP proved both tumultuous and transformational, ultimately inspiring the birth of Despair, Inc. in 1998.

He has been quoted by, appeared on, or written about in the *Wall Street Journal,* NPR's *Marketplace, Financial Times, Harvard Business Review, Washington Post, BusinessWeek, Time,* and many other outlets. He is married and lives in Texas.

About the Illustrations

INCLUDED THROUGHOUT THIS BOOK are illustrated renderings of several of Despair, Inc.'s popular Demotivators® designs. In their original photographic form, they serve as lucid rebukes to the platitudinous condescensions of the motivational poster world.

It is my primary hope that their inclusion has enlivened and even amplified the text of this work, as this book is engaged in a similarly noble enterprise—offering a reality-based rebuttal to the wildly popular (and equally patronizing) management books of the day.

Cynics may suggest that their placement is little more than a crass advertisement for the award-winning but surprisingly affordable products commercially available at our website, www.despair.com. As the patronage of such jaded minds has contributed to my own success, I tend to trust their judgment.

Observant readers will also notice that the illustrations have a stylistic familiarity to them. This is not a coincidence. I thought it was best to commission the originator of the *Wall Street Journal*'s signature portrait style to use that technique to render the illustrations. My hope is that the stylistic familiarity will provide a bit of psychological refuge for those executives who experience a measure of disorientation while in the process of being ripped from the ideological clutches of the Noble Employee Myth. Moreover, I also had my portrait done in the same style. Recognizing the transformational impact *The Art of Demotivation* is bound to have, I thought it was best to have a suitable portrait available—for obvious reasons.

About the Illustrator

KEVIN SPROULS is perhaps best known for creating the *Wall Street Journal* portrait style. Over the past two decades he has been a rather busy freelance illustrator.

His work has been featured in *Smithsonian Magazine,* an online exhibit of the National Portrait Gallery, and his pen is housed in the Newseum in Washington, D.C.

Kevin and his wife have two children and live in the New Jersey Pine Barrens.

His website is www.sprouls.com.

About the Type

THIS BOOK is typeset in New Baskerville, with display type for the title page and chapter openings in AT Sackers Gothic.

New Baskerville is a face derived from Baskerville, created by John Baskerville (1706–1775), a master printer and repeatedly successful entrepreneur. Tirelessly innovative, he was fiercely committed to advancing the science of printing and the art of typography. His spirit lives on in the elegant typeface that bears his name, and in the heart of executives who endeavor to live similarly worthy lives (and/or to die wealthy).